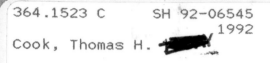

BLOOD
ECHOES

BOOKS BY THOMAS H. COOK

BLOOD ECHOES

*The True Story of an
Infamous Mass Murder
and Its Aftermath*

Thomas H. Cook

A DUTTON BOOK

For Debra, Glenn, and Daniel Furman
and for Otto and Carolyn Penzler
Family and Friends

DUTTON
Published by the Penguin Group
Penguin Books USA Inc., 375 Hudson Street, New York, New York 10014, U.S.A.
Penguin Books Ltd, 27 Wrights Lane, London W8 5TZ, England
Penguin Books Australia Ltd, Ringwood, Victoria, Australia
Penguin Books Canada Ltd, 10 Alcorn Avenue, Toronto, Ontario, Canada M4V 3B2
Penguin Books (N.Z.) Ltd, 182–190 Wairau Road, Auckland 10, New Zealand

Penguin Books Ltd, Registered Offices: Harmondsworth, Middlesex, England

First published by Dutton, an imprint of New American Library,
a division of Penguin Books USA Inc.
Distributed in Canada by McClelland & Stewart Inc.

First Printing, February, 1992
10 9 8 7 6 5 4 3 2 1

REGISTERED TRADEMARK—MARCA REGISTRADA

LIBRARY OF CONGRESS CATALOGING-IN-PUBLICATION DATA:
Cook, Thomas H.
  Blood echoes : the true story of an infamous mass murder / Thomas H. Cook.
    p. cm.
  ISBN 0-525-93399-9
  1. Mass murder—Georgia—Seminole County—Case studies. 2. Alday family.
3. Issacs, Carl Junior, 1953– . 4. Coleman, Wayne Carl. 5. Dungee, George
Elder. 6. Isaacs, William Carroll. I. Title.
HV6533.G4C66   1992
364.1′523′09758996—dc20   91–24901
                                                           CIP

Printed in the United States of America
Designed by Eve L. Kirch

Acknowledgments

First and foremost, the author wishes to express his abiding gratitude to Ernestine, Patricia, and Nancy Alday for their invaluable assistance in the writing of this book. The reliving of these events was understandably difficult and painful, but they never relented in their determination to see the task through to its conclusion.

In addition to surviving members of the Alday family, many others gave unstintingly of themselves, devoting many hours to the completion of this book.

Ronnie Angel, formerly of the Georgia Bureau of Investigation, worked tirelessly in helping me reconstruct the investigation that followed the murders on River Road. Others involved in the apprehension and early questioning of the suspects were equally forthcoming in detailing events from their particular perspectives, notably, Larry Good, L. D. Townley, F. E. Thomas, and Wade Watson. In addition, Robert Ingram, of the Georgia Bureau of Investigation, was vital in providing information regarding the prison breaks in which Carl Isaacs was involved.

Peter Zack Geer, Charles Ferguson, and Daniel L. Ricketson helped detail the prosecution of the Alday defendants.

Bo McLeod and the staff of the *Donalsonville News* were most generous in providing space, as well as access to their extensive file on the murders and the trials, with particular reference to their impact upon the community.

Numerous local officials in Donalsonville gave unsparingly of their time and services, notably John Godby and Hurbey Johnson of the

Seminole County Sheriff's Department, and Sylvia James, County Clerk of Seminole County.

At the Georgia Bureau of Corrections, John Siler and Fred Steeples arranged for inmate interviews.

Susan Boylen of the Georgia Attorney General's Office provided critical documents which pertained to the later appeals process and was always available to be of assistance in leading me through its thorny byways.

Tom West proved a devoted advocate of his client, Wayne Carl Coleman, and his willingness to assist a writer whom he knew to have a different perspective from his own will serve as a testament to his own self-confidence and certainty of purpose.

Starr Holland and others on the staff of the *Albany Herald* were painstaking in their efforts to provide me with articles and photographs pertaining to the long history of the case.

And finally, in New York, my editor, Michaela Hamilton, leveled a keen eye on the manuscript, providing not one suggestion that did not substantively strengthen and improve it.

To all these various individuals I offer my sincere appreciation.

Author's Note

This is a work of nonfiction. Although much of the dialogue in it is taken directly from court and police transcripts, there are numerous instances in which it has been reconstructed on the basis of the author's interviews with relevant individuals.

The real names of the people involved in this story have been used, except for Charlie Bowman, Steven Dennis, Tom Fitzgerald, Willie Flynn, Sarah Foster, Sam Hall, Theodore Hall, Bill Maddox, Eddie Phipps, Sylvester Pitts, and Judy Powell, whose names have been changed in the interest of privacy. Any similarity between the fictitious names used and those of living persons is, of course, entirely coincidental.

For them no more the blazing hearth shall burn,
Or busy housewife ply her evening care;
No children run to lisp their sire's return,
Or climb his knees the envied kiss to share.

Thomas Gray
"Elegy Written in a Country Churchyard"

FIRST BLOOD

Chapter One

River Road
Seminole County, Georgia

B y five-thirty in the afternoon, the smell of scorched gunpowder was thick in every room. No one knew exactly how many shots had been fired, only that the old man had required more than anyone else, rising determinedly from the bed, one side of his forehead already blown open, but rising anyway, as the bullets rained down upon him until he slumped back finally, still breathing, but only for a few seconds more.

Another body lay beside his, thick and husky, the arms made strong by the rigorous farm labor he'd done all his life.

In the next room, a third body sprawled facedown across the small sofa, the legs hung over the side so that the feet touched the floor. In the opposite bedroom, two more men lay on a tiny bed, the blue smoke from the pistols still curling out the half-closed door.

With five men dead, the only question that remained was what to do with the woman.

She lay on her back beneath the kitchen table, whimpering softly, but entirely conscious, her blouse pulled over her breasts, her panties in a crumpled mass beside her.

The four men who moved about the trailer hardly glanced at her as they rifled through the drawers and cabincts and closets, looking for guns and money.

From her place on the floor, it would have been hard to keep track of the men. The tiny windows of the trailer let in very little light, and that was further constricted by the curtains which hung over them. As for the lights inside the trailer, the men had not turned them on, preferring to skulk through the rooms in a gloomy shadow, muttering to each other about their next move, their eyes averted as if they did not want to remind themselves that she was still there, still alive, that there was one to go.

In the end, it was a topic that could not be avoided, however, and they discussed their options quietly while she continued to lie beneath the kitchen table, her eyes combing its low ceiling, or crawling along the walls and windows, lighting from time to time on some little knick-knack she'd bought across the border in Florida or in one of the small shops of nearby Donalsonville.

She'd married her husband, Jerry, only a few years before in a ceremony at the Spring Creek Baptist Church, a small, wood-framed sanctuary that sat on a shady hill a few miles from the trailer. All Jerry's relatives had crowded into the church that day, the whole Alday clan. Among them: Ned, Jerry's father, dressed in his Sunday best; Aubrey, Ned's brother, beaming from the front pew; Shuggie and Jimmy, the two brothers who kidded Jerry mercilessly, their faces grinning over their roughly knotted ties. All their bodies were with her now, their feet dangling from the beds or off the sofa, their shoes still encrusted with the rich topsoil of their farm.

The strangers told her to get up, and one of them stepped over and jerked her roughly from the floor. He was a short man, hardly more than a boy, with long dark hair that swept over one eye. Earlier, he'd called her a bitch and slapped her while the others looked on, waiting their turn. Then he'd forced her down, first to her knees, then on to her back, ripping at her clothes, his hands all over her, his teeth sinking into her breast, breaking the skin, leaving a jagged purple mark.

"Get dressed," he barked.

She'd worn turquoise pants and a matching sweater to work that day, and she put them back on slowly, already exhausted, standing completely still, except for the trembling, while the blindfold was pulled tightly over her eyes, then another cloth stuffed into her mouth.

A few seconds later she was outside, the last light of afternoon pouring over the undulating rows of freshly planted corn and beans and peanuts as they pushed her toward the waiting car.

Once in the car, she crouched down in the back seat floorboard, moaning softly, her knees against her chest, while the one black man among the three white ones held the gun on her, staring silently from over the barrel, his brown eyes wide and bulging behind the thick black-framed glasses.

The car moved in a zigzag pattern for a time, then turned off the road entirely and headed into the woods, its wheels bumping across the rutted ground, weeds and branches slapping noisily at its sides until it finally came to a halt.

In a moment she was outside again, first perched on the hood of the car, like an ornament for the men to gaze at, then on her knees, dragged to them by her hair, and finally on her back again, with the dark-haired man on top of her, the black man watching from above, while the other two moved quickly around and inside a second car, wiping it with brightly colored bits of cloth.

Soon the other two returned to the car, one of them sucking at a bottle of whiskey. The other one, blond and lanky, the youngest of them all, stood away, slumped against the back of the car, as if keeping his distance from the others.

She felt the dark-haired man pull himself off her, his eyes now trained on the others. He laughed and nodded toward her, his gaze still fixed upon the other men. "Any of you want some more of this?" he asked casually, as if offering his companions one last sip from the nearly empty glass.

Chapter Two

Several days before, on May 11, at approximately two o'clock in
the afternoon, Riley Miller walked into the headquarters of the
McConnellsburg Police Department and worriedly filed a Missing Persons report on his nineteen-year-old son, Richard Wayne Miller,
a senior at the local high school.

Police officials asked Miller the usual questions. Had the boy acted
strangely in recent days? Was he having personal problems? Had conditions deteriorated in his home life? In other words, was it possible
Richard had run away?

Mr. Miller was adamant. His son was a good student, a member of
the Future Farmers of America. He held down a job at the local Exxon
station. He was an all-American boy.

But he had not come home the previous night, and Riley Miller
wanted to know why. "I thought he might have gone to stay with a
friend," he told police.

But he hadn't, Mr. Miller went on, his voice darkening with each
passing second, a gloomy apprehension now rising in the faces of the
policemen who surrounded him. As they listened, Richard Miller began
to take shape in their minds, no longer a name on a form, but a young
man with an easy smile and helpful manner, friendly, modest, a perfect
son.

"I called all of Richard's friends," Mr. Miller insisted. "But none of
them have seen him."

Mr. Miller had also called the Exxon station where Richard worked, but none of his coworkers had seen him since his departure the previous afternoon.

"When did he leave the station?" one of the officers asked.

"Around the middle of the afternoon."

"What was he driving?"

"A green Chevy Super Sport," Mr. Miller answered. "He was going into town to buy some auto parts."

"Did he buy them?"

"Yes, he did. Then got in his car and headed down U.S. 30."

Down U.S. 30, and into oblivion.

At 9:00 A.M. the next day, Pennsylvania State Trooper Larry Good received an urgent telephone call from Riley Miller.

"Someone saw Richard," Mr. Miller told him.

"Who?"

"Her name is Deborah Poole. She's with me now."

Good drove immediately to Miller's house and listened as Poole told her story.

At around 12:30 P.M. on May 10, Poole told him, she'd been on her way to pick up her children at her mother's house just off U.S. 30 when she'd seen Richard Miller traveling west in his green Chevy Super Sport. As their two cars approached Patterson Run Road and slowed down to make a left turn, she and Miller had glanced to the left and seen three white men and one black one as they hustled around the cab of a pickup truck. Both Miller and she had recognized the truck as belonging to a local resident, Lawrence Schooley. But Schooley had been nowhere around the truck, Poole added, and so she had become suspicious.

"Why?" Good asked.

"Because of the men around it," Poole said. "They didn't seem like they ought to have been in Mr. Schooley's truck."

"What did the men look like?" Good asked.

"The black one wore thick dark-rimmed glasses," Poole answered. "And one of the white ones had long light-brown hair."

Miller had become suspicious of the men too, Poole added, and after they'd made the left turn, they'd both stopped on Patterson Run Road to look at what was going on around Schooley's truck. Poole had remained in her car, but Richard had gotten out of his and walked up to where she had stopped.

"Did he say anything to you?" Good asked.

"Yes," Poole answered. "He asked me if I knew any of the men we could see around Lawrence's truck. I told him that I'd never seen any of them before."

"Did he say anything else?"

"Yes," Poole said. "He told me that he was going to hang around and watch where they went. If they pulled away, he was going to follow them."

According to Poole, Miller had then returned to his car and backed down the road to U.S. 30, from which position he would be able to observe the men at the truck, then follow them should they pull back out onto the highway.

"And that's where you left him?" Good asked. "Sitting in his car?"

Poole nodded. "I didn't think anything else about it until I heard he was missing."

Later that same afternoon, Good consulted a recent Maryland State Police bulletin about a breakout at the Poplar Hill Correctional Institute, a minimum-security prison outside Baltimore. Three men had simply walked off the grounds at three in the morning on May 5. Two of the men, Carl Junior Isaacs and his half-brother, Wayne Carl Coleman, were white. The third, George Elder Dungee, was black. A fourth man, the younger brother of one of the escapees, was suspected of having joined the gang.

The next day, suspecting that the men Poole had seen around Lawrence Schooley's truck might be the same as those who had escaped from Poplar Hill, Good presented her with two separate photographic lineups. One consisted of six pictures of black men, all were wearing glasses. She identified George Elder Dungee as the man she'd seen sitting placidly in the back of Schooley's truck.

Next Good presented her with a second lineup consisting of seven photographs of young white males. Poole picked William Carroll ("Billy") Isaacs as the long-haired youth she'd seen three days before. Billy Isaacs was the fifteen-year-old brother of Carl Junior Isaacs.

Some time later, a second witness came forward. His name was Norman Strait, and he told Good that as he'd been coming down U.S. 30, he'd seen several men loading material from a blue Chevrolet into Schooley's truck. He'd stopped to observe them more closely, and taken his hunting rifle from the gun rack and drawn a bead on each of the four men. Through the powerful lens of his hunting scope, he had watched them haul things back and forth between the two vehicles. One had remained idle while the others hustled about, and Strait had been able to get a good look at him. He was short, with long dark hair that often fell over one eye.

In a photographic lineup, Strait identified Carl Isaacs as the man he had sighted through the cross-hairs of his hunting scope. "I guess I should have shot that son-of-a-bitch right there," he would tell Good only three weeks later. "It would have saved a lot of lives."

FREE AT LAST

Chapter Three

One thing was sure, and Carl Junior Isaacs must have known it as he led Wayne and George out of Poplar Hill on the morning of May 5, 1973. He was in command, a position he reveled in.

Born on August 9, 1953, Carl was the son of a father who abandoned him and a mother he despised. His father, George Archie Isaacs, had drifted up from Mountain City, Tennessee, where he'd worked as a delivery man and a service station attendant before finally coming north.

Once in Maryland, George took a variety of odd jobs, everything from working at a mushroom plant to plying his skills as a carpenter.

A woman proved his undoing, as far as remaining in the North was concerned. Her name was Betty, and when George met her she was already married to Carl Coleman, the father of her four children. Such incidental facts did not stop Archie and Betty from deepening their relationship, however, and when Coleman realized he was being cuckolded, he promptly signed a warrant against George, charging him with "breaking peace" between Betty and himself. As a result, George spent forty days in jail.

Once released, he went back to Betty. By then, Coleman had disappeared into the wilds of West Virginia, where he was later rumored to have been shot.

Though George would later describe Betty as a faithless wife who did "nothing but sit around and drink," he fathered so many children by her during the next few years that in 1988, when interviewed by a defense team psychologist, he could remember neither the names nor the exact number of his offspring. Their separate personal identities equally eluded him. "I'm just trying to remember which one that was," he said, when asked about the early life of Carl Junior, the son who would bring to the Isaacs name a singularly dark renown.

It wasn't very long before George had had enough of family life. Betty's own behavior toward him was bad enough, as he saw it, but even worse was her tendency to set the children against him. Egged on by Betty, they tormented him mercilessly, finally forcing him to do the "dirty thing," as he later described it, of abandoning them, the idea suddenly popping into his head as he sat in a diner after dropping Betty off at work. It was the kind of bizarre whimsy he'd already passed on to his eldest son, though in Carl it would take on a far grimmer character, horrendous acts committed with a shrug.

Once his father had deserted the family, and with his mother either drunk at home or holed up with her latest romantic interest, Carl and the other children were left to fend for themselves. Roaming in what amounted to a family pack, they moved along the streets while their neighbors watched them apprehensively from behind tightly closed doors.

What the neighbors saw was a collapsing family structure, its center gone, its sides caving in. Soon the Isaacs children were reduced to rags, though still wandering together, clinging to whatever loose strands of family life they might gather, particularly to such communal efforts as foraging for food in garbage cans.

But as the weeks passed, their lack of supervision finally drew the attention of various Maryland authorities. At the Hartford Elementary School, teachers noticed that the Isaacs children were unkempt, their teeth rotten, that they stank from unwashed clothes and poor personal hygiene. Called in to explain this condition, Betty Isaacs declared that it was up to the public school teachers to take care of her children, an attitude educational officials greeted with helplessness and dismay.

Over the next few weeks, the mischief and disorder of the Isaacs children grew steadily more severe, until, in April 1965, Maryland officials assumed full responsibility by declaring them wards of the state.

By that time Carl Junior, now eleven, had been caught stealing in his elementary school, as well as in Korvette's, a local department store. He was placed in a foster home, along with Bobby, his younger brother, and Hazel, his older sister.

For a time, the placement appeared successful. Carl joined the Boy Scouts and began playing trumpet in school.

By May of 1966, however, the darker angels of his experience had begun to reassert themselves. He was caught stealing again, first at his school, then at the construction site where his foster father worked. A psychologist declared the thievery, along with numerous other incidents of bad behavior and foul language, to be entirely consistent with Carl's background and advised against any form of therapy.

Predictably, the stealing continued. His schoolwork slumped as well, so that by December he was failing four subjects.

By May of 1967, Carl's behavior had darkened considerably. Now fourteen, he'd begun to resent the whole notion of school attendance. His bouts of truancy lengthened steadily, and even less taxing activities came to represent additional elements of the "straight life" for which he now harbored a growing contempt. Finally the Boy Scouts dismissed him, a circumstance that led to even more heated arguments with his foster parents.

Increasingly beyond restraint, Carl grasped the solution most ready-to-hand: flight. On May 22, he ran away from his foster home, though he seems to have had little idea of where to run. He wandered the streets until, two days later, he was picked up by authorities and placed in the Maryland Training School for Boys on Old Hartford Road. Two subsequent psychological examinations found him suffering from depression, a poor self-image, and pronounced inability to handle his increasingly angry and tumultuous feelings.

After a short stay at the Maryland Training School for Boys, Carl was placed in a second foster home in October 1967. Almost immediately after placement, he began to act out. His performance in school was poor, and his new foster parents found him a disruptive and uncontrollable presence in their home.

By January the situation had become intolerable, and Carl was committed to the Lapinsky Shelter Home until April 1968, when a third foster home was found. After a recurrence of the same behavior that had made the two previous placements unworkable, Carl was transferred to the Woodbourne Boys Home. A few weeks later he ran away, only to be picked up by police and returned to the Maryland Training School for Boys.

At fifteen, Carl was now in the full throes of adolescence. Yet another psychological examination revealed that ominous feelings had begun to emerge, particularly associated with hostility toward women. A report by a staff member of the Maryland Training School for Boys stated that Carl could not respond to female authority figures or accept discipline from women, an attitude that could only have been exacerbated when, during a prearranged visit with his mother, Betty Isaacs was unable to recognize him and had to be told by a staff member that the brooding young man who stood before her was her son.

In February of 1969, Carl was readmitted to the Woodbourne Boys Home, where he remained until the following June. During that brief period, he ran away many times. On June 2, after yet another escape, Woodbourne notified Maryland officials that they would not readmit Carl to the home.

Though missing for a month, Carl was finally picked up when police found him and another boy during the course of an assault upon a third boy. Both assailants were returned to the Maryland Training Center for Boys for reconsideration of their cases.

A subsequent investigation of Carl's whereabouts during his month on the streets revealed that he'd moved in with Charlie Bowman, an employee of the Burns Detective Agency, a homosexual whose taste ran to children. Carl had been one of several boys who'd lived with Bowman, providing sex in exchange for room and board. Unlike the other boys, however, Carl, when interviewed by a social worker, had asked to be placed officially and permanently in Bowman's foster care.

Such a placement was absurd, but state officials were unable to find much of an alternative. A social worker declared Carl to be ungovernable, and recommended that he be returned to the Maryland Training School for Boys.

On August 11, 1969, Carl once again took up residence at the school, and once again began a series of escapes. As a result, the state of Maryland formally declared that it had exhausted its resources in regard to him and promptly removed him from the juvenile system. From that time forward, there would be no more training schools or foster homes.

Carl Junior Isaacs had been set loose upon the world.

He reverted instantly to crime, stealing cars and burglarizing houses, while living a seminomadic existence, bunking with friends or the families of friends, sometimes for no more than a few days, at most a few weeks, then moving on to the next temporary shelter.

In 1970, he was arrested for breaking and entering and for car theft. Legally an adult, he was now ready for an adult institution, and after yet another arrest for car theft and breaking and entering in Maryland, he was sentenced to the Maryland State Penitentiary, arriving there on March 27, 1973.

Two days later, a riot broke out, and Carl, small, young, and to some eyes nubile, was raped by fellow inmates from 6:00 P.M. to 2:30 A.M., eight and one-half excruciating hours, while the riot swirled around him, engulfing the prison in a smoking whirlwind of rage and violence.

When it was over, Carl was removed from the penitentiary and on April 2 given yet another psychological evaluation. For the nervousness, depression, and insomnia it revealed, the doctor prescribed three hundred milligrams of Noludar, one tablet a night for ten days.

Two days later Carl was transferred to the Maryland Correction Camp, a far less grim institution than the Maryland State Penitentiary. On April 25, he was again transferred, this time to the minimum-security institution at Poplar Hill, outside Baltimore, a place at which he did not intend to remain for very long.

Chapter Four

The nineteen-year-old boy who arrived at Poplar Hill Correctional Institute on April 25, 1973, had lived most of his life under some form of official, rather than family, supervision. He was a dark flower grown in the hothouse of institutionalized care. But to the resentment and suspiciousness common in institutionalized personalities, Carl had added a critical element of his own, a dangerously romantic notion of the outlaw archetype.

During his years of petty crime, Carl had developed a vision of the criminal ideal which, by the time he was nineteen, had entirely captured him. His heroes had become the Wild West bad guys of comic book renown: Jesse James, Cole Younger, Billy the Kid, and other such repositories of outlaw legend. Short, and often ineffectual, fighting the fears of inadequacy that tormented him, Carl had created a similarly exalted outlaw persona for himself, then grafted it onto the drifting cloud of his personality. In a sense, the outlaw persona served as the only identity he had, and he used it like a mask to confront the world, a way either to frighten others or to gain their admiration.

But in Carl's case, admiration could be gained only from people who were susceptible to his own bloated vision of himself. His own half-brother, Wayne Carl Coleman, was just such a person.

Some months before, Wayne had been transferred to Poplar Hill, and once Carl had established contact with him, he began to enlist him in his escape plans, a systematic manipulation that Wayne had few resources to resist.

Twenty-six years old, the eldest son of Betty Isaacs and Carl Coleman, Wayne had been in and out of institutions for most of his life, usually for such relatively innocuous crimes as car theft and burglary, the same type to which Carl had become addicted.

Compared to Carl, he was timid, sluggish, and without direction. Consequently, he looked to others for leadership, since he was more or less unable to formulate even the most rudimentary schemes of his own. At five feet five inches, he was only slightly shorter than Carl, but he was considerably less intelligent, and frequently appeared disoriented, his mind prone to wander from one point to another, unable to focus for very long on anything but his most primitive needs. Shy and awkward, he had lived his life in a shadowy crouch, a figure on the periphery, waiting for someone to lead him to the promised land.

Within Wayne's limited scope, Carl was just that sort of person, and he could think of no one he'd rather follow through the vicissitudes of life than the wild and cunning half-brother who'd drifted back into his life. In Wayne's eyes, Carl was bold and resourceful, a fast talker with the perfect combination of guts and brains. Better yet, Carl didn't shamble through life as Wayne did. He took things by the horns, his head full of plans.

This was precisely the grandiose view of himself that Carl so actively promoted, and so, with very little effort, he quickly drew Wayne under his own fledgling wings.

While his older brother listened as attentively as he was able, Carl explained that he'd come up with a few ideas for the immediate future. Poplar Hill was for losers. It was also a minimum-security institution that only a jerk would hang around in. And Carl Junior Isaacs was no jerk. He was going to break out of Poplar Hill, he said, and he wanted Wayne to come with him.

Wayne easily fell in with the scheme, although he added a critical precondition. He would not go with Carl, he said, unless he could bring a fellow inmate along with him.

The inmate was George Elder Dungee. Thirty-six years old, innocuous and dim-witted, with thick black-rimmed glasses and a mind given to hilarious non sequiturs, Dungee had been incarcerated at Poplar Hill on a contempt of court citation for not paying child support, and while there, he had developed a homosexual relationship with Wayne. Gullible and trusting, Dungee had little ability to filter the varied data that came into his mind. Despite the fact that he was soon to be released from Poplar Hill, he was willing to go along with the escape for no reason other than that Wayne wanted him to.

Beyond its sexual component, the nature of Wayne's relationship with George Dungee would remain obscure, though it seems to have been composed of an odd combination of ignorance and amusement. Although of low-average intelligence, Wayne was clearly superior to Dungee, and their interactions often suggested a low-watt version of George and Lenny in Steinbeck's *Of Mice and Men.* Unable to conceive of Dungee's witlessness as the simple and regrettable product of an innately inferior intelligence, Wayne found his friend's bumbling manner, limited vocabulary, and disordered conversation funny and ingratiating. For Wayne, George was not only a source of occasional sexual release but a comic entertainment, a squat, bug-eyed clown whom he often treated like a small child, and for whom he seems to have felt less a deeply human than an oddly canine affection.

All of these vagaries were acceptable to Carl. He had not, after all, lived his life in a community of rational spirits. But there was one thing about Wayne's new companion he found intolerable. George Dungee was black, a circumstance Carl found highly distressing, since only a few days before, he'd spent eight and a half hours being raped by black prisoners during the riot at the Maryland State Penitentiary. That, as he would say later, had "turned him racist," and he was in no mood to have a black face staring, perhaps a bit lustfully, at his behind.

At first Carl had refused to include George in his plans for escape, firmly insisting that it be an affair of brothers, like the James boys and the Youngers, the first exploit of the Isaacs-Coleman Gang. But Wayne remained adamant, his own needs for once triumphing over his general lack of will in the face of such a commanding presence as his daring younger brother. He would not go without George, he told Carl bluntly; it would be the three of them, or it would be Carl alone.

In the end, the prospect of a solitary escape did not appeal to Carl, and so, after some thought, he grudgingly accepted Dungee, though he continued to hold him in the utmost contempt.

The escape was carried out at three o'clock on the morning of May 5. It had not been a very complicated matter, the three of them merely crawling out an open bathroom window, then disappearing into the sparsely populated area surrounding Poplar Hill.

For the next few hours, they skulked among the trees and shrubs, virtually in sight of the prison lights, and reveled in their freedom while the custodians of Poplar Hill maintained their loose vigilance through the night, unaware that an escape had taken place at all.

After a period of somewhat compulsive and erratic movement, however, the three escapees finally settled on a destination, drifted down into the neighboring community, and from there made their way toward Baltimore.

Not far from the Bay Bridge, they spotted a blue Ford Thunderbird in a motel parking lot, stole it with the same ease with which they'd walked out of Poplar Hill only a few hours before, and headed, as if following the mesmerizing drone of a homing device, into their native city of Baltimore.

By then the morning shape-up had been called at Poplar Hill, and the authorities had at last become aware of the escape. A review of the escapees' yellow-sheets, however, could hardly have been expected to cause them any serious alarm. Though embarrassed by the escape, there was nothing in the criminal histories of the three men that could have alerted Maryland authorities to the grave public danger now at large in nearby Baltimore. If anything, they appeared relatively mild-mannered, their prison breakout as uncharacteristic of their general behavior as a sudden act of violence would later prove to be. With few or no violent offenses in their backgrounds, their escape emerged as the most surprising thing any of them had ever done, an impulsive act which could be dismissed as little more than one of those sudden bursts of the unfathomable which periodically rocked the otherwise routine workings of the Maryland Department of Corrections.

The first taste of freedom was exhilarating, and for a time Carl, Wayne, and even George, in his own hazy fashion, rode it like a high, white wave. For nearly two days following the escape, they aimlessly bummed around Baltimore, roaming its dilapidated neighborhoods until Carl decided that the city was probably getting a bit hot for them to remain any longer.

Even so, they did not leave the city in a rush of sudden flight. Despite the steadily increasing official heat, the call of blood was just too strong. Thus, instead of leaving Baltimore immediately, Carl and Wayne, with Dungee mindlessly in tow, headed out into Baltimore County. Carl had decided that he wanted to drop in on Billy, his younger brother.

They found him in the Towson area of Baltimore County, where he'd been living with a female friend.

In Billy, Carl had once again located a near perfect boost for his continually flagging ego. Even more than Wayne, Billy idolized Carl as a creature of heroic dimensions, one who occupied the revered role not only of older, but of outlaw, brother. He saw him as bold and resourceful, a pint-sized Jesse James, a criminal so agile and elusive that he could slip through the tightest net, outsmart the wiliest lawmen. Carl, like no one else, injected excitement into the air around him, a seductive, tingling aura. It was a feeling Billy, a bit of a self-styled outlaw himself, openly relished and did not want to live without. Besides, when compared to the flat plain upon which he now lived, its dreary landscape of rusty cars and dilapidated houses, its suffocating sense of hopelessness and entrapment, Carl's vision of life on the run presented itself as the ultimate escape hatch, a point of light beneath the concrete wall.

Chapter Five

A t around three o'clock on the afternoon of May 6, sixteen-year-old Lori Levine and twelve-year-old Jennifer Lyons were lounging on a rundown street outside Baltimore when a car suddenly pulled up to them and stopped.

Inside, Jennifer glimpsed her boyfriend, Billy Isaacs.

Billy nodded to the dark-haired boy behind the wheel. "This is my brother, Carl," he said proudly. "He's just broke out of prison."

Jennifer's eyes drifted over to Carl, then on to the two other men, one lanky and unkempt, the other a black man with thick glasses. "Hi," she said.

Carl took the spotlight at once, his eyes fixed on Lori while he told the two girls about the escape, a real blood-curdling tale, with himself as the criminal mastermind of the whole brilliant scheme.

The girls were very impressed, and their attention spurred Carl on. "We're going south," he said boldly. "Maybe to Mexico." It was going to be a life of high adventure, and Carl took pains to paint a glowing picture of it, days of leisure, plenty of drugs. When he was sure his description of life on the road had captivated them, he popped the question. "You girls want to come along?"

Trapped as they were in the bleak tenements of suburban Baltimore, Jennifer and Lori were easy marks for Carl's tall tales. Mexico, with its wide haciendas and glittering tropical lagoons, sounded like Paradise.

"Yeah, okay," Lori said, then with Jennifer directly behind her, she slid into the car and headed toward the blue unknown.

*   *   *

But if Mexico lay in Jennifer and Lori's future, it was certainly not in the immediate one. For instead of making a wild dive south, the warm wind in their hair, Carl hesitated, as if unsure of his next move. Typically, The Big Plan shriveled into an aimless wandering of the same old streets and towns Jennifer and Lori had already had enough of. Carl remained behind the wheel, sometimes blowing off about all he'd done, sometimes simply driving on silently, sullenly, his eyes locked on the road.

Thus, for the first few hours after getting into the green Chevrolet, Jennifer and Lori experienced nothing even remotely similar to the southern escape from the confines of Baltimore that Carl had so cavalierly promised. Instead, they drifted through an assortment of small towns in the Baltimore area, sleeplessly cruising through Hillendale, up and down Taylor Avenue, while Carl jabbered about his innumerable triumphs over the various authority figures who'd tried to tame his wild spirit.

For Carl, the girls were a captive audience for his breast-beating fables of criminal exploit, and he railed at them ceaselessly while the sweltering interior of the car grew increasingly disgusting with the smell of smoke, cheap beer, and unwashed bodies. Hour after hour, the cruising dragged on, until night finally fell, and Carl parked along the unromantic stretches of Notch Cliff Road.

This first, uninspired day on the road was followed by a second of pure tedium. After a cramped night, Carl was in no mood to entertain the girls with more tales. Besides, he was running out of stories, his limited imagination depleted by many hours of spinning lies and fantasies.

In addition, the girls were getting cranky. Something had to give.

For Carl, crime had always served as a quick relief from boredom, as well as a way of reasserting his authority. He decided to pump things up a bit by stealing a car.

He found one in a parking lot in Hillendale, hot-wired it, then waved the girls over. He could tell that the strategy had worked by the way the girls tumbled in delightedly, thankful for even this limited change in their surroundings. After that, the "gang" enjoyed a nutritious breakfast of cakes and coffee, all their combined finances could afford.

Once breakfast was over, the drifting began again. It lasted until around 9:00 P.M., when Carl, bored again, stole a second car, a bluish-green Buick. It was late by then, and with no other plan in mind, Carl fell into his usual pattern, drove up to Notch Hill Road, and parked again, just as he had the night before, as if his mind were trapped in its own circular ruin.

The second night was no less wretched than the first. Carl remained in his bizarre holding pattern, a cycle of aimless cruising that wore on more than the collective psychology of the people crowded in the bluish-green Buick. It was also taking its toll on the group's dwindling finances.

The solution was predictable, of course, but it was also enough to pull Carl from his robotic, perseverating tendencies. No money meant no gasoline, which meant no cruising, which meant that something different had to be done, a break in the iron recapitulations that gave his actions their only discernible structure.

Thus, toward afternoon, Carl and Billy broke into a house while everyone else waited in the car. Approximately twenty minutes later, the Isaacs brothers returned to the car, their arms filled with shirts, watches, radios, and several rifles. For a time, there was general jubilation at the ease with which the burglary had been committed, the loot passed around and fondled lovingly, the totemic objects of their outlawry.

Once the initial thrill was over, however, the incessant cruising began again. Back and forth, the bluish-green Buick lumbered heavily along the bleak suburban streets like a gray fish in a tank of murky water while Carl fought to keep up his flagging self-esteem by conjuring up increasingly outrageous tales of derring-do.

There followed a second burglary, this time with all the men disappearing into the house while Jennifer and Lori remained in the car, their eyes searching the streets for that lone police patrol car that could bring the whole fantastical enterprise to an abrupt and dreary end.

Soon Carl and the others shot back to the car, their arms filled with the latest addition to the group's accumulating assets, a camera, binoculars, ammunition, and to everyone's delight, a bag of mixed nuts.

After a quick meal at Gino's Pizza, Carl and Wayne burglarized yet another house, this time netting an assortment of jewelry, shirts, cassette tapes, guns, ammunition, and, best of all, forty dollars in cash.

With a third burglary completed in a small radius of towns, Carl decided that things were probably getting too hot to remain in Maryland any longer and so crossed the border into Pennsylvania.

In Falls River, he contemplated another burglary, but the sound of a woman calling frantically for her husband forced him to reconsider. As they drove away, Billy could see the woman standing in full view on her porch. A burst of bravado seized him, and he grabbed one of the rifles they'd stolen the day before.

"Want me to pluck her off?" he asked Carl, who alone had the power to answer questions of such profound consequence.

Carl shook his head. "No," he said casually. It was the last time he would lift a restraining hand.

The next few days saw a few more burglaries, none of which added very much money to the collective coffers. Stolen articles like binoculars and cameras were nice enough, but they were hardly legal tender. Only cash bought the necessities of life on the run, particularly beer and cigarettes. Carl decided that the time for kidding around was over.

In more ways than one.

By then, the girls had become a nuisance. The crowding was bad enough, but the problem was deeper than that. The girls had seen a great deal, knew a great deal, and Carl began to think about the danger involved in letting them go.

Billy could see the tumblers moving in Carl's mind, but felt powerless to do anything about it. As for Jennifer and Lori, they appeared oblivious to the dark web Billy could see descending over his older brother.

Still, it was the shortage of cash that remained foremost in Carl's mind. The girls were tiny glitches on a big screen. The real problem was money. To travel very far, he needed a lot more money than could be had by breaking into penny-ante suburban homes.

This meant armed robbery, a crime distinctly more serious, and far more dangerous, than slipping into empty houses, grabbing shirts and peanuts.

Carl was determined to do it, and it was easy to convince the others that it was necessary.

Except for Jennifer and Lori. The lark had not been exactly thrilling so far, but at least no one had gotten hurt. And that's the way they wanted to keep it. They told Carl they would have nothing to do with an armed robbery.

Carl made no effort to persuade them otherwise. He had run out of fairy tales with which to amuse them. More burglaries and car thefts would not impress them. His bag of manipulative tricks was empty. It was time to part company.

He let them out on a deserted street corner, telling them that the rest of the gang would carry out the robbery, then return for them, a pledge he had no intention of fulfilling.

"They said they were going to come back for us if nothing went wrong," Jennifer told police the next day, May 10, 1973, when she and Lori were spotted loitering on a local street corner, questioned vigorously by the officers who had spotted them, then returned to their fretful mothers. "Well, they didn't come back, so I guess something went wrong."

SOMETHING
WENT WRONG

Chapter Six

Traveling south through the steadily flattening expanse of the southern coastal plain, you reach it by way of roads where the tractors, agricultural combines, and dusty, late-model cars politely pull onto the shoulders to allow the faster cars to pass. On all sides, white, long-necked cattle egrets rise over broad fields of peas, beans, and cotton. In the distant woodlands, there are hints of Spanish moss. Towns called Cuthbert, Lucille, and Blakely spring up from the surrounding fields. In one courthouse square, the citizens have erected a granite monument to the peanut, the area's most lucrative crop. Everywhere the pace is leisurely, amiable, a world where people nod to strangers in a gesture that seems almost archaic, gone with the wooden plow. In Bluffton, a hand-lettered sign hawks the town's best barbecue, then adds, "If you don't have time to stop, wave." As far as the horizons stretch, the land seems curiously open, innocent . . . vulnerable.

Seminole County, Georgia, rests at the center of this world. Bordering Alabama to the west and Florida to the south, it is a region of marginal farms, understaffed government offices, and underfunded schools. As late as 1990, it had yet to produce a written history of itself. Some of the bank branches even maintained their offices in tiny converted house trailers. In its library, located in a small brick building behind the Piggly Wiggly supermarket, shelf after shelf was filled with scores of worn paperbacks, romance novels decidedly the winner in the quest for space.

Of the county's population of nine thousand, almost twenty percent received food stamps. In taxable sales Seminole ranked 102nd, near the bottom, in the state, and its yearly expenditure for education amounted to a mere $2,725 per student.

An area of farmland and uncultivated woodlands, Seminole County was merely part of that "second Georgia" which has always existed south of Athens, and which has been viewed by the far more developed northern part of the state, particularly its urban center of Atlanta, as intractably lost to the forces of intellectual sophistication and economic development.

As a consequence of this perennial underdevelopment, Seminole County would not have ranked high on any tourist's list of places to go. There were no museums, race tracks, nightclubs, zoos, or amusement parks, and even the official Georgia State Guide listed as its notable local events only Independence Day, Labor Day, and an "Old Fashioned Halloween." In summer, there was the broad green expanse of Seminole Lake for fishing and swimming. Winter, when it came, offered nothing to relieve it, no motion picture theater, civic center, swimming pool, or even one of the small "outlet malls" which had sprung up in other, less remote, rural communities to lure the bloated tourist buses from their more established routes.

Thus, on Monday, May 14, 1973, few people in Seminole County would have argued that their region had much to recommend it to those occasional traveling strangers who sometimes found their way into its tiny county seat of Donalsonville.

But to those who had lived in the region for generations, Seminole County and its environs represented a style of life that conformed to their own vision of decency and neighborliness.

No family embodied those modest virtues more than that of Ned and Ernestine Alday. They had married in 1935, together eking out a bare living even during the darkest days of the Depression. It had not been easy. For the first years of their marriage, they'd had no fixed home at all, but had been moved about by the sawmill for which Ned worked, their tiny house jacked up and transported by truck from one milling site to the next.

After many years, Ned and Ernestine had accumulated enough money to buy a small house in Donalsonville, then worked on until there was at last enough money to buy a farm of their own, complete with a large farmhouse on River Road where, during the next few years, the family grew steadily. In the end, there were eight children, equally divided between boys and girls.

By 1969, Norman, the oldest son, had made a career in the military and was living abroad, the first of the family ever to do so. Patricia, the eldest daughter, had graduated from college, the first of the children to receive a college degree, and had taken a job in social work at the Seminole County Department of Family and Children Services. Two other daughters, Nancy and Elizabeth, had married and moved to Augusta, while their brother, Jerry, had married Mary Campbell and moved into a trailer only a few miles down River Road from the family homestead. Fay and Jimmy, the youngest of the Alday children, still lived with their parents, while Shuggie, their older brother, lived with his wife Barbara in a trailer parked only a few yards from the homestead.

Despite the fact that Norman lived in Europe and two of the Alday daughters had migrated to Augusta, the lives of the farming Aldays continued without disruption.

The work was backbreaking, of course, but rewarding nonetheless. There were no bosses or time clocks, so that the Aldays raised their animals, plowed their fields, seeded and harvested their crops according to the slow dance of the seasons as one generation passed unobtrusively to the next.

Through the generations, they had lived so steadfastly according to the strictures of their religion and the customs of their region that as late as the summer of 1973, no psychological evaluation had ever been done on any member of the Alday family, nor any letter written by a concerned schoolteacher or probation officer. No police or court officer had ever entered the Alday home in an official capacity. No Alday had ever been on welfare, disturbed the peace, or violated the dignity of the community. Not one, in almost two hundred years.

"Beefeaters," Carl smirked to the other men in the car as he headed down the narrow back country road. "Nothing but beefeaters everywhere you look."

Since the flight from Pennsylvania, the mood in the latest of their stolen cars, a Chevy Super Sport, had darkened considerably. Billy particularly was ill at ease. He had not counted on following Carl over the dark abyss toward which he seemed driven since the events in McConnellsburg. Nor could Wayne or George be expected to stop him. Wayne appeared perfectly content to ride shotgun in the front seat, satisfied with his role as Carl's trusty henchman. And as for George, he remained as oblivious as ever, doing what he was told, sluggish, dependent, obedient as a child.

They were in Seminole County, Georgia, now, having just crossed over the Florida state line after a short stay in Jacksonville. Though by no means a high point on their tour, Carl was convinced that it had much to recommend it. It was remote, its spacious fields crisscrossed by obscure, unpatrolled back roads, its isolated farmhouses perfect for what he had in mind. In addition, with dreams of Mexico now faded, penniless and nearly out of gas, the Super Sport already beginning to fall apart, it offered nothing more threatening than a redneck police department Carl was certain he could outsmart.

Ezell Spencer was perhaps the first to see them. It was nearly one in the afternoon, and he'd been working at his job at Jimbo's Drive-In in downtown Donalsonville all day, taking the usual midday orders of fast food from the local farmers and workmen. He knew most of the people who came by Jimbo's, but he did not recognize any of the four men who pulled into its gravel parking lot that afternoon in a dark green Chevy Super Sport stuffed to the gills with men and supplies. They ordered quickly in Yankee accents, then sat talking to each other while they ate their burgers and fries.

To Spencer, glancing out at them from behind Jimbo's large picture windows, they appeared rootless and road-worn, and it crossed his mind that they might be headed toward the small hippie community that had lately sprung up near Americus, and which the people of Seminole County regarded with a xenophobic caution and distrust. Certainly the younger ones, the dark-haired youth behind the wheel and the blond boy in the back seat, possessed that dusty, hippie look of long-haired scruffiness that Spencer associated with San Francisco and New York.

If not hippies, he concluded as he watched them pull out of Jimbo's parking lot, they were certainly drifters of some type. It was a suspicion that seemed confirmed about two hours later when he saw the same green Super Sport cruise slowly through the back lot of Jimbo's once again, this time without stopping, but with the same four men sitting silently inside, staring straight ahead, still looking, it seemed to him, for a place to stop.

Twenty-three-year-old Sarah Foster was the next to see them. She'd lived many years in Donalsonville, Georgia, the small county seat of Seminole County. Accustomed to its slow, rural pace, she was surprised to see the dark green car as it barreled toward her from down the road. As she neared the Oak View Church, the car suddenly swerved toward her. To avoid collision, she jerked the wheel to the right, then held on to it tightly as the car slammed into the shallow ditch just beyond the road's narrow shoulders. The other car was far ahead by then, but she'd gotten a quick glimpse of it as it had hurtled by her, enough to notice the four men inside. They had not even looked back to see what had happened to her as their car bulleted on down the road, a green speck disappearing into an even greener landscape, leaving her shaken and slightly injured behind the wheel. Local boys would have stopped, she thought; only outsiders would have driven on heedlessly as they had done.

A little over ten miles away, Ernestine Alday had been working since just after sunrise. Large-boned and physically strong, she was a farm woman, born and bred, and she had never wanted to be anything else. The call that sometimes drew the seniors of Seminole County High School to the urban jungles of Dothan, Albany, and Atlanta had never sounded in her ears. "The family," she would say many years later, "was always the most precious thing I ever had."

That family was gathered closely around her, both in terms of relationship and physical proximity, a closeness whose most visible manifestation was the midday meal.

Ernestine prepared it every day, cooking all through the morning while she completed other chores. By noon it was ready, the table completely stocked with beef or chicken, corn, peas, potatoes, cornbread, and iced tea. As they had for generations, the Alday men arrived right on time, seated themselves around the table, and bowed their heads for the traditional noontide blessing in a portrait, as someone later observed, that Norman Rockwell could have painted without the loss of a single stroke.

After the blessing, the talk turned to the farm, as it always did. Ned, neatly dressed in flannel work clothes, shunning, as all the Alday men shunned, the baggy denim overalls more common to the area, had been working with Jerry, the two of them plowing a distant field, though at a slower pace than they liked, since the ground still contained muddy patches from the late rains. It had been particularly arduous that morning, and Jerry's boots were encrusted with the dark soil he'd been slogging through since first light. As for Jimmy and Shuggie, they had already mapped out their activities for the afternoon. Jimmy would be plowing the fields behind Jerry's trailer on River Road, while Shuggie intended to join his Uncle Aubrey, borrow some equipment from a neighbor, and work a different field to the west.

By one in the afternoon, the men had finished their meal and were on their way out of the house. As she cleared the table, Ernestine watched as each one of them went through the screen door, made his way down the short flight of steps, then vanished, as it would later seem to her, into the blinding light of the midday sun.

While the Aldays were routinely moving through a typically uneventful working day, Carl was in crisis mode. The immediate trouble was the car. It had begun to act up. And although he and Wayne agreed that it was probably caused by some malfunction in the carburetor, neither knew what to do about it, except to keep the motor running continually. Thus, even when they stopped to get something to eat or go to the bathroom, the engine churned greedily, incessantly guzzling gas hour after hour.

By late afternoon, they were nearly out of gas again, and with no way of refueling, since they were also running out of money. "We were always out of money," Coleman would say a few days later. "We were spending a lot, mostly on booze and gas. We usually had booze, but we were always running out of gas."

Curiously enough, gas was harder to come by than a car. To break in and hot-wire a car took only a matter of seconds. To siphon gas took a great deal longer. Some rudimentary technology was required, along with a few cumbersome devices. To score well with gas, it was necessary to find a tank in some remote field or behind an isolated house. Thus, unable to shut the motor off, the broken carburetor greedily pumping gasoline into its churning engine, their wallets empty of everything but gas receipts, they began cruising the back roads in search of just such a tank.

By mid-afternoon Ned and Jerry were having machine trouble too. After the midday meal, they had headed back to a parcel of land they'd leased from Otis Miller. These were good fields, but they'd been made difficult by the wet, muddy ground that still lingered in the wake of recent rains. Consequently, not long after they'd begun plowing, the tractor had bogged down, and they'd returned to the Alday homestead and picked up a jeep they intended to use to pull the tractor from the bog in which it had become mired.

After several unsuccessful attempts to pull it free, Ned and Jerry decided to get more help. They drove out of the field and headed down River Road, hoping to find a few of the other Alday men to lend a hand. In the bright mid-May sun they could see the broad fields of their neighbors, the green leaves of their budding crops, even from time to time the slender fronds of the small palm trees that had managed to sprout in this northernmost corner of the semitropical zone. But as they continued up the narrow paved road, they found no one who could help them free the tractor, and so they returned to it for yet another try.

At about the same time that Ned and Jerry were returning to the stranded tractor, Jimmy was finishing up his day's plowing in a long flat field only a mile or so from his brother's trailer. He had only a few more chores before he could head over to Jerry's trailer, where the men often met to plan the next day's farming while Mary worked in her flower garden in the front yard. It was always something he looked forward to at the end of the day, a rural version of winding down.

At around 4:00 P.M., Carl spotted a tank sitting by itself in a field about fifty feet from the road. Carl slowed the car, then eased it onto the shoulder of the road. From the passenger side, Wayne slid over so that he could keep his foot on the accelerator while Carl checked it out.

From their places in the back seat, George and Billy watched as Carl trudged out to the tank, his short legs slogging over the still damp ground. They could see him circling the tank slowly, stopping to fiddle with it from time to time, before he shook his head and returned to the car.

"It's gas, all right," he told them, "but it's diesel. We'll have to keep looking."

He pulled in behind the wheel again as Wayne slid back over to his usual place, riding shotgun against the passenger door. They would have to keep looking, Carl told him, as he pressed down on the accelerator, moving the car back again onto the road, his eyes sweeping left and right, searching with increasing desperation for a place to hit.

Some fifteen minutes later, they settled motionlessly on what everyone agreed was a perfect mark.

At approximately four-thirty in the afternoon, Bud Alday was heading toward his house on River Road when he saw his nephew, Jimmy, pull his tractor up into the driveway of Jerry Alday's trailer. He called to him briefly as he passed, and Jerry waved and called back before heading on up into the drive. As he continued down River Road, Bud could see other vehicles around the trailer, Jerry's blue jeep in the driveway, and almost out of sight, parked just behind the trailer, a dark-colored car he didn't recognize. Two miles farther down the road he glanced over his shoulder and saw two other relatives, his brother Aubrey and nephew Shuggie, at work in the fields. He waved to them broadly and continued down the road toward home.

For a time after Bud passed, Shuggie and Aubrey continued to work in the fields. Earlier that day, they had borrowed some farm equipment from Otis Miller. With light now growing dim, they off-loaded the borrowed equipment and returned it to the Miller farm. It was a little after five, and, tired and thirsty, they decided to drop by the local grocery. They bought soda and crackers and Shuggie bought a pack of cigarettes. For a few minutes they chatted with Leonard Roberts, the owner. Then they left, telling Roberts they were off to feed their hogs.

Later, finished with the hogs, their day's work done, they headed back down River Road. On the way, they passed Jerry's trailer and noticed the various Alday vehicles parked in its driveway: Jerry's green John Deere tractor, Jimmy's blue jeep, Mary's blue and white Chevy Impala. It had the look of a family council. They decided to pull in.

About twenty minutes later, Benny Alday drove past Jerry's trailer on his way home. The driveway was crowded with vehicles, Mary's blue and white Impala, Jerry's jeep, Jimmy's truck, the Alday family tractor, all of them parked in the wide open spaces around the Alday trailer. He did not see the dark green car Bud had previously glimpsed, or notice that for all the people who must have been gathered together inside the trailer at that moment, none of its interior lights had been turned on.

By six o'clock the first blue haze of evening was beginning to settle over the coastal plain, but as long as some light remained, Mrs. Eddie Chance continued to work in her garden. She had nearly finished the day's weeding when she glanced up River Road toward the trailer of Jerry and Mary Alday and saw two cars pull out of the driveway. She recognized one of them as Mary Alday's, but the other was not familiar, and, as she would later say, it left her with only the vague impression of something dark.

A short way down River Road, fifteen-year-old Michael Jackson was watering flowers in his front yard when he saw two cars move slowly past his house. He recognized the first one as Mary Alday's, but noticed that it was being driven by a long-haired young man he did not recognize, and that a black man sat hunched slightly forward in the back seat. Directly behind it, he saw a dark-colored Chevrolet Super Sport with two long-haired boys inside. It cruised very near the Alday car, and Michael got the impression that it was carefully following it. Both cars drifted past him slowly, then returned about five minutes later, moving in the opposite direction, as if heading back to Mary Alday's trailer down the road. Five minutes later they passed a third time, moving once again down River Road, the same people, the same cars, only this time they were going very fast.

Still farther down the same road, Jerry Godby was busy filling a chemical tank on the back of a 3020 John Deere tractor when he glanced up and saw two cars traveling down River Road. The first car had rushed by too quickly for him to see it very well, but he saw the second very clearly. It was a dark green Chevrolet, and as it passed, the driver, a young man with shoulder-length hair, waved at him politely, and Godby waved back.

Only a few minutes later, as Godby was spraying the peanut field on the north side of Hamock Springs Road, he again saw the same two cars, one so close behind the other that for a moment Godby thought they might be about to begin a drag race. One was green, and he recognized it as the same car he'd seen only a few minutes before. The other was blue with a white top, a Chevrolet Impala that reminded him of the one driven by a neighbor down the road. He squinted to see if he could make her out, but he only saw two men, one in front, driving, one in back, sitting off to one side. It was an oddly formal configuration in a part of the country where chauffeurs were unknown, and because of it, he decided the car must belong to someone other than his neighbor. Besides, as he continued to watch the cars move down the road, there was no sign at all of Mary Alday.

At approximately 6:30 P.M., Barbara Alday, Shuggie's wife, left for her job at the Dairy Bar Restaurant in Donalsonville. On her way, she passed Jerry's trailer, and noticed that Mary was not working in her flower garden as she usually did this time of day.

That wasn't the only thing she noticed, however.

The tractor was pulled up onto the carefully maintained lawn and parked in an odd position, one she doubted Jerry would have parked it in, since he'd always been very careful about damaging the lawn. For the briefest instant, she felt that something was wrong in the Alday trailer, then dismissed the thought and continued into town. Once at work, the thought returned to her, and at around 7:00 P.M., she began calling the trailer. Finally, after several attempts, she called a friend, Bill Woods, and asked him to go to the local high school and find out if there was a Young Farmers' meeting, the only local gathering, other than church services, that the Aldays were likely to attend. Woods did as Barbara asked, then called her back to report that no meeting was being held.

By ten o'clock the same night, Inez Alday, Aubrey's wife, had also begun to worry about her husband. Earlier in the day, Aubrey had told her the exact location of where he intended to work that day, and so, with her son, Curtis, she decided to drive down to the area of the farm he'd indicated. They reached it a few minutes later. It was a clear night, and she could see a long way out into the distance. If anyone had been working out there, she would have been able to see the lights from the tractor and go out to them. But there were no lights, and so for a time she and her son remained by the road, staring out into the empty silence of the nightbound fields.

Nearly a hundred miles to the west, at the Riverside Restaurant in Elba, Alabama, Mrs. Birdie Kieth saw a blue and white Chevrolet Impala pull into the restaurant's parking lot. Two men got out of the car, a tall man in his mid-twenties and a black man with thick, dark-rimmed eyeglasses. The black man seemed to position himself by the door while the white one sauntered up to the counter and ordered coffee and barbecue sandwiches. After a time, the black man stepped over and played the jukebox, while his friend remained at the counter, eyeing the cash register each time Mrs. Keith opened it.

While the black man swayed to the music of the jukebox and the white one waited for the sandwiches he'd ordered, Mrs. Kieth disappeared into the back of the restaurant, retrieved the pistol she always kept there, and gave it to Mrs. Jacobs, one of her employees. "Stay behind the curtain," she told her, "and keep an eye on those guys."

A few minutes later, after joking with one another boisterously for a while, the two men paid the bill, left the restaurant, and disappeared down the road, leaving nothing behind but the money they'd paid the bill with. But like the two men themselves, that was odd, too. She could not remember ever having been paid such a substantial bill with nothing but coins, especially these coins, all of them the same, all of them Kennedy half-dollars, the sort you expected to find in a little household bank.

Chapter Seven

At about the same time Inez Alday was returning with her son from the empty fields, Ernestine was also beginning to worry about her family. She had long ago gotten used to the long hours the Alday men kept during planting season. And when that planting season came late, as it had this year because of the incessant and unseasonably late rains, the hours grew even longer, stretching into what rural people call "can see to can't see" working days.

On the Alday farm, just as in industry, time was money. What could not be planted could not be harvested and later brought to market. Because of that, much had to be done to ensure that the 552 acres of Alday land were fully planted, and to do it required that the men work from dawn to dusk to make up for the valuable time the rains had stolen. At the noon meal, Ned had even warned her that he and the boys might well be working late into the night.

Consequently, for the first few hours, as supper grew cold on the table and she continued with her other chores, Ernestine had allowed for the lateness by reminding herself of what Ned had told her. By nine o'clock, however, with the late-spring air pitch-black outside, she could not imagine that the Alday men were still at work, and she began to talk to Fay about what they might do to find out where the men were.

Nor was Ernestine the only Alday woman who had begun to grow concerned. At nine-thirty Shuggie's wife, Barbara, came over to ask if Ernestine had seen or heard from any of the men.

Ernestine shook her head. "I haven't heard from any of them," she said.

Barbara then told Ernestine that earlier she'd become sufficiently concerned to take a drive down River Road in search of Shuggie. She'd driven by Jerry's trailer and seen something that made her worry even more.

"There were lots of cars there," Barbara said, "just about everybody. Jerry's jeep and Jimmy's pickup truck, along with the family tractor."

But the one vehicle that should have almost certainly been there was missing.

"Mary's car was the only one that wasn't there," Barbara said.

The fact that Mary Alday's car was not among all the other vehicles Barbara had seen around the trailer caused the women to theorize that something might have happened to one of the men, a sudden illness or a farming accident that would have caused everyone to pile into Mary's car and head for the nearest hospital.

As a theory, it sounded plausible enough, so Ernestine began calling the hospitals in the area. The results were disheartening. None of the hospitals had listed any Alday as having been either treated and released or admitted as a patient. It was as if they had all disappeared into thin air.

Something was wrong, but Ernestine could not imagine what it was. She knew that wherever the Aldays were, they were certainly together. Other than that, she knew only the places where they would not be found. Since the Aldays did not drink, they would not be off drunk somewhere. Nor would they be apt to lose themselves in the nearby tourist traps of Panama City. There were no church, town, or Democratic Club meetings scheduled for that Monday evening.

In light of all this, only one conclusion seemed possible.

Something was wrong.

But what?

Repeatedly Ernestine called other members of the family in the hope of locating Mary and the missing Alday men, but none of them had heard or seen any of them since earlier in the day. Throughout the night she, Barbara and Fay continued to discuss the various possibilities, one by one dismissing each while hoping that at any moment they might hear the familiar sound of the jeep or the tractor, or Mary's missing blue and white Chevrolet Impala, the one the rest of the Aldays seemed to have packed themselves into late the preceding afternoon, before disappearing without a trace.

Finally, at approximately 2:30 in the morning, Ernestine gave up. She had called everyone she knew, exhausted every avenue in her search for her missing family. Fay and Barbara had gone back to Jerry's trailer and knocked at both back and rear doors, but no one had answered. In addition to the calls and visits to the trailer, various members of the family had meticulously searched very inch of the Alday land, moving into the fields and woods, endlessly driving the many roads that skirted around and through the farm, everything from county highways to obscure wooded paths. But all of this searching had turned up nothing, not so much as the faintest suggestion of where Mary and the Alday men might be.

It was time to take the next step.

With Fay and Barbara still at her side, though growing more frightened every minute, Ernestine called the only son she still had of whose whereabouts she was absolutely certain, Bud Alday, who'd seen Jimmy pull into the driveway of the trailer many hours before.

He arrived at Ernestine's a few minutes later. By then his son-in-law, Roy Barber, and his nephew, Andy Alday, had also arrived. Together with Barbara and Fay, the five Aldays drove to Jerry's trailer on River Road, determined once and for all to find out what had happened to their missing relatives.

The area surrounding the trailer was completely dark when they arrived. The yard lights had not been turned on, and inside the trailer they could see only a soft, yellowish glow, as if a single small light were burning somewhere in one of its tiny rooms.

In the driveway and around the trailer itself, the jeep, tractor, and truck remained as they had been on the afternoon of the previous day. Nothing appeared to have been moved during the ten long hours which had passed since Bud had first seen Jimmy steer his tractor into the driveway. Everything was the same. Except the eeriness of the dimly lit trailer, and the hollow silence.

Slowly, Bud and the others got out of Bud's truck and moved to the trailer's back door. It was very still, the wide, recently planted fields a smooth, black slate all around them, the atmosphere utterly motionless until Jerry's dog suddenly rushed around the corner, whimpering softly as it turned and followed them around the edge of the trailer to where they gathered at the back door.

Roy reached for the door and turned the aluminum knob slowly. It rotated smoothly. The door had not been locked. He tugged it open partially, then drew back. Bud stepped over to it, opened it a bit further, and silently peered inside.

What he saw, although innocent enough on its face, sent a wave of terror over him. It was a single Pabst Blue Ribbon beer can sitting upright on the kitchen counter, and the very sight of it stunned him nearly speechless. Because the Aldays did not drink and so never kept liquor in the house, he knew that people very different from them had found their way into Jerry Alday's trailer, and he felt instantly that something terrible had happened to Mary, his father, his uncle, and his brothers. For Bud Alday, a beer can resting on Jerry's kitchen cabinet was as alien and incongruous a sight as a severed head might have been, or a rock brought from the moon.

"What is it?" someone asked.

Bud did not answer. He let his eyes drift downward and saw a rumpled pair of white panties lying loosely under the kitchen table. He took a quick, shallow breath, then drew his eyes to the right, where, in the bedroom at the north end of the trailer, he could see four legs dangling motionlessly from a bed, all in farm work clothes, all dusty from the very fields that surrounded him at that moment.

He stepped back instantly and closed the door. "We got to get some help," he said. "Something's happened."

The Aldays returned immediately to the homestead, where Bud called Seminole County Sheriff Dan White, and a neighbor, Hurbey Johnson.

"There's something happened up at Jerry's trailer, Hurbey," Bud said. "Mary's car is missing, and there's a light on in the trailer. Can you meet me at Ned's?"

"Yeah, Bud."

"And bring a gun with you," Bud told him.

Johnson hung up, dressed as quickly as he could, and made his way toward the front door. On the way out he picked up a twelve-gauge shotgun.

Bud was waiting in Ned and Ernestine's driveway when Johnson pulled in.

"Something's happened up at Jerry's trailer," Bud repeated. "Everybody's missing."

Johnson looked at him, astonished. "Everybody? Who?"

"Everybody," Bud answered. "Daddy and Shuggie and Chester. Jerry. Jimmy. Mary. Everybody."

"Missing?"

"Nobody's heard from them since yesterday afternoon," Bud went on, "and all the cars, the tractor, Jerry's jeep. They're just sitting in the driveway. Mary's car. That's the only thing that's not at the trailer."

Johnson felt his hand tighten around the shotgun. "Have you been in the trailer yet?"

Bud shook his head. "Not all the way in," he said, unable to add anything else.

Johnson glanced around at the large assembly that had gathered in Ned's driveway. Ernestine, Fay, and Barbara were there, their faces ghostly white in the moonlight, along with a neighbor, Eddie Chance, the long stock of a shotgun cradled in his arm.

"Roy and Andy are up at the trailer," Bud said. "They're watching the front and back doors in case anybody tried to come out."

Johnson nodded.

"And I called Dan White, too," Bud added. "He said he'd be there in a minute."

"Okay," Johnson said. "Let's go."

The men drove the short distance to the trailer and got out of the truck. Roy Barber and Andy Alday converged on them, their shotguns at the ready.

It was now 2:45 on the morning of May 15, 1973, and as the men advanced on the trailer, they could feel a thick and terrible dread coagulating in the air around them. In response, they fell completely silent.

"There was not a sound," Johnson recalled, "not a word spoken. We just got out and headed toward the trailer. On the way, you could hear us racking shells into our shotguns."

Once again, as he had done only a few minutes earlier, Bud Alday made his way to the back door of the trailer, shoved the door open, and stepped back, unable to go in.

Johnson stepped around him and headed into the trailer. To the right, he could see a beer can on the kitchen countertop. Across the room, he noticed a few items that appeared to have been scattered across the small dining room table, and which looked like the general contents of a woman's purse, a compact, a mirror, hair brush, tube of lipstick.

His eyes drifted downward, lighting on the white panties beneath the kitchen table, then further to the right into the trailer's north bedroom, where he saw four legs hanging off the side of the bed.

"We knew something real bad had happened in there," Johnson recalled, "and we didn't want to mess anything up. Roy and Andy had already took up positions to guard the back and front of the trailer. We just waited, then, for the sheriff to get there."

Dan White pulled into the driveway five minutes later, and taking Johnson and Eddie Chance with him, moved decisively into the trailer.

What they saw during the next five minutes as they trudged from room to room inside the trailer was unimaginable.

In the bedroom to the right, just off the kitchen at the south end of the trailer, Ned and Shuggie lay facedown on the bed. Shuggie's face was pressed deeply into the bed, while Ned's was turned slightly to the side, revealing what appeared to be several wounds running in a jagged line down the right side of the face.

Following White, Johnson and Chance headed back through the kitchen and into the living room. On a sofa by the window, they found Jimmy Alday lying facedown, one long leg slumped off the edge of the sofa so that the left foot touched the floor.

White then proceeded back toward the far end of the trailer, while Johnson and Chance remained in the living room. They could see him standing in the doorway, staring down. "Here's Aubrey and the other one," he called, the only words spoken in the trailer.

By the time Sheriff White and the others made their way out of the trailer, all the missing Alday men had been accounted for.

Except for Mary.

Under other circumstances, she might have become a suspect in the murders, a distraught woman who'd suddenly snapped, shot several members of her family, and fled in her own car from the scene of the slaughter.

But then there were the panties, plain and white and lying where Mary, a very neat and very modest woman, never would have left them, crumpled and exposed beneath the kitchen table.

Wherever the killer or killers were, the men outside the trailer reasoned, if she were still alive, she was with them.

It was now past three in the morning, and as he stood beside the closed trailer door, Johnson could see Sheriff White talking to Bud Alday.

Inside the trailer, Ned, his brother, Aubrey, and his three sons, Shuggie, Jerry, and Jimmy, lay motionlessly in the darkness, a family's heart and soul. Alive they had done the heavy labor of the farm, cleared the land, plowed the fields, driven and repaired its cumbersome machinery. But they had done more than that, as Ernestine and the surviving wives and children would always remember. Ned had lit a thousand smiles with his good humor. Aubrey, with his broad red face, had never let a chance for laughter pass him by. Shuggie, stout and huggable, seemed always to have someone beneath his outstretched arm. Jerry, reticent and reserved, the least boisterous member of a boisterous family, had brought only Mary into his deepest confidence. And Jimmy, youngest of them all, a high school prankster renowned for his "dirty tricks," had just begun to throw off the last vestiges of boyhood.

Now they were all dead, and for the first time, the very traditions that had made the Alday family strong—particularly the sexual division of labor common to agrarian life—began to weaken it, while other, even more sinister, elements began to gnaw ceaselessly at its vital center, like a worm at the core. The saga of the farming Aldays had ended, and the saga of the "Alday victims" had begun.

Chapter Eight

During the early hours of May 15, the heartrending business begun just outside the Alday trailer as Sheriff White spoke to Bud Alday continued one phone call at a time.

At approximately 3:00 A.M. the telephone rang in the home of Patricia Alday Miller, Ernestine's thirty-two-year-old daughter.

"Patricia, this is Mama," Ernestine said in a voice that remained very firm, unshaken. "Something's happened. You need to come home."

"Home" meant the family homestead on River Road, and the tone in her mother's voice convinced Patricia that something dreadful must have happened. Quickly she roused her husband, the two of them throwing on the clothes they'd worn the day before, and headed for the door. On the way out, Patricia instinctively looked in on her sleeping children, the warmth of their room, the look of their bodies safe beneath the blankets already suggestive of a security and contentment she would never know again.

Outside there was a chill in the air, though enough light had broken for her to see a clear sky overhead, the promise of another bright spring day. The prospect of enjoying it had already dimmed in her mind. Her mother's voice had replaced it, cool, strained, female. *Why didn't Daddy call?*

She tried to press any further direct questions from her mind as the truck backed out of the driveway and headed toward River Road. On the way, the truck racing through the early morning mist, she kept her eyes straight ahead while her mind moved through a grim catalog of possibilities, images of death and injury in a steady stream of horrible conjectures. "It only took a few minutes to get to River Road," she remembered later, "but it was the longest drive I ever took."

At last, as they neared her brother Jerry's trailer, Patricia could see several cars lined up and down both sides of River Road. Her husband slowed down as the truck neared the trailer, then stopped dead on the road in front of it.

From her place in the passenger seat, Patricia could see Sheriff White standing a few yards from the trailer itself. He saw her, too, and strode down to where she sat nervously in the truck.

"They're all dead, Patricia," White told her solemnly. "And Mary's missing."

Patricia couldn't speak. She stared mutely at White, totally unable to imagine the "dead" he was referring to. The only name he'd mentioned was Mary's, the fact that although the others were dead, Mary was not among them. Her first thought would later astound her with its irrational oddity: *What has Mary done to my family?*

The truck eased on through the line of official vehicles toward the Alday homestead on River Road, Patricia now entering a state of near paralysis, her mind unable to arrange the disjointed information it had received during the preceding minutes.

Once at home, she found Ernestine seated at the dining table, utterly still, her hands folded in her lap, her gray hair neatly combed, as it always was, with little to betray the unimaginable blow she had received nearly an hour before.

For the next few minutes, as Patricia listened in disbelief, Ernestine related the evening's events, the nightlong search for Ned and the others, then the discovery of their bodies in the trailer. Through it all, she remained entirely controlled, holding her emotions in with a monumental determination.

"Mama was determined to be strong for the rest of us," Patricia remembered, "and she was strong, very, very strong. I think the fact that she didn't fall apart that night was the one thing that held us all together."

Still, it finally fell to Patricia to alert her two sisters, Nancy and Elizabeth, both of whom lived in Albany, and neither of whom had telephones. The only thing to do was to call the Albany Police Department and have one of its officers deliver a message to her sisters.

But what kind of message?

Barely able to conceive of the murders herself, and not knowing how to break such news to her sisters, Patricia penned an oblique note, one that gave no details as to what members of the family had been killed and made no reference whatever to the fact that they'd been murdered.

Once the message had been received, the Albany Police Department dispatched two officers to the home of Nancy Alday, the older of the two sisters.

"It was about five in the morning, and we were all sound asleep, of course," Nancy later remembered. "There was a knock at the door, and two Albany police officers were standing there."

As she glimpsed the two officers through the screen door, Nancy suddenly felt that sense of dread which had earlier seized Patricia when the phone rang in her bedroom.

"Is your husband here?" one of the officers asked.

"Yes."

"Can we speak to him?"

Nancy summoned her husband Paul to the door, then eased away, wondering, against all reason, if Paul were in some kind of trouble.

From her place a short distance away, she could hear the policemen speak to Paul for a moment, before returning to their car.

Paul approached her slowly and handed her the note the policemen had given him.

"It's from Patricia," he said.

Nancy read the note quickly, then looked up at Paul, still puzzled. "It just says that people in the family have been killed," she said. "Who? How?"

Paul shrugged. "We'd better go tell Elizabeth."

They dressed quickly and drove the short distance to the small house where Elizabeth lived with her husband, Wayne. While the two sisters sat in the living room, their husbands walked to a nearby store and called the Alday homestead in Donalsonville. Patricia answered the call, and told Paul and Wayne all she knew about the murders. Stunned, the two men walked dazedly back to Elizabeth's house. On the way, they agreed that they could not tell their wives what Patricia had told them. At the time, Elizabeth was seven months pregnant with her first child, and because of that, they were afraid that such a shock might bring on a miscarriage.

"Patricia had told our husbands everything," Nancy remembered, "but when they got back from the store, they just told us that some people in the family were dead, and after that they wouldn't say anything."

As a result, for the next hour and a half as Nancy and Elizabeth rode through the early morning light toward Donalsonville, they assumed that some of their first cousins, younger, teenage Aldays, had perhaps been killed in a terrible traffic accident. It was not until they reached Jerry's trailer that a considerably grimmer possibility entered their minds.

"There were police cars all over the place by the time we got to Jerry's," Nancy recalled, "but we kept going until we got to Mama's house."

Fay Alday met them in the driveway, standing grimly in the morning light, her face streaked with tears, as she ticked off the names. "Daddy's dead," she said. "And Shuggie. And Jerry. And Jimmy. And Uncle Aubrey." Then the final, unbelievable detail: "Somebody killed them."

At that moment, Nancy and Elizabeth felt as if the world had suddenly turned upside down, all the rules by which they'd lived, the little certainties of life, spilling into the void.

"I didn't know what to do or say," Nancy later remembered. "And it was like that for a long time. It was like you just couldn't absorb it, couldn't believe that it was really true."

By approximately 7:30 A.M., the focus had turned from identifying the dead and informing their relatives to a desperate search for their murderers, and for Mary Alday, who was still missing.

After talking to Bud Alday, Sheriff White had secured the crime scene from any intrusion. He'd summoned help from the Donalsonville police, from the sheriff's department in neighboring Decatur County, and had informed the Thomasville office of the Georgia Bureau of Investigation that a multiple homicide had occurred in Seminole County. GBI Agents T. R. Bentley and B. A. Turner then made the inevitable call to the GBI's Major Crime Squad in Atlanta, a newly created special division headed by a thirty-two-year-old agent with the unlikely name of Angel.

Of moderate height by law enforcement standards, his body compactly built, Georgia Bureau of Investigation Lieutenant Ronald Eugene Angel hardly looked angelic. He kept his hair in a close-cropped military style, dressed neatly but without ostentation, and let his smile do what it could to relieve the bulldog look of his face.

Born in Evansville, Indiana, on February 2, 1940, he had not lived an idyllic life. His family had come south after the small building his father had once maintained as a woodworking shop had been occupied by United States Government war industries during World War II.

Financially at sea, Angel's father spent the next twelve years wandering from town to town before settling in Chattanooga, Tennessee. As a result, Ronnie Angel had attended seven different schools before finally graduating from Rossville High near Chattanooga.

Added to this rootlessness was another problem, his mother's alcoholism. In later life, as he looked back upon his childhood, Angel could not remember a time when his mother had not needed a bottle. Thus, with his mother drunk most of the time, his father helpless to do anything about it, Angel grew up as "poor white trash," living in what amounted to shacks, one with an asphalt floor, others without indoor plumbing, all of them growing filthier by the hour as Angel's mother focused her attention on the bottle. "Even some of the moves were just because the house would get so dirty," he recalled years later. "I mean, it got so bad, my father would just say to hell with it, and we'd just pack up and move."

Within the turmoil of his early life, Angel found aid and comfort almost exclusively from people in uniform. In the fourth grade it was a traffic officer who would let him sit in his car and listen to the police radio. Later it was the men in the local fire station who always put him up when things at home disintegrated into unendurable chaos. "They always had a bunk for me when things were really bad at home, or when my parents split up, as they often did," Angel recalled. "I don't remember a time when the firemen ever turned me away."

At fourteen, Angel went to work as a soda jerk in a local drugstore in Rossville, Georgia. The pay was thirty-five cents an hour. Two years later, he went up a notch, working as a darkroom assistant to a local photographer.

In 1958, a tree-climbing incident forced Angel to give up his job as a medical photographer. Subsequently, he took a job as a radio dispatcher for the Fort Oglethorpe Police Department, and still later hired on as a security officer at a sprawling amusement park not far from Chattanooga.

Quickly bored with such a lonely vigil, Angel applied for a job with the Georgia State Patrol. He was hired the following year, then steadily rose from driver's license examiner to trooper, and finally into the more prestigious ranks of the newly formed Georgia Bureau of Investigation.

The GBI had been created specifically to deal with a form of gang activity that was peculiar to the rural South, and, like its considerably more sophisticated northern counterpart, had its roots in Prohibition. By the mid-sixties, parts of northeastern Georgia were almost entirely controlled by redneck gangs. Brutal, ruthless, and infinitely resourceful, these gangs were usually concentrated within a dense family structure that was all but impenetrable to undercover agents or informants.

Assigned to the Gainesville office of the GBI, it was Angel's assignment to move against the gangs with full force. He did so, going undercover to arrange illegal liquor buys in an effort that resulted in the destruction of fifty-four bootleg operations. In response the gangs decided to assassinate Angel and a local district attorney. In the latter case, they were successful.

At 7:00 A.M. on August 7, 1967, Angel was put in charge of coordinating the investigation into the district attorney's murder. He did not return to his home again until November 24. The result was four arrests, four convictions, and three death sentences, "just what they deserved," as Angel thought of it, for the crime they had committed.

That "people" should get what they deserve was a notion Angel had never doubted. Methodical and dedicated, honed sharp by his long experience with southern violence, he moved determinedly against those whose malignancy seemed as obvious to him as any hope for their eventual rehabilitation seemed futile. Taught by his own early deprivations that bad experiences did not necessarily create bad people, he was the sort of man in whom the quality of mercy could fairly quickly become strained. He did not like sob stories, and hardly ever lingered in rooms where they were being told, and even the fact that over the years he had adopted numerous foster children, rescuing them from backgrounds markedly similar to his own, had not softened the bedrock of his ideological conservatism. He believed that children needed love, stability, and the presence of authority figures worthy of their affection and respect. In the service of that belief he was willing to make grave personal and financial sacrifices. Nonetheless, he did not believe that the absence of these positive forces were in themselves responsible for creating depraved and murderous human beings, or that such absence could be used to justify their acts.

"My own early life was a lot like theirs," he would say years later of the Alday killers. "Now, I'm not a saint by any means, but I didn't walk into a trailer in Donalsonville, Georgia, and kill six people who had never done me the slightest harm. The Isaacs bunch did that because they were no damn good . . . period."

Nothing in the characters or backgrounds of the four men he would later arrest for the Alday murders would serve to change his mind.

PURSUIT

Chapter Nine

When Ronnie Angel arrived at the state headquarters of the Georgia Bureau of Investigation in Atlanta at nine o'clock on the morning of May 15, he realized immediately that something very serious had happened, and that it was probably a good deal more than a departmental purge or administrative shake-up. The people he saw scurrying along the corridors or gathered in small groups in the adjoining offices were on full alert, as if in response to a sudden alarm. There was a dark humming in the air, along with that peculiar excitement which always signaled a sudden gearing up of the agency's staff and resources. Angel had been around long enough by then to know that it was the sort of atmosphere that could only be generated by one thing: somewhere during the night or early morning hours a very serious crime had been committed in the state of Georgia.

"It was obvious that something terrible had happened," he remembered years later. "But even I couldn't have guessed just how bad it was, that it was the single most heinous crime that had ever been committed in the history of the state."

He was about to find out.

Within moments of his arrival, Deputy Director Jim Stanley came into Angel's office and told him that there had been what he called a "major homicide" in Donalsonville, Georgia. Stanley went on to say that Major Beardsley, the GBI director, had decided it would be handled by the Major Case Squad, the division Angel now headed, and that Angel would be in charge of the investigation.

Angel dispatched Agent Jim Duff to Donalsonville by car, then headed for the local airport to meet Dr. Larry Howard, the forensic pathologist who'd been assigned to the case.

When he reached the small airport on the outskirts of Atlanta, Angel could hardly believe what he saw, a rickety, moth-eaten old wheezer of an airplane that Dr. Howard owned and that he fully intended to fly to Donalsonville himself. The whole structure of the plane looked alarmingly unsteady, and the windshield was so old, cracked, and stained that Howard could not even see through it. Instead, during the long, uneasy flight to Donalsonville, he leaned out over the side of the plane in order to navigate it, staring at the blue expanse before him and the steadily flattening farmland several thousand feet below.

On the way, Angel went over what was known about the case so far, amazed at just how little it was. Some people had been murdered, but no one at GBI headquarters had been sure of just how many, whether they were male or female, young or old, or even precisely when or how the murders had taken place. As to the critical issues of suspects and motivation no one had a clue, and the only thing Angel had been given to understand was that a hippie commune was situated not too far from the murder site, and that some "hippies" had been seen in the area not long before the murder. Just what he needed, Angel thought wearily as he glanced toward the ground below, some Charles Manson type on the loose in southern Georgia.

He looked at his watch. It was 10:00 A.M. He would not sleep again for four days.

Meanwhile, in Donalsonville, Mary Alday was still missing. As he stood near the Alday trailer, watching Mary's dog as it darted back and forth from the driveway to a spot down River Road, Jerry Godby recalled the two cars he'd seen the preceding afternoon. He was reasonably sure that one of them had been Mary Alday's, and after a moment, he decided to take a drive down the road in the same direction as that strange convoy had taken not quite twenty-four hours before.

Once in his truck, he drove slowly, glancing left and right, not quite sure what he was looking for, but only looking, hoping that something would strike him as he tried to retrace the route of the cars. He passed the Alday homestead, its yard and driveway now cluttered with the cars and trucks of their neighbors, then on along their recently planted fields until he reached the peanut fields he'd been spraying when the cars had passed him the final time. This was the last time he'd seen them, but he had noted their direction, and now he decided to drive on down the road, following it as far as the cars would have had to follow it before turning left or right at the nearest crossroads.

He was drifting even more slowly now, his foot barely touching the accelerator as he glanced about, meticulously searching the bordering woods. They were thick with summer growth, the tall oaks and pines towering above the forest understory of dogwood and gallberry, sweetleaf and greenbrier, all so dense that Godby could only see a few yards before everything disappeared behind an impenetrable wall of broad green leaves and brightly colored wildflowers.

Even so, the outer reaches of the forest were visible, and it was a sudden disarray within them that drew Godby's attention as he continued down the road. At first it was no more than a few broken branches, slender tendrils of weed and vine that looked as if they'd been snapped nearly in two and now hung perpendicular to the ground. But as he approached them, he could see a set of tire tracks that led down a narrow, rarely traveled dirt road and into the deepening woods. He pulled onto the shoulder of the road, stopped, and peered down the wooded path. It was scarcely larger than a footpath, but the tire tracks disappeared down it anyway, as if whoever had taken the route had been determined to see it to the end. All along its narrow route, he could see more broken branches, along with a scattering of weeds that looked as if they'd been pressed down into the soil as the car's tires had moved heavily over them. Beyond that, there was only the lush green of the deepening forest, a familiar, pastoral landscape that he had never feared before but that now filled him with a sense of icy dread. He decided not to venture farther into the woods alone.

Mary's dog had been shut up in a barn by the time Godby got back to the trailer, and the area around the trailer seemed curiously silent without its frantic barking. There was no shortage of people, however. They were everywhere, some huddled about the various vehicles that filled the driveway and lined both sides of the road, others in small knots in the yard or out in the surrounding fields. If he wanted to assemble a party to help him search the woods, he had plenty of people to choose from. As he approached the house, he saw Espy Gray, Max Trawick, Wayne Easom, and Ray and Rudolph Spooner. He'd known them all for quite some time, and it struck him that they were exactly the kind of men he could depend on, courageous, but not reckless.

"I think I may have found something," he told them, "down a little road in the woods, not far from where I saw Mary's car go by yesterday.

I think we should go down there and check it out."

None of the men hesitated. Fully armed, the black barrels of their rifles weaving gently in the summer sunlight, Godby and the others immediately made their way back to the small dirt road where Godby had first noticed the tire tracks and broken undergrowth.

"Right there," he said, pointing to the strange indentation in the woods. "What do you think?"

The men agreed that it was worth pursuing. Fanning out slightly so that they walked in a short flank rather than a column, they advanced through the thickening brush, their eyes carefully surveying the area, their ears attuned to the slightest sound from anywhere around them.

For a time, the men saw nothing. The woods were quiet except for the summer birds and the whir of insects. Here and there slender columns of bright sunlight fell through the dense overhanging foliage. Nothing looked out of place.

Then, at a spot about a hundred feet from the road, Godby approached a pine tree that appeared to have been recently damaged. A large section of bark had been stripped away, leaving the pale white wood fully exposed. From its height and appearance, it looked to Godby as if the tree had been raked by the bumper of a car. But where would a car have been going? And why would it have been moving so carelessly? He glanced about, his eyes searching for the car, but saw nothing further, and so he walked on.

He'd only moved fifty feet deeper into the woods when he heard Espy Gray's voice ring through the trees, calling tensely for the others.

Angel let out a long sigh of relief at approximately 11:00 A.M. when he stepped out of Dr. Howard's tiny Cessna and let his feet touch the earth again. He walked shakily to the waiting car and pulled himself in beside the trooper who sat behind the wheel. The radio was alive with traffic about a mysterious car that several local residents had located in the woods of the Cummings estate.

"Cummings estate?" Angel asked one of the local lawmen. "Is that anywhere near the Alday place?"

"About six miles from it."

"Let's go check on the car first then," Angel said.

Twenty minutes later he arrived at the small dirt road identified in the radio dispatches, and headed down it. He'd only gone a short distance when he realized that the radio traffic had purposely concealed the profound nature of Espy Gray's discovery. A car had been located. That much was true. But it had not been found alone.

Sprawled across the forest bramble in an area incongruously adorned with the bright buds of summer wildflowers, Mary Alday's nude body lay facedown, her head turned slightly to the left, her hands tucked just beneath her breasts so that both elbows were nearly parallel to the upper part of her rib cage. The stark, midday sun fell so brightly on her pale skin that her body appeared to glow luminously from out of the deep shade that surrounded her, an eerie patch of blinding white that rested motionlessly on a sea of green.

As he drew nearer, Angel could see how her dark hair lay in a tangled mass on her bare shoulders, her body's only cover. All her jewelry, if she'd had any, had already been stripped from her hands and neck and ears.

Angel knelt down for a closer look. He could see no ligature marks on her hands or legs to indicate that she'd ever been forcibly restrained.

As to the cause of death, it could hardly have been more obvious. Dried blood had caked in a broad swath from a large wound in her upper back. A second gunshot wound was clearly visible near the back of her head. The rest of her body had been so ravaged by ant bites that for an instant she appeared to Angel, as he stared silently at her, as if she'd been raked repeatedly by distant shotgun fire.

Only a few yards from the body, Angel noticed a few pieces of clothing scattered across the forest floor. One by one, he examined them before dropping them into evidence bags. There was the bottom half of a turquoise pants suit that appeared damp and soiled in the crotch. A few feet away, its matching checkered blouse, grimy with dirt and forest debris, lay in a tangled mass amid a scattering of leaves. A white bra rested nearby, but as he glanced about, Angel realized that there were no panties to go with the bra, nor any other female underwear in the vicinity either of Mary Alday's body or her other discarded clothes. Their absence suggested that unlike her male relatives, Mary Alday had been subjected to even more than murder.

After his initial observation of the body and clothing, Angel paced the area carefully, concentrating on the scene as minutely as he could, pointing out and gathering up various items that appeared to have been abandoned at the murder site. Up ahead, at a distance of perhaps a hundred feet, obscured within the shadowy light of the woods, he saw a car, its dark green exterior blending almost seamlessly into the surrounding woodlands. As he neared it, he could see that it was a 1968 Chevrolet Super Sport and that it bore a temporary Pennsylvania license plate, number 2029-301. Pennsylvania was far to the north, hundreds of miles away, and as Angel began circling the car, gathering what little information he could before the lab crew arrived, he sensed that what he'd already been told about the murders was probably true, that no one from Seminole County would have wished any harm upon the Aldays, that their killers had been strangers who'd swept in from afar, the kind of wanton, shiftless drifters who emerged from time to time to carry out some appalling act on villagers who still insisted, despite all his advice to the contrary, that they need not lock their doors.

For the next hour or so Angel continued to process the green Super Sport. Nick Campbell, the chief of the Latent Fingerprints Section of the GBI, had arrived from the Alday trailer by then, and Angel assisted him in lifting various prints from the car's interior. After that, he repeated his initial search of the area around Mary Alday's body, looking for the slightest hint of something the killer or killers might have left behind.

In the meantime his associate, Agent Horace Waters, was doing the same at the Alday trailer. It was now almost noon, and the heat in the trailer was stifling, but Waters moved slowly and meticulously from room to room, his disbelief mounting with each successive step.

In the north bedroom he found the bodies of Ned and Shuggie Alday as they lay facedown on the bed. A camouflage jacket had been flung over Ned's shoulder, but with the body turned slightly to the left and the side of his head exposed, Waters could see several gunshot wounds that moved in a tight pattern along the side of his face.

Shuggie Alday lay beside his father, but at an angle, so that his feet lay across Ned's legs, as if draped over them. A small towel had been wrapped around his head and was now encrusted in dried blood.

In the living room, Waters found Jimmy Alday's body, also facedown, with what appeared to be a single wound in the back of his head.

After a moment, Waters headed back into the south bedroom where Jerry and Aubrey Alday lay side by side, facedown on the bed. As his eyes lingered on them a moment, he noticed that Aubrey's fingers lay folded over Jerry's, as if, in the last moment, he'd reached out to hold his nephew's hand.

* * *

The bodies had been removed by the time Angel arrived at the trailer, and yet, as he moved through its small rooms, it was not difficult for him to imagine the lives of the people who had arrived there the previous afternoon, or how crowded with death the trailer must have seemed to those who had toured it while the bodies were still inside. It was very small, a miniature house, with everything scaled down in a radical compactness. The bedrooms barely provided space to walk around the beds, and Jerry and Mary Alday had crowded them even more with their few possessions. There were tiny bureaus and an old-fashioned sewing machine on top of which Mary's modest sewing kit rested, still open, its tiny interior chambers crowded with needles and multicolored threads. The bedroom closets were stuffed with work clothes, but only a few suits, the couple's "Sunday best" relegated to a single narrow section of the closet's limited space.

Judging from the trailer, Jerry and Mary Alday had lived a modest, pared-down life, but a neat, orderly, decent one. Within their small cabinets and dresser drawers, Angel found no drugs, no pornography, no hateful letters, no bills that had not been paid. He found nothing locked away or covered up or in any way concealed. "With the Aldays," he would later say, "what you saw was what you got, the salt of the earth."

By early afternoon, the Pennsylvania license plate had been traced and Angel was on the phone with Sergeant Larry Good of the Pennsylvania State Police.

According to Good, three inmates had escaped from the Poplar Hill Correctional Institute in Wimpimco, Maryland, on May 5, 1973. Later they had picked up the younger brother of two of them, fifteen-year-old William Carroll Isaacs, known as Billy, in Baltimore. After that they'd added two young girls to their party, and subsequently gone on a protracted spree of petty crime, burglarizing an assortment of houses before finally abandoning the girls on a street corner.

It was presumably at that point, Good went on, that things had gotten meaner. The four men had stolen a truck in McConnellsburg, Pennsylvania. But the theft hadn't gone smoothly. They'd been spotted and followed by a nineteen-year-old boy named Richard Wayne Miller.

"Where'd he see them go?" Angel asked.

That was a question Pennsylvania authorities had not yet been able to answer, Good replied, because Miller had not been seen since he'd disappeared down the road behind the stolen truck.

"He just vanished?" Angel asked.

Without a trace, Good told him, despite considerable local efforts to locate him. In fact, Good added, the discovery of the green Super Sport in the Georgia woods was the first lead he'd gotten in many days, since the car was the one Richard Miller had been driving as he'd followed the four escapees down U.S. 30 the day he'd disappeared.

"And nobody's spotted Miller since then?" Angel asked.

"No."

"So it's possible he's still with them," Angel said.

"It's possible."

"But that would be against his will, right?" Angel asked. "They're not the type he'd have gone off with."

"Absolutely not," Good said. "He's a very clean-cut type of kid."

"All right," Angel said, "let's go on with the three escapees."

For the next few minutes, Angel took careful notes as Good gave him full physical descriptions of the Isaacs brothers, Coleman, and Dungee. To Angel, they seemed small in more ways than their size. They were stunted men with stunted lives, petty offenders, dropouts, losers, the northern urban equivalent of the rural redneck outlaws he'd been tracking all his life.

Still, for all their shiftlessness and criminality, they had committed no acts of violence so far, a fact that Angel found surprising. It was as if something had suddenly snapped in them, shot them up to a terrible slaughter that nothing in their backgrounds could accurately have predicted.

And yet the escape Good had described struck Angel as equally arbitrary and illogical, the same irrational quality at work, though with none of the reckless, annihilating violence that now gave a sudden, terrible urgency to his pursuit. Clearly, the Maryland escapees were precisely the kind of men who had lost all sense of proportion, the type for whom the ordinary limits of human behavior were mere spindly, insubstantial obstacles in the path of their flight. As long as they were at large, he thought as he hung up the phone after his conversation with Larry Good, not one person in the whole vast country was entirely safe.

At approximately 10:00 P.M. Dr. Howard finished the autopsies he'd been conducting on the six members of the Alday family. He'd been working at the Evans Funeral Home in Donalsonville nearly all afternoon and evening as one body after another was wheeled into its small embalming room.

The final results of his autopsies indicated that Ned Alday had been shot six times with two different pistols, .22 and .32 calibers. Aubrey Alday had been shot once with a .38. Shuggie Alday had been shot once with a .380-caliber pistol, Jerry Alday had been shot four times with a .22-caliber pistol, Jimmy Alday had been shot twice with a .22-caliber pistol, as had Mary Alday, who, Dr. Howard concluded, had also been raped, probably more than once.

Angel was standing in the room when Howard finished the last of the autopsies. By then it was awash with the results of the ones that had gone before. The heavy stench of the bodies hung in the air around him. But it was the ravaged appearance of the room that affected him the most. It looked like an army field hospital, a place where, after battle, the bodies had been brought back to lie, gutted and alone, until they could be hauled away. That they were all members of a single family struck Angel as nearly beyond belief. He could not imagine the level of grief and loss that he knew must now be sweeping down upon the Aldays who remained alive.

Eleven miles away, in the Alday homestead on River Road, the remaining members of the Alday family were dealing with the murders as best they could. While scores of neighbors gathered inside the house or poured out onto the porch and surrounding yard, Ernestine worked to comfort her children. Elizabeth, fearing a miscarriage, had been heavily sedated, while the others fought their grief by busying themselves with the huge amounts of foods their neighbors had been showering upon them for the past few hours. No one in Seminole County could remember ever having seen anything like it. On tables throughout the house, scores of cakes and pies, along with all manner of meat and vegetables, had been brought in by a community that had decided to extend itself fully in a family's time of unimaginable trouble. It was the one bright spot in those first dark days, and in the years that followed it would surface from time to time in the minds of Ernestine and her children. "If you can say that anything good can be taken from all this," Nancy would say in July of 1990, nearly seventeen years after the murders, "it was how we felt about what our neighbors did for us."

All through that long day and deep into the night, they continued to arrive at the Alday home, bringing with them what they could, offering whatever help they might extend from their own marginal existences. Late on the evening of that first day, one of them, Eunice Braswell, drew Ernestine away from the others and solemnly pressed a five-dollar bill into her hand. "This is for you," she said. It was a gesture Ernestine would never forget, something that seemed to rise like a flower from the richest soil on earth.

In Colquitt, Georgia, however, things took a different turn. In the small town approximately eighteen miles from where their daughter's body had been found, the mother and father of Mary Alday were receiving friends and neighbors much as the Aldays had been doing for the last two days in Seminole County. Mary's death had sent shock waves through that community as well, but the agonizing details of Mary's last hours had been concealed from Mary's mother. Although only sixty-two years old, Mrs. Campbell had been in failing health for several years, and because of that it had been determined that the actual circumstances of Mary's death would be too much for her to bear. Consequently, she had been told only that Mary had been shot and had died instantly from the wound.

But at some point during the evening, a neighbor unintentionally revealed as much as was known about Mary's last moments, including the fact that she had been the last to die, having witnessed the murders of her husband and in-laws, and that she had been found nude in the woods and had probably been raped.

Shortly after being told the horrifying details of her daughter's torment, Mrs. Campbell sank into a diabetic coma. Only a few hours later, she died of what her doctor later described as the combined effects of "a diabetic condition and grief over her daughter's slaying."

It was a determination of cause of death with which Ronnie Angel wholeheartedly concurred. "I always thought of her as the seventh Georgia victim," he would say years later, "because, really, it was just like those boys put a gun to her head, too."

Meanwhile, as the night was steadily deepening along the Mississippi-Alabama border, Wesley Williamson decided to go into Livingston, a small town just inside the Alabama state line and almost 275 miles west of Donalsonville. As he headed toward town, he saw what appeared to be a dark-haired man and a slender, blond-haired young girl as they trudged wearily along the shoulders of the road. They looked tired, and Williamson particularly felt bad for the girl who, from a distance, seemed very thin and gangly. He slowed as he went by them, then swung over to the side of the road to pick them up. From the dusty glass of his rearview mirror, and through the scarred wooden stocks of the hunting rifles that hung in a gun rack over the back seat, he could see them rushing toward him eagerly, their lean figures faintly illuminated by the red glow of his taillights. As they neared, he noticed that the blond-haired young girl was, in fact, a boy, and something in the way he and the other man came rushing toward him, the cold, hungry look in their eyes, warned him off immediately. He turned back to the wheel, and without so much as a backward glance, plunged his foot down on the accelerator and sped away, leaving the still rapidly pursuing men in a cloud of yellow dust behind his spinning tires.

Several hours later a solitary police cruiser turned onto the Boyd Cutoff as it made its nightly rounds along the back roads of Sumter County. Up ahead, just off to the right near an abandoned construction site, the car's lone patrolman could see a blue and white 1968 Chevrolet Impala as it rested motionlessly along the narrow shoulders of the road. He drew his car over to the right and pulled in behind it. The car bore Alabama license plates, and before getting out, the officer recorded the number in his notebook. Then, his flashlight held loosely in his hand, the other dangling freely at the grip of his revolver, he slowly advanced on the car, shining his light into its dark interior. There was nothing inside to identify the car in any way, so he returned to his patrol car and radioed in the make, model, license, and serial numbers. There was nothing to do now but wait for the report to come back. Only five minutes later, it did. The car he'd discovered was registered to Mary C. Alday of Route 3, Donalsonville, Georgia, the report informed him, and was wanted in connection with her murder.

Chapter Ten

A ngel and Waters were just leaving the Evans Funeral Home, on their way to their motel room to go over the day's findings and plan an investigative strategy for the next day when they were notified to call Sheriff Melvin Stephens of the Sumter County Sheriff's Department in Livingston, Alabama.

Angel returned the call immediately and listened, both surprised and exhilarated by the rapidity with which the case was breaking, as Stephens told him about the blue and white Impala which had been found during a routine neighborhood patrol only a hour or so before.

"One of our patrolmen just spotted it sitting on the side of the road," Stephens said. "Then we ran it through NCIC, and it came up that you were looking for it, that it was connected to a homicide in Georgia."

"Six homicides," Angel said.

"Six?"

"Yes."

"So, the report was right?" Stephens asked. "This is the car you're looking for, the one involved in the Alday thing, the one that's all over the news?"

"Yes, it is," Angel said.

For a moment, he entertained the faint hope that the Maryland escapees might actually have been spotted.

"Did any of your people see anybody around the car?" he asked quickly.

"No."

If the men were not there, Angel thought, perhaps they might not be far away. "How about the car?" he asked. "Did anybody have any idea how long it might have been there?"

"No," Stephens said.

"Where's the car now?"

"Right where we found it," Stephens said. "Once we knew you wanted it, I mean, for a homicide, we just posted a guard out there."

Stephens had done the right thing in not ordering his own men to process the car, and Angel was glad of it. "We're on our way," he assured him, "we'll be there as soon as we can. Just keep the whole area secure."

"Nobody'll get near it," Stephens assured him.

Angel immediately dispatched Agent Jim Duff in a crop-duster biplane to Livingston to secure the Impala, while he, Waters, and several Crime Lab officials followed by car. Officers of the Alabama State Patrol met them at the Alabama state line and escorted them for nearly four hours as they moved the rest of the way across the state to Livingston.

"It was like a whirlwind from then on," Angel remembered. "Things breaking almost every second. There was no time to get tired, no time to come up with a theory or a plan of action, no time to do anything, but just stay on top of all that was going on."

Several hours before the discovery of Mary Alday's car, as soon as it had gotten dark enough to move out of the woods surrounding the Boyd Cutoff, Carl had finally decided to make a move, and had roused Wayne, Billy, and George from the idleness that had overtaken them for the past few hours. Far in the distance, they could see the lights of Livingston flickering brightly through the night, and it was not hard to surmise that somewhere along its streets there might be a car too carelessly surveilled. It had already been determined that strolling through a quiet southern town with an arsenal of weapons might draw a certain amount of unwelcome attention, so most of their more obtrusive weapons, particularly their assortment of rifles and shotguns, had already been jettisoned at the Boyd Cutoff, while several of the remaining ones were abandoned in the hills above Livingston.

Traveling light, now armed only with those few weapons that could be nestled beneath their jackets, Carl led his ragtag army out of the woods and down into the dark, nearly empty village. With the Impala now abandoned, his first order of business was to find another form of transportation. For even without a weaving array of black rifle barrels, they would look suspicious enough, as Carl well knew, three white men and one black, all of them hunched and unwashed, straggling along narrow village streets or winding country roads. Under such conditions, a car was their only hope.

As he walked, Carl kept his eyes on the alert for an easy mark, a car parked in an empty parking lot or sitting alone on a quiet street.

To his delight, he found one within a few minutes. Turning a corner onto one of the residential blocks directly off the downtown streets, Carl saw something glint in the silvery street lamp that illuminated the area. It was a set of keys dangling innocently from the ignition of a two-toned Chevrolet Caprice. His eyes shot over to Wayne, back to the keys, and back to Wayne again. Then the two men smiled at each other as George, dazed as usual, and Billy, now beginning to crumble, still staggered by the violence he had witnessed at the Alday trailer, straggled up behind.

It was nearly dawn on the morning of May 17 when Georgia officials began processing the scene in Livingston, Alabama. While the lab crew powdered Mary Alday's deserted Impala, trying to pick up latent fingerprints, Angel and Waters searched the surrounding area for any indication as to where the men had gone after abandoning it.

Not far from the car, on a gently sloping downgrade, they saw a piece of cloth hanging from a rickety barbed wire fence. They headed down the slope and into the woods where they found several items of clothing scattered in the brush. One of them caught their attention instantly. It was a high school jacket shaped like the varsity jackets Angel remembered from his own days in high school. On the front, it bore the insignia of the Future Farmers of America, along with the letters FFA. It was the sort of jacket worn in rural areas throughout the United States, but as he turned it around, Angel saw that this jacket had come from a particular place, its town of origin written in large block letters across the back of the jacket:

McCONNELLSBURG, PENNSYLVANIA

It could hardly be doubted that this was Richard Wayne Miller's jacket, and since he had last been seen pursuing the Maryland escapees, its presence in a field near Mary Alday's abandoned car indisputably linked the Isaacs brothers and George Dungee to the Alday murders. Certainly it left no lingering doubts in Angel's mind as to the identities of the men who had stolen Mary Alday's car after wiping out nearly an entire family.

The question now was where exactly were the men from Baltimore?

This was not the only question, however. For the fate of Richard Miller had not yet been discovered either. It was unlikely that he was still alive, Angel thought, but if dead, where was his body? Pennsylvania authorities had described very thorough and extensive efforts to locate it, all of which had been unsuccessful.

Since Miller's body had not been discovered since his disappearance, it was conceivable that he had still been alive during or immediately after the Alday murders. If so, then the killers might have decided to dispose of his body in Livingston just as they had disposed of so much else.

After gathering up the evidence found near the barbed wire fence, Angel and Waters headed farther out into the woods in search of Miller's body and other evidence that might have been left behind by the Maryland escapees. They had gone only a few yards when they came upon an astonishing scene. In a small clearing, still in sight of the road, they found evidence that the Maryland escapees had waited many hours in the woods near Mary Alday's car. Scattered all about were cigarette packs, soda cans, potato chip and other junk food wrappers, and an impressive assortment of weapons.

The discovery of this campsite virtually within view of Mary Alday's car was important. It clearly indicated that the wanted men had not had a second car with them at the time the Impala had been abandoned. Because of that, Angel guessed that they had remained in the woods until nightfall, at which time, in all probability, they had gone in search of another car. Following these assumptions, Angel quickly contacted police officials in Livingston in an effort to find out if anyone in the area had reported a stolen car. The answer came back very quickly in a call from Larry Moody, chief of the Livingston Police Department. Between 8:30 and 9:30 P.M., he told Angel, a car had been reported stolen by P. C. Mincus, Jr., a resident of Livingston.

"What kind of car?" Angel asked.

"A 1973 Chevrolet Caprice."

"Color?"

"Dark green with a bronze top."

"Where was it stolen from?"

"From in front of a residence. Mike Wise's residence."

"Is that anywhere near the Boyd Cutoff?"

Yes, Chief Moody told him, no more than a few blocks away.

With the discovery of the stolen-car report, Angel now felt certain he knew exactly what car the Maryland escapees were driving. He transferred that information via NCIC, and a nationwide alert was put out for the recovery of P. C. Mincus's car.

"At that moment, I thought it was only a matter of time before we had them," Angel said later. "They were just a few hours ahead of us, just a few hours, and we knew who they were, what they looked like, the car they were driving. I could almost feel them in the palm of my hand."

Judging from their actions, neither Carl nor Wayne felt the slightest intimation of impending capture. Instead, they obliviously continued the same erratic movement that had characterized their journey since leaving Maryland. As they drove, they talked about various destinations, shifting radically from one moment to the next, dreams of California or Mexico or Canada flashing through their collective imaginations like images projected from a magic lantern.

In the back seat, George hummed to himself or stared vacantly at the whizzing landscape, while Billy sat frozen beside him, his own mind now repeatedly playing over its own terrified scenario, as he wondered if perhaps he had already been selected as his brothers' next victim. Certainly his own edginess had served to make them edgy, as well, and Billy had had enough recent experience with his older brothers, particularly Carl, to know just how wired for sudden violence he already was. To completely break down in front of him might result in more than a loss of face. There was something in the furtive glances and low muttering he had observed between Carl and Wayne that suggested to him that he might be just as expendable to them as the Aldays, and because of that, he labored as best he could to keep his self-control.

Meanwhile, through the long aimless night following the murders, Carl and Wayne jabbered incessantly as the stolen green Caprice crossed and recrossed the Georgia-Alabama line, before, without any stated reason or explanation, Carl suddenly veered it westward into Mississippi.

Nor had these ramblings been uneventful. Just on the western outskirts of Jackson, as they had found themselves cruising along a deserted two-lane blacktop road, they'd seen a car approach, slowing as it neared them.

As it drew closer, they could see that it was a Mississippi State Patrol car. Carl continued driving, staring straight ahead until the two cars passed. Then, from the rearview mirror, he could see the patrol car come to a sudden brake-slamming halt, then make a hard doughnut turn in the middle of the road.

"They spotted us," Carl said to Wayne who sat, as always, in the shotgun position of the front seat.

Billy and George, both still drowsy with the long ride, straightened up immediately, their eyes darting toward the rear where they could see the patrol car closing in behind them, its lights flashing.

Wayne glared at Carl. "What are you going to do?"

Carl slammed his foot on the accelerator. "Let me know the first road you see coming up on the right side," he said grimly.

It came up only a few minutes later, a dirt driveway that led up to a rickety, unpainted wooden house. Just behind them, the patrol car had disappeared behind a curve in the road just long enough for Carl to make a hard, brutal turn into the drive, skidding wildly as the back tires spun to the left, lifting clouds of grit and dust as they churned up the dark driveway before coming to a stop.

Once the car slid to a halt, Carl and Wayne leaped out and took up positions behind it, their guns already leveled at the driveway, while Billy and George hunkered down, cowering together in the back seat, both too petrified to leave the car.

Seconds later the patrol car sped by, its siren blaring as it raced past the driveway before disappearing entirely into the night.

Carl lowered the shotgun and laughed. "That's one lucky bastard," he told Wayne.

Only a short time later, still vaguely heading west, the green Caprice pulled into yet another small Mississippi town. As it approached a four way stop, the men inside saw a police car edge its way into the intersection. Glancing to the right, they saw a second patrol car ease into the intersection, then to the left, a third.

Genius was hardly required for Carl and the others to suspect that more than mere coincidence was necessary to explain such a sudden convergence of law enforcement on a single, isolated intersection.

In the complete silence that fell inside the Caprice as it continued to roll toward the intersection, Billy and George remained in the back seat, sitting motionlessly while waiting to see what Carl and Wayne would do.

In the front seat, neither of the two men discussed the issue. Instead, they sat stiffly and silently, staring straight ahead as Carl gently pressed down on the accelerator and let the car cruise smoothly through the intersection.

Any relief that might have swept through the shadowy interior of P. C. Mincus's Chevy as it glided through the intersection was to be short-lived. For in a gesture fully characteristic of the reckless bravado with which Carl attempted to live out his fantasies of outlaw grandeur, he suddenly punched the accelerator, cut the wheels to the right, and careened so violently around a nearby corner that the car had gone up on two wheels for an instant before slamming back down on the hard pavement once again.

From the back window, a thunderstruck Billy and George could see one of the patrol cars jerking forward and backward as it struggled to maneuver itself out of the narrow street and give chase. Then it suddenly came to rest, its flashing light finally blinking off, leaving nothing but the lights of the small town disappearing behind the men in the green Caprice, and only the dense rural darkness up ahead.

Once again Carl felt the exhilaration of escape, the high rapture of thumbing his nose at the law. To Wayne and George, it was an outrageous exploit that served to demonstrate not only Carl's daring but his invulnerability. To Billy, however, it had demonstrated something else, the terrible depth of his brother's self-destructiveness, his Bonnie-and-Clyde urge to die in a hail of gunfire, even at the cost of taking the rest of them with him. Carl, it seemed, was on a suicide mission, and as Billy watched his brother's dark hair slapping in the wind that rushed through the car's unlighted interior, it struck him that in all likelihood he was destined to die with him, all of them together, to pay the debt they had incurred on River Road. There was no talking to him or reasoning with him. Carl Isaacs was now on autopilot, his mind entirely propelled by its wildest and most reckless fantasies, a death ship rushing toward the rocky bar.

And yet, as the Caprice sailed on through the thick southern night, even Billy had to admit that Carl had done it again, spit on the sheriff and lived to tell about it.

The mythical sheriff, however, was not finished yet.

Chapter Eleven

On the morning of May 17, the community's only newspaper, the *Donalsonville News*, a weekly published each Thursday morning, began its coverage of the murders with the bold headline:

COMMUNITY SHOCKED BY MURDER OF
SIX MEMBERS OF THE ALDAY FAMILY

The following story related the murders and the discovery of the bodies, along with police speculation that based on the condition of the interior of the trailer, the Alday victims had been killed without a struggle, probably immediately upon entering the trailer. Only Mary, the paper noted, appeared to have been "running from someone" at the time of her murder.

The paper went on to quote Gil Kelley, foreman of the coroner's jury, to the effect that Mary Alday had probably been followed home by "four or five hippie-type men" who'd been seen pulling into her yard late Monday afternoon.

The paper noted that Governor Jimmy Carter had dispatched officials to Donalsonville to work on the case, and went on to speculate that police were searching for several escapees from a Maryland prison camp in connection with the murders. According to the director of the Georgia Bureau of Investigation, William Beardsley, the paper said, so much evidence linked the escapees to the murders that at the present time there was "no point in looking for anybody else."

* * *

At about the time the people of Donalsonville were reading their first local reports of the murders, the Isaacs brothers and George Dungee stopped for breakfast at a small restaurant in northern Alabama. By then they had crossed and recrossed into Mississippi several times, moving randomly, their vision of a western escape decidedly dulled by the two near-captures in Mississippi. While Wayne went into the restaurant, Carl remained behind the wheel, glancing occasionally into the rearview mirror where he could see Billy and George staring vacantly ahead.

Minutes later, Wayne scrambled quickly back into the car. While in the restaurant, he told the others, he'd seen a customer reading a local newspaper. "It was all about the killings," he said excitedly. "I couldn't see what it said, but I figured it might have our pictures in it, so I got the hell out of there."

Carl nodded, but said nothing. Certainly he could not have been disturbed by the newspaper story, since he could feel his criminal fame building by the second.

Criminal fame had never been his younger brother's life ambition, however, and while Wayne and George seemed content with the situation as it had developed, Billy had begun to crack up.

"I want to go home," he said at last.

Carl looked at him darkly. "What do you mean, go home?"

"I can't take this anymore," Billy said, though already terrified of Carl's response. Still, he had no choice but to hold to what he'd already said. He'd had enough of Carl's exploits. The long night of narrow escapes, with Carl increasingly out of control, had entirely unnerved him, and even at the grave risk of his own life, he found himself unable to shore himself up, to keep the outlaw pose which alone ensured his survival. He began to cry. "I can't take this anymore," he repeated brokenly. "I just can't."

Carl's eyes swept over to Wayne, as if for a signal, some sign that he might join him in the murder of their younger brother.

But Wayne did not give it. Instead, he made a mundane suggestion. "We could put him on a bus."

Carl nodded obliquely, his eyes returning once again to the wheel. "Yeah, okay," he said with a shrug. "We'll just have to find one."

Wayne glanced back at Billy. "That okay with you, Billy?"

"Yeah, okay," Billy said softly, fighting to regain control of himself. "A bus, yeah."

"That's what we'll do then," Carl said to Wayne as he hit the ignition and guided the car back out onto the road. "We'll find a place for Billy to catch a bus."

Billy nodded silently, though for the rest of the trip, he believed that his two brothers were not looking for an appropriate bus stop, but a place where they could kill him.

In any event, they headed north, back toward Baltimore along a random assortment of obscure state and county roads, finally crossing into Tennessee. As they traveled, they tried to keep their ears tuned to the local radio stations in order to keep abreast of whatever news was breaking about the murders. But they were moving so quickly, flying from town to town, county to county, that they could only catch small bits of their own story as it was unfolding over the airways. Hearing only snatches here and there before the story dissolved in clouds of static, they could only grasp that it was a big story, immensely big. It seemed to pervade the very air around them, reports of the murders pursuing them like angry, hissing ghosts down every country road, through every jerkwater town, over the densely forested hills and valleys, extending on and on, it seemed to them, toward the farthest edges of the world.

Toward noon that same day, ten-year-old Rhonda Williamson went for a walk in the woods around her father's home in Sumter County, Alabama. The shade kept her cool in the terrible heat that envelops the Deep South by mid-May, but that was not the main reason for her jaunt into the woods around her house. The day before, she'd seen an enormous amount of activity around a blue and white Impala that had been found on the Boyd Cutoff, and since then the neighborhood had been buzzing with tales of a murderous band of escaped convicts. There'd been talk of a body that might have been thrown into the lake or dumped off in the woods. In addition to these sizzling stories, she'd also heard tales of sinister discoveries, guns and ammunition hidden in the tall weeds that grew everywhere in the area. If the escapees had come through the woods near her house, she reasoned, then they might have dropped such dreadful wares in them as well. She decided to find out.

For a long time, she strolled aimlessly, enjoying the cool as she rambled among the trees, her eyes following whatever attracted them, a play of light, some small movement in the leaves or along the ground. After a time, she came to an old barbed wire fence, its rusty strands just high enough for her to crouch and go under them. As she straightened again, her eyes swept the forest that spread out beyond the fence until they caught suddenly on something dreadful.

Several yards ahead of her, just at the edge of a narrow culvert, she saw something so frightening and macabre that she froze for an instant before screaming loudly for her father. He heard the scream from his house down the hill, bounded over the little fence, running as fast as he could through the bramble until he reached his daughter's side. Once there, he stood motionlessly beside her, his eyes staring out in the direction toward which she pointed.

In a large tree several yards away, he saw four shirts hanging several feet above the ground. They had been methodically stuffed with leaves so that they appeared to him exactly as they had appeared to his daughter seconds before, as headless bodies dangling from the limbs.

By early afternoon, Angel had arrived once again in Donalsonville. By then he'd accumulated a massive number of case notes, and he was busily transcribing them when the phone rang. It was Chief Melvin Stephens from Livingston, Alabama, again. A little girl had found something, he told Angel, something Georgia authorities would certainly want to see.

"So I need to come back?" Angel asked unbelievingly.

"I guess so," Stephens said.

Angel hung up, drew in a long, deep breath, and headed for his car for the long drive back to Alabama.

He arrived nearly four hours later, then accompanied Sheriff Stephens to a narrow wooded area at some distance from where the Alday car had been abandoned.

The four stuffed shirts still hung eerily in the trees as he and Stephens began gathering up the odd assortment of items that lay scattered beneath them. To one side, in a pile at the base of a large tree trunk, he found what appeared to be about $30.00 in pennies. He shook his head wonderingly. Pitching pennies, he thought, that's how they must have killed time during the afternoon, just sitting around, pitching pennies.

Not far from the pennies, he found several unopened cartons of cigarettes, which they'd obviously decided not to bother with anymore.

But of far greater interest was a single black suitcase which had not yet been opened. When he opened it, he discovered all the evidence he needed in order to determine where it had come from. Inside, he found Georgia hunting and fishing licenses made out to Shuggie Alday, along with his temporary driver's license and two dental appointment cards. He also found Barbara Alday's fishing license and a yellow Instamatic camera box with a packet of undeveloped film inside.

Not far away, but still at some distance from the original campsite, Rhonda Williamson continued to patrol the forest. She could see thirty to forty men as they inched their way among the trees and undergrowth, slipping up and down the culvert, meticulously combing every inch of the woods for anything the escapees might have left behind. They'd gathered up a great deal, she noticed, and she presumed that there was little left to find, until her eyes swept down to the ground a final time, and she saw a few bits of paper blowing idly in the summer wind. She knelt down, gathered them up, and looked at them closely. They appeared to be torn parts of a black-and-white Instamatic photograph, and she now sat down on the ground and began to piece them together. One by one she shifted the parts, fitting their jagged edges together, until the picture was finally made whole. She would never be able to forget what she saw. It was a crude black-and-white photograph of a dark-haired woman who lay on her back, nude, her body spread across the ground, her still living eyes staring up toward the camera at the man who no doubt stood above her, grinning as he took the picture. It was Mary Alday minutes before her death as she lay on the ground of the Cummings estate six miles from her trailer. She appeared dazed, almost lifeless, though unquestionably still alive, her terrible visage captured in a photograph taken by her tormentors at the moment of her deepest anguish.

"I've never been able to forget it," Rhonda Williamson would say nearly seventeen years later. "I've never been able to get it out of my mind."

Over two hundred miles away, as the tide of investigation continued to sweep rapidly from Georgia to Alabama, all the varied social and commercial activities of Donalsonville and Seminole County came to a complete halt for the Alday funeral.

Heeding the mayor's call for a day of mourning and commiseration for the Alday family, the stores of the downtown area closed for the funeral. Its streets deserted, with little moving other than the steady blinking of its few traffic lights, Donalsonville looked like a town that had been swept by plague.

By 3:00 P.M. almost all the townspeople, along with hundreds of others from the surrounding counties, had gathered to attend the funeral services for Ned, Shuggie, Aubrey, Jimmy, Jerry, and Mary Alday, which were being held at the Spring Creek Baptist Church only a short drive from the Alday family home.

For many years the spiritual center of Ernestine Alday's life, Spring Creek had also become the church of her family. Ned had helped to build it, and all of her slain sons, as well as Mary, had either been officers in the church or teachers in its Sunday school.

But if the Spring Creek Baptist Church had sustained the Alday family in life, it was physically unable to accommodate the enormity of the deaths that had suddenly swept down upon it. Over a hundred years old, and in serious disrepair, its small, modest sanctuary was incapable of handling the six full-sized Alday coffins, along with the incalculably large crowds that were expected to attend the funeral. As a result, Ernestine had already decided that the funeral would be held on the cemetery grounds so that everyone who wanted could attend the full service, rather than the burial alone.

Consequently, the coffins were brought to the cemetery and arranged side by side, then decked with the enormous number of flower arrangements that had been arriving with steadily increasing frequency at both the church and the Alday home since the murders.

"It was probably the biggest funeral ever held in Georgia," Nancy remembered. "I'd never seen anything like it. People everywhere, hundreds of them, and flowers stacked on flowers around the caskets and the graves."

Over the next hour, eulogies were given by four separate ministers while a crowd, which included various state dignitaries along with both Governor Carter's special assistant and his mother, Lillian, listened quietly.

As the service progressed through the long afternoon, each of the murdered Aldays was given his or her moment of remembrance in simple eulogies that recalled their hard work, their service to their church and community, the devotion they had shown to their families. Ned was remembered for his liveliness and humor; Aubrey for his skills as a farmer; Shuggie for his strength and comic zest; Jerry for the quiet dignity with which he'd lived his life; Mary for her work in social service and devotion as a wife; Jimmy for his energy and youth; and all of them for their service to the church and their community, the long stewardship they'd maintained as husbands, brothers, sons, and wife.

These eulogies would be among the last times that Ned, Aubrey, Shuggie, Jerry, Jimmy, and Mary would be presented as individuals with separate and distinct identities. Increasingly from this point onward, they would be fused together, their personalities melded by a single phrase used repeatedly to describe them: *the Alday victims*. It was as if a single bullet had felled them all, pulverizing their individualities by reducing them to lumps of flesh spread over beds, couchs, a forest undergrowth.

"I remember that at one of the trials," Nancy said years later, "they were showing the jury a picture of the trailer, and in the background, you could see Mary peeping out the front door. The defense objected to the picture right away. They didn't mind the trailer, they said, but they didn't think the jury should be allowed to see Mary Alday's face."

Hundreds of miles away from Mary Alday's trailer, a dark green Chevrolet Caprice was winding northward along the back roads of northern Virginia. Behind the wheel, Carl felt he had done very well indeed so far. Since Mississippi, he'd moved everyone forward without a hitch by keeping to the back roads as long as possible, hour after hour effectively concealing their northbound flight.

But now, once again, they were growing short of cash. Without a new influx of gas and money, even continuing along the back roads would be impossible. Because of that, Carl told the others that it would soon be necessary to strike again, even at the cost of revealing where they were.

Chapter Twelve

At approximately 4:15 on the afternoon of Thursday, May 17, the dark green Chevy Caprice, which had been stolen in Livingston, Alabama, nearly twenty-four hours before, pulled into the driveway of Mullins Grocery, a remote country store at Slate Fork, a tiny commercial crossroad near the town of Grundy in Buchanan County, Virginia.

Utterly isolated on a winding country road, it was perfectly situated for what Carl had in mind. Having successfully eluded an impressive array of redneck cops, he had grown increasingly confident that he could make it back to Baltimore, drop Billy off, then head farther north, Canada now replacing Mexico as the ultimate refuge.

For a moment after Carl pulled into the driveway, he, along with the others, lingered in the car, carefully observing the store. Several customers were inside, more than expected in so remote a place. There were a man, two women, and a couple of teenagers, certainly a number sufficient to deter any but the most reckless kind of man.

By that time, of course, Carl had had a considerable amount of experience in dealing with unexpected crowds, and the few isolated individuals he could see moving idly along the store's narrow aisles hardly served to threaten him. He was soaring on a wild wind by then, and five people in a grocery store only meant the robbery would require the full team's active participation. Neither he nor Wayne could pull it off alone.

Accordingly, all four eased themselves out of the car and made their way into the store. For a time they casually cased it, standing together around the soda machine as their eyes swept here and there about the store's cluttered interior.

Then, without giving any signal to either Billy or George, Wayne stepped forward and made the first move.

Standing by the door, Billy could see him advance on the sole adult male in the store. When he reached him, he thrust a pistol into his face.

Instantly Billy and George pulled their weapons and brandished them before the remaining, now utterly terrified, customers while Carl moved haphazardly about the store, firing orders in all directions. Billy was commanded to stand lookout while Dungee was told to begin the rather daunting task of tying up all the store's customers.

They obeyed without hesitation, and while George struggled with the petrified customers, Carl walked to the cash register, popped it open, and extracted its modest contents. He was methodically counting it when yet another customer entered the store. Billy let her in and stepped aside while Wayne turned his pistol on her, marched her over to George, and watched a few feet away while he tied her up.

George had just completed the task when still another customer entered the store, this time an older woman in a trenchcoat. Quickly robbed, then tied up, she was lowered to the ground, where she watched helplessly as the men continued to fumble about the store, their movements typically disordered and time-consuming, as if they'd learned nothing from their disastrous experience in the Alday trailer.

Still posted as lookout by the front window, Billy, now frantically concerned that another slaughter was about to take place, glanced back and saw George inexplicably disappear into the rear of the store. Moments later he heard Dungee calling nervously for Wayne. In response, Wayne also disappeared into the rear quarters of the store to confront a scene that would have been comical had it not been so perilous to those involved.

In the store's crowded stockroom, George had stumbled upon an additional three people, a young woman and two children, one a toddler, the other no more than ten months old. The baby had begun to cry loudly as it squirmed in its mother's arms, an unexpected and uncontrollable response that had thoroughly unnerved the far from resourceful George. Unable to think through to his next move, he had called Wayne for the necessary assistance.

It had not been the best of choices. Equally confused, and apparently just as unable to deal with the complications Dungee had suddenly flung upon him, Wayne simply stared in disbelief at the crowded room.

"Jesus Christ," he muttered. "It's like we can't get out of here."

"What are we going to do?" George sputtered.

For a moment, Wayne seemed lost in a vague trance, as if unable to find a way out of these new complications. Then he suddenly snapped out of it and set to work, moving as quickly as his own mental disarray would allow, first tying up the young woman, then returning to the front of the store, where he grabbed the older woman, dragged her back into the rear of the store, and laid her out beside the younger one.

It was only then that the four men headed out of the store, all of them running at a frantic pace that captured the attention of two other men who'd just pulled into the store's now crowded parking area.

Both supremely suspicious and heavily armed, the new arrivals called to the four men they saw running toward a green Caprice, and when they received no answer, drew their rifles from their truck and fired upon them.

Once inside the car, and while still under an unexpected barrage of gunfire, Carl slammed into reverse, hurled backward onto the main road, and raced northward, taking a narrow, winding road that led almost immediately across the state line into West Virginia.

As the road began to twist and turn, Carl eased off the accelerator to accommodate their increasingly tortuous route. They were rising into the mountains now, the dense wooded ridges pressing in toward them from all sides. Unable to negotiate the curving road at high speeds, Carl continued to ease his foot off the accelerator so that when he saw a West Virginia State Police patrol car approach from ahead, he was traveling well within the prescribed speed limit.

The officer behind the wheel of the patrol car was Hoyt C. Ryan, and by the time he glimpsed the Caprice heading toward him, he and his partner, D. J. Meadows, had already been advised that an armed robbery had been committed in nearby Slate Fork, Virginia, and that the suspects had been seen heading west on State Route 83. The all-points bulletin Ryan and Meadows had just heard included a description of the car, which matched in every detail the one that had just drifted past them, and Ryan slammed on his brakes, made a tight U-turn, and began his pursuit.

Up ahead, the Caprice speeded up, swerving from one side of the road to the next as it rocketed along the winding mountain roads before making a hairpin turn onto the even narrower and more remote mountain road known as Route 16. For a time, Ryan was able to keep it in view, but finally lost sight of it as it disappeared into a shady labyrinth of twisting roads and tight, bone-crunching curves.

Then, suddenly, the green Chevy Caprice appeared again. Only this time, rather than careening from side to side in its wild dash through the hill country, it was pulled alongside the road, its occupants nowhere to be seen. Ryan and Meadows knew that the suspects had to be somewhere in the surrounding countryside, since there was nothing but thick woods from where they'd abandoned their car to Yukon, West Virginia, the nearest town.

For the next few minutes, Ryan remained in the area, his eyes fixed on the abandoned car, while Meadows radioed for additional assistance. Within minutes, other troopers had arrived, along with police officers from the nearby town of War, West Virginia.

By then, Ryan and Meadows had been told that the men in the car were very heavily armed, and that they should proceed against them with extreme caution. While other officers secured the car, Ryan, Meadows, and two local constables headed down Route 16, moving slowly along its forested edges toward the general area in which local residents had seen the men flee after abandoning the car. They had not gone far before they saw three men dart across the road. They called for them to halt, and when they didn't, chased them into the woods, firing as they ran. In the distance, over the barrels of their guns, they could see the three men's heads bobbing in the brush, but by the time they'd reached the place where they had crossed the road, they had disappeared into the surrounding woods.

Rather than returning to their car, however, Ryan and the others, realizing that the fourth man must still be hiding somewhere in the hills above the road, recrossed Route 16 and fanned out into the woods. Only a few seconds later, at a distance of little more than one hundred yards from the road, they found a black man crouched in the bushes, frantically fumbling to load a pistol, the heavy shells dropping like enormous raindrops on the forest floor beneath him.

Ryan leveled his rifle at the man's head. "Don't move," he said.

The black man froze.

"Now, put your hands on your head," Ryan commanded.

Trembling, the man let the pistol and ammunition drop to the ground, and raised his hands into the air.

While the other officers stood by, Ryan quickly handcuffed his prisoner, read him his Miranda rights, and after that, began going through his pockets. They were empty, except for a small Timex watch with

Roman numerals. Ryan looked at it closely, then back up at his prisoner. He wondered what such a man was doing with what was obviously a woman's watch.

After gathering the pistol and ammunition, Ryan led Dungee back up the road. On the way it struck him that his prisoner had to have been frightened out of his wits at the time of his arrest, because he'd been trying to do the impossible, load .380-caliber ammunition into a .32-caliber revolver.

Once back at the roadblock, Ryan placed Dungee in the back of his patrol car and radioed patrol headquarters that an arrest had been made. While he waited for further instructions, he slid in behind the wheel. In his rearview mirror, he could see Dungee trembling almost uncontrollably in the back seat.

"What's your name?" Ryan asked.

"George Dungee."

"Where you from, George?"

" 'Round Baltimore."

Ryan radioed to headquarters and requested an NCIC report on Dungee. Within minutes NCIC had responded, and Ryan learned that the cowering little man in the back seat of his car was a prime suspect in the murder of six people.

"You're in a lot of trouble, George," Ryan said to him after listening to the NCIC report.

Dungee nodded softly, but did not reply.

At approximately 8:15 P.M. Ryan arrived at his headquarters in Welch, West Virginia, with Dungee still sitting silently in the back of his patrol car. Dungee was then turned over to the local sheriff, at which time he was read his constitutional rights once again.

In the meantime, Ryan called Wade Watson, the assistant district attorney of McDowell County. He told him that Dungee had been captured, and that he'd indicated his willingness to make a statement.

Watson arrived at the Welch headquarters fifteen minutes later. He glanced through the building's back rooms until he found a small wood-paneled office that had what he was looking for, a desk with a typewriter. Then he summoned other officers to escort Dungee to the room.

Dungee appeared a few moments later, and as Watson observed, the considerable time that had passed since his capture had done nothing to relax him. He looked utterly panic-stricken, his eyes darting about in all directions until, at his first remark, the source of Dungee's terror was entirely revealed.

"Do they have the death penalty in West Virginia?" Dungee asked.

"In West Virginia?" Watson said. "Well, I'm not sure you've done anything in West Virginia that would call for the death penalty anyway."

Dungee nodded silently.

"Of course," Watson added, "Georgia has the death penalty, and there might be some things down there you'd be worried about."

Dungee said nothing, and while he remained silent, Watson ordered that he be handcuffed in the front, rather than behind his back, and asked him to sit down.

"You got a cigarette?" Dungee asked as he took his seat. "And something to drink?"

Watson supplied both, his eyes still trained on the small, terrified man before him.

"I understand you're ready to make a statement," Watson said.

"Yes, sir."

Watson read Dungee his constitutional rights, the third time he'd heard them in less than two hours. In response, Dungee signed a waiver of those rights, after which he indicated that he was now ready to begin his statement.

Watson pulled up a chair and looked closely at the small, curiously inconsequential man before him. It hardly seemed possible that such a person could have committed the acts of which he was accused. He was small, his voice soft and somewhat whining, so that in general he gave off a sense of innocence and gentleness that was even further supported, as Watson noticed, by the odd fact that bits of forest debris were still clinging to his hair.

"I was never in no trouble before," Dungee said.

"Well, you'd escaped from a prison in Maryland, hadn't you?"

"Yeah, but I was just in there for not paying child support," Dungee said. "That's all I ever done 'til we ducked out of there. Then there was some things."

Watson raised his fingers to the typewriter. "All right, Mr. Dungee," he said, "let's hear it."

Two hours later, Watson felt certain that he'd gotten as much of the complete story as Dungee was likely to tell at the moment. It was a horrible tale of mass murder, rape, and both psychological and physical torture, all of it told in a flat, emotionless voice that neither rose nor fell as it related the terrible details. Only at the very end had Dungee indicated any feeling whatsoever concerning the events he had so meticulously related. Then, suddenly, he'd looked at Watson almost plaintively, his large, slightly bulging eyes even larger behind the thick lenses. "I haven't been able to sleep since what we done to the woman," he said.

Watson nodded, but said nothing, since his only concern after hearing Dungee's hellish tale was that he do absolutely nothing that might hinder for the briefest instant his full and forceful prosecution.

Chapter Thirteen

By the time Angel reached Donalsonville at just before dawn on the morning of May 18, he'd already been radioed that the car which had been stolen in Livingston had been recovered in West Virginia, and that one of its occupants, George Dungee, was in custody in the little town of Welch, West Virginia.

As he began making plans for an immediate flight to Welsh, he was informed by Director Beardsley that several high officials of the Georgia Department of Public Safety had decided to go along as well.

As Angel well knew, none of these officials had ever gone to Donalsonville. In fact, they had scarcely communicated with the agents assigned to the case, and knew nothing of the subsequent investigation. Still, they had determined to go to West Virginia for the capture, and as a result, Angel's more immediate travel plans were put on hold so that the considerably more complicated travel arrangements and security measures of the accompanying officials could be made. Angel could see the writing on the wall. A criminal investigation was about to turn into a media event.

While Dungee was narrating his version of the last few days' terrible events and Angel was frantically trying to leave Georgia, West Virginia authorities were in the process of concentrating and enlarging their effort to capture the three other men who were still at large.

By early evening, scores of men and women were pouring into the area of the abandoned car, and shortly after 8:00 P.M., a command post to control and alert them was set up in the offices of the Olga Coal Company in Caretta, West Virginia.

Using topographical maps, West Virginia officials established checkpoints at every imaginable point in the area around and between Caretta and Yukon, where the men had last been seen. By 9:00 P.M., roadblocks had been set up throughout the adjoining counties, while specifically designated road patrols fanned out in all directions from the central site of P. C. Mincus's green Caprice.

An hour later, after creating search grids of the entire region, full police dragnets were launched on foot into the surrounding hills. For the next few hours, perhaps as many as a hundred men and women, scattered at various points over many square miles, began moving through the thick darkness that had by then descended over the West Virginia borderland.

All through the night, in sortie after sortie, they pushed through the thick summer undergrowth toward a group of heavily armed men they could but faintly hope to glimpse before being seen themselves and fired upon.

At the same time as foot and automobile patrols continued to search the difficult terrain of the West Virginia hill country, Ronnie Angel was literally in the air. Having obtained warrants for all four fugitives, along with an array of forms related to their formal extradition, he was now on route to West Virginia.

He was not alone, however. The "Uniforms," as he called them, were everywhere, and although they'd assured him that they had only come along to assist him, Angel continued to worry that they might do or say something which might endanger the case, a possibility he wanted to avoid at all cost. Accordingly, he had determined that neither he nor any of the agents under his command would attempt to question any of the fugitives until they were in formal custody in Georgia. Instead, they would limit their activities to the gathering of physical evidence, the processing of the crime scenes, and the final provision for the transfer of the Isaacs brothers, Coleman, and Dungee to Georgia.

Meanwhile, by the time the first morning light had broken over southern West Virginia, almost two hundred men and women had gathered either for direct action or to hold on standby for a full-scale, inch-by-inch search of the wooded area into which the Isaacs brothers and Wayne Coleman had disappeared. All during the night they had been marshaling their forces. Helicopters and small planes had been brought in from nearby bases for airborne searches to be conducted at first light. Scores of patrol cars cruised the winding roads, while perhaps as many as a hundred officers gathered at grid points to await the final assault, their rifle barrels forming a stiff, black thicket against the morning sky.

While additional forces had been massing during the night for a sweep far more extensive than the ones that had been launched late the preceding afternoon, other officers had been moving relentlessly through the nightbound woods since sunset.

Still others had arrived somewhat later. Two of them, Harold Hall and L. D. Townley, had come with Prince, a prize tracking dog they'd brought with them from the Bland Correctional Institute in Whitegate, Virginia, a town nearly two hundred miles away.

At around midnight, Price, his handlers, and Troopers F. E. Thomas and L. R. Bailey moved into the woods. Some minutes previously, Prince had been allowed to sniff his way through the abandoned car, and had then shot off across Route 16, entering the woods at full run at exactly the spot where, hours before, Officer Ryan had seen the fugitives disappear into the undergrowth.

For the next four hours, Prince continued to bound through the heavy brush, but in a pattern that began to concern Thomas and the dog's handlers. He would run up and down the hills, moving back and forth from the woods to the command headquarters in Carreta in a way that suggested he might not be trailing the fugitives at all, but rather some particular police officer. In other words, Prince had perhaps begun to follow the posse that was following him, literally chasing his own tail.

At three in the morning, with Prince still moving in this confused pattern, Thomas and Prince's handlers, now utterly exhausted by the long slog through the dark undergrowth, decided to return the dog to the original site of the abandoned car, then make a wide arc around the area to avoid his picking up any scent other than those he'd picked up in the car.

The results were immediate.

"It was like everything just suddenly came clear to him," Thomas recalled. "He just took off into the woods and kept going for the next few hours without any letup at all."

Suddenly, Prince's large black muzzle rose into the air, the indisputable sign that the fugitives were near at hand, that the dog no longer needed to trail them over ground, but rather that their scent still hung in the air around him.

The men continued to follow him through the brush, now tensed and watchful, their guns at the ready. Within a few minutes, Prince began to froth at the mouth, barely able to contain his excitement as he closed in upon his targets, yet still carefully obeying the foremost law of his training, never, under any circumstances, to bark unless commanded to do so by his handler.

Convinced that they were now very close to the fugitives they had been tracking for eight hours, the men began to move more slowly, their eyes darting about constantly, searching for the first sign.

It was a shirt, and they all saw it at exactly the same time. Through a clearing, approximately a hundred yards away, they could see several figures lying on the ground beneath a granite overhang that jutted out at the base of the mountainside.

Instantly, the four trackers dispersed around the cove, silently taking cover in positions that matched the remaining three points of the compass, thus blocking all avenues of escape for the men who slept obliviously beneath the overhang.

Once the officers were in place, Thomas called to the prone figures he could see sleeping on the ground some forty yards away. They did not rouse themselves in any way, and when he saw no response, Thomas decided that a more determined effort to get the sleeping men's attention was required. He emptied a twenty-round clip from his AR-15 into the mountainside above their heads.

As the men stirred within the cove, Thomas called to them again. "This is the West Virginia State Police," he cried. "Lay down your weapons, and stay on your stomachs."

The stirring stopped.

"Now, the one closest to us, crawl out and down this way with your hands over your head," Thomas commanded.

One by one the men followed Thomas's instructions until they all lay flat on the ground, one behind the other, in a strange human line, fingers touching feet, faces in the dirt.

Once they'd been handcuffed and read their rights, Thomas and Bailey searched the cove, while Hall and Townley kept the prisoners covered. The searches completed, it was now time to move the prisoners out of the woods.

But there was a problem. Since Thomas and the other trackers had been following Prince through a solid darkness, they now found themselves in a completely unfamiliar terrain.

"We were lost," Thomas remembered. "We were just in the woods somewhere with four prisoners who had killed six people, but with no idea exactly where to take them."

Their only hint was the sound of traffic. It was sporadic and very distant, but from time to time a car could be heard moving along a mountain road. Each time they heard it, they moved in its direction, while at the same time vaguely following the meandering course of a little mountain stream.

At last, it led them home, and through the trees Thomas and the others could see people gathering on the road above them.

Waiting on that road, stretching out in all directions, some in uniform, others in plain clothes, scores of officers and local residents watched as Thomas, his beleaguered but triumphant posse, and the men they had captured, slowly ascended the hill toward them. When they were about halfway up it, still trudging wearily through the heavy brush, they heard the first gentle round of what would be a long applause.

Chapter Fourteen

A ngel's plane touched down at just after dawn on the morning of May 19. From his window, he could see a large contingent of West Virginia State Police, including several of its highest officials, all in full uniform, waiting for their Georgia counterparts to stride down the gangway for a hearty salute.

Within minutes, the plane had emptied, and a long line of police vehicles pulled out of the small airfield near Welch, West Virginia, and headed toward the command post that had previously been established in the offices of the Olga Mining Company in Caretta.

Angel presumed that after checking in at the command post, he would be escorted to the site from which the manhunt was set to be launched within only a few minutes.

While on the way to Caretta, however, he and the other Georgia officials were notified that the three remaining fugitives had been captured nearly at the exact moment their plane had touched down in West Virginia. At present, the report continued, they were on their way to the state police barracks in Welch, still in the custody of the officers who had captured them. The report added that none of the three had been injured in any way. They had immediately surrendered upon being confronted by police, and no shots, other than those used to awaken them, had been fired during their apprehension.

A few minutes later, when Angel arrived at the barracks in Welch, his worst suspicions were confirmed. Several dozen law enforcement officers were crowded outside the barracks' main building, their own substantial numbers swollen by an almost equal number of people from the print and television media. Camera crews, television newsmen, newspaper and magazine reporters swarmed over the grounds of the barracks, their equipment vans and cars lined up in all directions along the road which led to the barracks' entrance.

Angel had just begun to elbow his way through the crowd when several police cars made their way to the front of the barracks. Inside one of them, he could see the men he'd been sleeplessly pursuing for four days. They looked worn out, depleted, sapped of even enough energy to hold up their heads. It was the way captured people often looked, helpless, almost pitiable. But as Angel leveled his gaze in their direction, he felt no pity whatsoever. He had seen pictures of Ned, by then, and Shuggie, Jerry, Jimmy, and Aubrey. He had seen Mary sprawled across the forest ground, the hard sunlight on her nakedness. The distress and weariness of the men who glanced toward him from the shadowy depths of the patrol car did not impress him. He simply waited for them to be delivered into his custody.

Their hands cuffed behind their backs, escorted by a police officer on either side, and surrounded by fifty to sixty others, Carl and Billy Isaacs and Wayne Coleman were led into the barracks where yet another swarm of law enforcement officers anxiously waited for them.

Angel drew back reflexively, the atmosphere already a bit too hungry for his taste. It was worrisome as well, the kind of three-ring circus that could undo the most meticulous of investigations. People who knew nothing about the murders, the investigation, the physical evidence or anything else having to do with the crime were now in control. The "Uniforms" were yapping to reporters who were as ignorant about the facts of the case as they were. It was the sort of situation that could destroy a case, and Angel wanted nothing to do with it.

As a consequence, he decided to carry through the plan he had outlined during the plane ride from Atlanta. Thus, during the next eight hours, he permitted himself to do nothing more than answer questions from various officials who were interviewing the fugitives, while staying decidedly clear of them himself. Instead, he and Waters concentrated on gathering and securing the physical evidence. P. C. Mincus's car had by then been impounded, and for several hours, they searched it meticulously, inventorying and bagging everything they could find that might later help to build the prosecution's case. They also examined an assortment of items which had been taken from the fugitives after their arrest, all of which had, in the heat of the arrest, been tossed into a cardboard box with no effort made to associate any item with the particular individual from which it had been seized.

To prevent such clumsiness from vitiating his investigation, Angel worked at full speed to gather up the evidence and complete the paperwork necessary for extradition. Only then could he take them back to Georgia, bring them fully under his own scrutiny, and begin the grueling process of finding out what had actually happened in that trailer on May 14.

Nearly ten hours after their capture in the West Virginia hills, the men from Baltimore were finally taken aboard a twenty-seat aircraft for the flight back to Atlanta, and Angel could begin to think of how to deal with them once they were exclusively in his custody.

Sitting only a few feet away, the Isaacs brothers, Coleman, and Dungee all seemed utterly exhausted. As Angel watched them, they appeared silent rather than sullen. Throughout the early-morning flight, they remained awake, but motionless, while just a few feet beyond them, near the front of the plane, the "Uniforms" snoozed sweetly in their seats, as if resting up for the supercharged media reception that was expected to greet them at their arrival in Atlanta.

But it was a grand reception that was not to be, as Angel already knew even as he and Waters sat together, talking quietly of the long day's work. For not long before takeoff, he'd called Director Beardsley and warned him of the security problems that might arise from such an extravaganza. Beardsley had agreed, and with his permission, Angel had secretly rerouted the plane to a remote airport, little more than a runway in a cornfield, where the entire contingent could deplane in total obscurity, the Big Noise now reduced to a whistling in the corn.

The plane arrived a few hours later on a dark field surrounded by a scattering of unadorned GBI field automobiles.

While Angel watched from a few feet away, each of the four prisoners was carried to a separate car and driven, with yet another escort car behind, to one of four separate jails within the state.

Within two hours of their departure, Angel, now once again behind his desk at GBI headquarters on Confederate Avenue, had been notified that all four prisoners had been safely transported to their respective places of incarceration, and that there had been no incidents on the way.

Then, after four relentless days, Ronnie Angel went to sleep.

* * *

He awakened early the next morning, headed back to his office, and waited impatiently for something that had by then seemed forever in coming, his first interrogation of one of the Alday suspects.

Wayne Carl Coleman, who'd spent the night in the county jail in Gainesville, Georgia, was the first to arrive.

With the swirl of officialdom now dissipated, Angel could carry out an interview in his own quiet style. After conducting Coleman into a small room adjacent to his own office, he and Waters watched silently as Coleman made himself comfortable behind the room's single wooden conference table.

Prior to this time, Angel had assumed Coleman to be the group's indisputable leader. At twenty-six, he was seven years older than Carl, and eleven years older than Billy. In addition, he was a more seasoned convict, his yellow sheet considerably longer than any of the others. Coleman had therefore taken the central position in Angel's mind as the gang's brutal chief.

But on the morning of May 19, as he began to interview Coleman for the first time, Angel experienced his initial doubts about Coleman's capacity for the kind of forceful, even vehement, leadership that would have been required to carry out the desperate acts that had taken place in Maryland, Georgia, and West Virginia.

Rambling in his speech and, after a brief period of reticence, curiously nonchalant in his attitude, Coleman appeared almost as a clownish, bumbling figure. As he narrated the events following the Poplar Hill escape, he exhibited none of the terror which had been the hallmark of Dungee's presentation. Nor did he seem particularly concerned that he'd been caught, an attitude distinctly different from that of both Carl and Billy Isaacs as Angel had observed them on the plane ride back to Georgia.

"He acted like the whole thing, the escape, the murders, everything was just a lark," Angel remembered. "The way he described it, it was just the boys out for a little wild time that sort of got out of hand."

Leaning casually back in his seat, one leg slung over a chair arm, a slender grin forever sliding onto his face, Coleman told Angel that it had all started with a simple burglary. While traveling the back roads of Georgia, they'd come upon an isolated house trailer, knocked at its back door, and, when no one had answered, they'd stepped inside and begun rummaging about for any valuables they could find.

In a tone that suggested he was incapable of grasping the enormity of what had taken place in the trailer on River Road, Coleman presented Angel with a flat, narrowly anecdotal account of a burglary that had gotten out of hand, accident following accident, until, at the end of the chain, six of the Alday family lay dead.

The first accident, the one that presaged all the others, according to Coleman, was little more than an inopportune arrival.

While still ransacking the trailer, Coleman told Angel, he and the others had spotted a jeep with two men in it as it pulled into the driveway of the trailer. They'd waited until the men had come to the door, then brought them inside at gunpoint, robbed them, and finally forced them to sit on the floor.

It was after that, Coleman continued, that things had begun to get out of hand. Realizing that if Jerry and Ned Alday were allowed to live, he and the others would never be able to get out of Georgia, Coleman had finally decided to kill them. After that, it was only a question of how to do it. Finally, he'd marched one man into each of the bedrooms at the opposite ends of the trailer, forced each of them to lie down on their respective beds, and shot them to death.

These murders were followed by the unfortunate arrival of Jimmy Alday, and subsequent events quickly turned into a merry-go-round of murder. "Here comes another damn tractor," he told Angel expansively, like someone narrating a television show he'd found curiously entertaining. "And pretty soon the house is filling up on us. There wasn't no way of getting out of there."

After the third murder, with one body in each of the bedrooms and a third, that of Jimmy Alday, now lying facedown on the small sofa in the living room, Coleman told Angel that he'd become somewhat anxious to leave the trailer. But at that point, he said, the others had resisted his advice and had chosen to linger a while longer.

"Why is that?" Angel asked.

"Because of the woman," Coleman replied. While Jerry Alday was still alive, he added, Carl had asked him if he were married. Alday had replied that he was, and that his wife would soon be home. He'd then pleaded with Carl not to hurt her, adding that if robbery were the motive, then the men need not wait for his wife, since she never carried more money than was necessary for her to go back and forth to her job in Donalsonville. However, the men had decided to wait anyway, Coleman added, even though he had protested the decision.

"I said, 'Shit, I'm leaving,' " Coleman told Angel. But still the others had refused to join him.

"Why?" Angel asked.

Coleman shrugged. "Those pussy-hungry motherfuckers, they said, 'No, stay around, wait for her,' " he told Angel. And in the end, that is what they'd done.

"So they waited for Mary Alday," Angel asked. "That's why they hung around?"

"Yeah," Coleman said.

But it was not Mary who'd next arrived at the trailer on River Road, Coleman went on, it was two men in a pickup truck who'd suddenly driven into the now crowded Alday driveway. In response, Coleman said that he and the others had remained inside the trailer and watched as the two men approached its rear door. They had allowed them to open it, and only then pulled their guns and forced them to come inside.

"What'd you do to them?" Angel asked.

"We robbed them," Coleman answered.

"Then what?"

After the robbery, Coleman replied idly, he had walked each man into the opposite bedrooms, just as he had done with the first two, and had murdered them.

A short time later, Coleman went on, Mary Alday had arrived just as her husband had said she would, her arms wrapped around a bag of groceries. For a time she was held captive in the kitchen while the men continued to burglarize the trailer. Later, while still in the trailer, Carl Isaacs had raped her, Coleman added.

Although rape had not occurred to Coleman before he saw Carl's assault on Mary Alday, it had been enough to convince him to "get some too," and after waiting for Carl to finish, he'd crawled on top of Mary and raped her on the kitchen floor while the others watched from various positions in the room.

Once the rapes were completed, Coleman said, Mary Alday was told to get dressed again. After getting dressed, she'd been taken to her car, where she was forced to crouch in the floorboard of the back seat while the men, now in two separate cars, Mary Alday's Impala and Richard Miller's Super Sport, drove her to a wooded area several miles from the trailer. There, according to Coleman, the Super Sport was abandoned, and Mary was raped again, first by Carl, then by George. After that, Coleman added, the men had "pushed her around a little bit, touched her ass and everything," while discussing whether or not to have her run about in the woods for a time while they shot at her. In the end, Coleman said, they had finally grown tired of playing with Mary, and at that point "since I had done shot everyone else," Coleman said to Angel, he had walked Mary a few yards further into the woods, ordered her to lie down on her stomach, and had shot her twice in the head.

And that in a nutshell, Coleman told Angel, was the way it had gone down. The story over, Coleman slouched back in his chair, took a long draw on his cigarette and smiled.

Standing only a few feet away, Angel felt his skin like a tightly drawn cord. "There are times when you really have to control yourself," he recalled, "and watching that grin on Coleman's face, the way he bragged about all he'd done . . . well, that was one of those times."

As a narrative of the murders, Angel had to admit to himself that Coleman's story had been plausible enough. At the same time, however, there were a few problems with it.

Coleman had told his tale in the tone of boastfulness, as if he were proud of his cruelty and brutality, and almost eager to make himself appear even more irredeemably evil than the events themselves suggested. Thus, as he watched Coleman saunter out of his office after finishing his story, Angel wondered if the narrative he'd just heard would be supported by the other Alday suspects, if Coleman would still emerge as the chief evil agent of all their deeds once the others had been led into the same room, slouched down in the same chair and told their separate versions, while he stood nearby, rigidly controlling himself again.

Although Angel might be wondering who the leader of the gang actually was, Frank Thomas was not. He'd already received some unsolicited information that left him with little doubt. Even before their capture, on the night of May 17, a phone call had come into the offices of the West Virginia State Police from a woman who claimed to be Betty Isaacs, the mother of three of the four Maryland escapees. Her tone was emphatic. "Carl is the one in charge," she told Thomas. "And he's a killer. He's the only one who's like that, but Wayne and Billy will go along to impress him."

"She was very impressive," Thomas remembered years later. "She knew it was her sons we were looking for, and she didn't want any police officers to be hurt."

And the one they should be wary of, she told Thomas, was Carl.

* * *

Within three days of the capture, Angel had plenty of confirmation
for the assessment Betty Isaacs had given Frank Thomas over the phone
that night, and which argued determinedly that Wayne Coleman was
neither the evil chief he'd claimed to be in his initial statement, nor the
agent of all six of the murders.

By that time he'd interviewed each of the four men who'd entered
the trailer on that fateful afternoon. Although similar in many substantive details, the four accounts had all varied in other, equally significant
aspects.

Whereas Coleman had confessed to killing all six of the Aldays,
Dungee had admitted to shooting Mary Alday himself, although pointedly adding that he'd only done so because he'd feared his own murder
at the hands of the others had he refused to do so.

In addition to this profound difference, there were other notable
discrepancies between the two men's stories. Not only had Dungee
claimed that he had killed Mary Alday, but he said that Carl had
actually murdered some of the men in the trailer, and Coleman had
murdered others. According to Dungee, only Billy Isaacs had murdered
no one.

Added to the contradictions regarding the actual murders, Dungee
and Coleman had also told widely differing accounts of the sequence
of the murders. Coleman had insisted that Mary was the last to arrive,
whereas Dungee claimed that the two men in the jeep, whom Angel
now knew were Aubrey and Shuggie Alday, had been the last to arrive
at the Alday trailer. Mary had arrived before them, Dungee said, although, in the end, she had been the last to die.

Finally, there was Coleman himself. Although Coleman had made
every effort to make himself the malignant center of the group, the man
in charge, he had delivered his narrative in a rambling, disorganized
manner, in the process exhibiting a level of ignorance and incompe-
tence that remained highly at variance with any capacity whatsoever to
lead anyone, except possibly George Dungee. Several times Coleman
had appeared utterly baffled by, and out of touch with, the group's
frantic movements. His knowledge of details involving such issues as the
number and caliber of the guns used and the positioning of the bodies
in the Alday trailer was at times equally hazy. Worst of all, Coleman
gave the overall impression of a man totally at sea even in regard to the
most rudimentary knowledge of American geography. Once, he'd actu-

ally stopped to ask Angel if Georgia were a part of Alabama, while on another occasion he had seemed to think Louisiana a county within Mississippi.

As for Billy Isaacs, his story had followed Dungee's general description much more closely than it had followed Coleman's. Still, in essence, it struck Angel as a self-serving version of events, one that worked utterly to exonerate Billy from having directly killed anyone, despite the fact that ballistics tests had already demonstrated that the murders had been committed using four, rather than three guns, and that one of them had belonged to Billy.

And last there was Carl Junior Isaacs. In almost every version, he'd seemed to be in charge of the group's activities. It was Carl who'd convinced Coleman and Dungee to escape from Poplar Hill although neither man had long to wait before release. It was Carl who'd decided to pick up Billy on Old Hartford Road. It was Carl who'd wanted to head south, Carl who'd chosen the trailer, Carl who'd waited for Mary, Carl who'd been the first to rape her. Even the incidental detail that it always seemed to be Carl who was driving the cars and making such otherwise insignificant decisions as where to eat, sleep, or buy gas argued that he was, in fact, the man in charge. At every corner, it seemed to Angel, it was Carl, Carl, Carl.

But if Carl were being talked about, he certainly wasn't talking himself, and so, as Angel prepared to make his last direct efforts in the case, he wondered if the truth would ever really be known about what had actually taken place in the modest sixty-foot trailer Jerry and Mary Alday had placed on their neatly pruned yard on River Road, or in the terrible woods six miles ways. As for Carl, he seemed determined to keep his own discussion of that day confined to a brief weather report. He remembered May 14 all right, he told Angel, but only that it was "a pretty May day."

TRIAL AND
TRIBULATION

Chapter Fifteen

On May 24, clothed in prison uniforms and bound in shackles and handcuffs held together by large leather belts, Carl and Billy Isaacs, Wayne Coleman, and George Dungee arrived at the Seminole County Courthouse in Donalsonville. Under the protection of a massive security force, they had been brought in from four separate jails to be arraigned on what the *Albany Herald* had already dubbed "the most brutal mass slaying in Georgia history."

The items in the arraignment included six counts of murder, along with an assortment of lesser charges, ranging from such very serious felonies as rape and kidnapping, through armed robbery, and finally ending in the relatively inconsequential offense of stealing Mary Alday's Chevrolet Impala.

As they were hustled into the courthouse, the Alday defendants had only the briefest instant to glance about at the scores of spectators who silently lined the streets in front of the building. Had their eyes been able to linger on them, they would have seen precisely the kind of people Carl Isaacs would later call "the type of society I don't like."

It was a hardworking and religious society of predominantly independent farmers, and in a bygone age, it would have been held up as nothing less than the Jeffersonian ideal of a broad common people, virtuous and independent, the bedrock of American life.

But much had changed since Jefferson, along with a host of largely aristocratic literary agrarians, had rallied to the cause of the country folk. Almost none of it for the better. As a consequence, rather than being romanticized, rural Georgia had over a period of many years become an object of metropolitan scorn and ridicule.

As a result it had, to some extent, even come to view itself as a poor and underdeveloped backwater world, one that had long ago been supplanted by the more industrialized northern part of the state. Held in contempt by its own capital city of Atlanta, the butt of a thousand redneck jokes, Seminole County and its environs was a region in a state of siege, an area under ideological and economic assault by the larger, more sophisticated world beyond its borders. Its pace was the pace of the seasons, rather than the financial markets, and its old-time religion was an object of contempt and rebuke. As to its marginal, no-frills lifestyle, every television program and motion picture declared it flat and lusterless, if not entirely irrelevant.

As a people then, Seminolians were portrayed by the outside world as not so much rooted in the land as helplessly trapped by it, their customs and beliefs less quaint than anachronistic. Consequently, the ordinary respect that was generally accorded to the working world—or that had been forced upon it in the past by the pride and power of industrial trade unionism—was denied to the people of Seminole County by a combination of their limited economy, closed ideology, and undramatic geography, along with the cultural aridity that was the inevitable result of everything else. "What did they ever do?" Carl Isaacs would later ask about the Alday family. "No one would have ever paid any attention to them, if I hadn't come along and killed them."

Isaacs' cruel question was merely the latest expression of an attitude the people of Seminole County had heard and felt before. Who are we? Nobody. Though we help to feed a world vastly larger than our own. Though we grow and cut the timber for its houses and its paper. Nobody. Though we do no harm—perhaps *because* we do no harm— we are nobody.

Under such conditions, it could be expected that the four men from Maryland would come to symbolize in the most graphic and horrendous manner the violation from outside that the county had been feeling for as long as anyone could remember. They were not only Yankees, but urban Yankees from cosmopolitan Baltimore who had invaded the region much as General Sherman had a hundred years before, destroying a helpless civilian population, killing wantonly and without regard, then moving north again, leaving everything behind in ravaged disarray.

Year after year, the people of Seminole County had been made to feel inferior, had been shunted aside and dismissed as hicks and rednecks who were little more than the farm animals the greater society used to plow its fields. Now they had within their grasp the living embodiment of that other world which had so long regarded them with disdain, so long offended and degraded them. Now, at last, there was a chance to get even, actually to see the face of the enemy, a treat few people wished to miss on the morning of May 24 when the Alday defendants arrived in Donalsonville.

Thus, dressed in their everyday work clothes, they had begun gathering early that morning, first in small knots, then spreading out along the small courthouse square until it was entirely filled. Carefully kept at a distance from the courthouse itself, they had nonetheless insisted on making their presence felt. Although they did not hoot or jeer, their stern, unsmiling faces testified to the outrage that had been sweeping the community since the murders.

For although this was their first appearance in Donalsonville since the murders, the defendants had come to occupy the minds of the local people with an intensity unprecedented in the region's history. In fact, so much outrage had already been voiced in the community that on May 24, only ten days after the killings, the *Donalsonville News* had taken pains to point out that, although profoundly offended, the people of Seminole County remained law-abiding, and thus capable of rendering the accused a scrupulously fair trial. "The four suspects cannot get a passive, indifferent trial here," Bo McLeod, the newspaper's editor, wrote, "but they could get a fair one."

A fair trial was all the Alday family expected for the men who had killed their kindred so wantonly. Still numb from the catastrophe that had overwhelmed them, they stayed to themselves in the weeks following the murders, often gathering together on Sundays in the family homestead as they had done in years past. "We just wanted to be quiet," Nancy remembered, "to be together and go through it the best way we could."

But the unearthly quiet that pervaded the homestead on River Road during those interminable Sunday afternoons when the family sat in stricken silence, or shuffled back and forth among the home's varied, and now largely unoccupied, rooms, was in marked contrast to the boisterousness and vituperation that had steadily engulfed their surrounding community.

Sitting at the nearly empty dining room table, or in the numerous unoccupied chairs that bedecked the house's expansive front porch, Ernestine, Nancy, Patricia, and Fay, the last of the Alday women who remained in Donalsonville, could sense the rising tide in every newspaper that fell into their hands. Reading them was an agonizing experience, compounded by the fact that it would have been impossible to find a local paper that did not remind them of the murders, as well as of their community's ferocious reaction toward the four men accused of committing them.

The *Camilla Enterprise* stated what it considered to be that community's feelings in no uncertain terms. "We kill rattlesnakes," the paper declared in a reference to what could hardly be mistaken for anything but the Isaacs brothers and Dungee. The *Bainbridge Post-Searchlight* was even more emphatic in its expression of disgust. After noting that in earlier editorial parlance American newspapers had often declared that a particular criminal "should be shot down like a dirty dog," the paper went on to say that in the case of the Alday killers, "such a comparison would be speaking disparagingly of dogs." The *Houston Home Journal* wrote that the Alday murders served as the best argument imaginable for the reinstatement of the death penalty. For its part, the *Baxley Banner News* dropped even the pretense of presumed innocence. Declaring that the case proved the need to extend statewide arrest powers to the Department of Investigation, the paper noted specifically that such powers were needed "to track down the escaped convicts who brutally killed six members of the Alday family," so that they could be "brought back to Seminole County to face the life-long friends and relatives" of the people they had murdered.

Local newspapers, of course, were not alone in their call for the execution, and day after day, Patricia in her office, or Nancy and Ernestine on River Road, listened as such local officials as Sheriff Dan White declared that he would "precook" the defendants before throwing the switch on the electric chair.

Although Ernestine and her daughters might have expected a fierce community reaction toward the men accused of the murders, others found the equally negative response of the very attorneys who had been appointed to defend them genuinely alarming, suggesting the possibility that a fair trial might not be possible in Seminole County.

Within days of their appointments, most of the eight attorneys who had been selected to defend the accused had either publicly or privately discussed their unhappiness with the appointment. Some, such as Julian Webb, who'd been appointed to defend Billy Isaacs, and J. William Conger, who was one of two attorneys assigned to defend Carl Isaacs and had publicly declared that he'd "rather take a whipping" than carry out that defense, were eventually granted their requests to be removed from their respective cases.

Other defense attorneys, while willing to carry out their court appointments, were quick to point out the odiousness of the task before them. Harold Lambert declared the defense of Wayne Coleman to be "the worst thing that's ever happened to me professionally," while Tracey Moulton, Coleman's other attorney, called his appointment to the two-man defense team a "terrible financial burden" that would also cause a "loss of friends" in the community.

According to a May 25 article in the *Albany Herald,* Lambert's, Webb's, Conger's, and Moulton's publicly expressed distaste for defending their clients was privately shared by all the other court-appointed attorneys. Although quoted as saying that they planned to provide their "best courtroom defense," they also told reporters that they would do so with "reluctance."

Though the tone of various public officials and officers of the court in Seminole County rose to a certain pitch, it was relatively mild compared to the response of the general public. A feeling of lost security had generated "sky-rocketing" increases in gun sales in Seminole, according to some reports. It had also darkened the mood of a region whose citizens had suddenly been made to feel terribly vulnerable to the sort of people Bo McLeod called "sorry and shiftless," and against whom the people of Seminole County could be expected to react in a spirit of shock, grief, anger, and, just as predictably, revenge.

Within the small community, the news of the murders spread, as one local observer said, "like fire in broom sage." During the following days it was the supreme topic of local discussion. So much so, as one Seminole County woman put it, that any local resident would "have to have had lockjaw" not to have discussed the case by the time of the arraignment. By then the discussion had shifted from the crimes themselves to the men who had been arrested for committing them and, inevitably, to the consideration of their punishment.

According to the *Atlanta Constitution,* local authorities in Seminole County believed that "lynching has crossed the mind of everybody" in that community. The specter of lynching was ever present in the public mind once the prisoners were returned to Georgia, and although publicly denied, it must have played a part in the final decision to house each of the defendants in four separate jails, all of which were outside Seminole County and at some distance from each other.

Nor was the notion of lynching merely a figment of official imaginations. Only a few years before his death, Bud Alday told reporters that he'd been approached by several men who'd told him that they were prepared to raise a lynching party. He'd forcefully resisted the idea at the time, he continued, then added that he'd later come to support it, although only after it was too late. Although several members of the Alday family privately doubted the veracity of Bud's claim, and in later months even came to resent his emergence as the family's self-appointed media spokesman, there could be little doubt that public sentiment in Seminole County was at a boil during the weeks immediately following the murders.

Predictably, the pervasive appetite was for swift and final justice, albeit through legal means. According to Ms. Lucille Bennington, the words "fry 'em" and "electrocute 'em" saturated the air of the county. "That's about all I heard," she told a local television reporter, "and that's what should have been done with them."

Atlanta Journal reporter Bill Montgomery remembered much the same atmosphere. "The general attitude was that if they were guilty, they should be executed," Montgomery recalled.

Dave Harrison, of the *Albany Herald*, heard much the same sentiment. "The people were very angry," he remembered years later. "They wanted revenge."

For some, according to UPI reporter Bill Cotterell, that revenge could not be carried out quickly enough. "I heard frequent expressions of an attitude like 'isn't it too bad that when they get these guys and when they're convicted it's going to take forever for justice to be done, and wouldn't it be better if we could just do it on the spot.' " The general feeling, Cotterell recalled, was that the presiding judge should simply release the defendants on their own recognizance, and that "justice would then be swiftly done within the community."

Added to this pervasive sense that the killers should be executed was the equally widespread conviction that the men who were about to be arraigned in Donalsonville on May 24 were, in fact, the men who had murdered the Aldays ten days before. According to Bo McLeod, the general feeling in the community was that "the law enforcement officials had arrested the right people, and that the persons who had been charged with the crime were the ones who had committed it."

With their guilt more or less decided in the mind of Seminole County, with much of the evidence against them already visible in the local press, with the defendants' own, however confused, statements and confessions steadily warming in the hands of state authorities, it was now only a matter of going through the legal motions in a formal process whose first slow turns began on the morning of May 24, 1973, as Carl and Billy Isaacs, Wayne Coleman, and George Dungee were escorted into the Seminole County Courthouse to hear the terms of their arraignment.

Although the community's outrage was so intense that defense attorneys could feel it powerfully as they began to assume the responsibilities of the defense, the demeanor of the defendants themselves, when they appeared for the first time at the Seminole County Courthouse, appeared directly opposed to the mood that surrounded them, cool, composed, almost entirely silent.

During the brief arraignment proceedings, Carl emerged as cool and self-contained. While Coleman appeared slightly nervous, Dungee half-dazed and emotionless, and Billy utterly broken, his head bowed deeply toward his chest, Carl gave an impression of icy indifference, his head high, his eyes staring directly at the judge, an attitude which, once struck, he would maintain forever, as if through such posturing alone he could grasp some notion of himself.

To the state's charges, each of the defendants replied, "Not guilty." They were then hustled out of the courthouse and into waiting vehicles while the crowd of several hundred spectators watched from a distance, but made no attempt to intervene, as the *Donalsonville News* was quick to point out, in the orderly processes of the law. "Our people in this county are good people," it quoted Bud Alday as saying. "They just want to see justice done. I believe the court will take care of that."

Of course there were other things in Seminole County to take care of as well. Because for the last thirty years Ned, Ernestine and their sons and daughters had worked exclusively as members of a farming family, the division of labor among them had been based almost entirely on sex, the women assigned the less muscular tasks of cooking and cleaning while the men carried out the heavy labor of the fields. The murders had removed all the male Aldays from that labor. Ned was no longer there to supervise his sons. Jerry was not there to run the tractors and combines and other heavy machinery. Shuggie would never again feed his hogs. Jerry's blue pickup sat idle in the driveway on River Road. Thus, although at the time of their deaths the men had finished planting the crops, they were not available to tend or harvest them. Now, though only a few weeks after the murders, the crops planted earlier in the season were beginning to emerge from the soil. Unfortunately, so were the various grasses and assorted weeds that would easily reclaim the fields, robbing the crops of light and water should they be left untended.

As the days passed, Ernestine watched the first weedy sprouts rise determinedly from the dark soil. Soon they would consume the vast acreage Ned and her sons had planted. It was like watching the land begin to drown, its brown surface sinking slowly beneath the surging green.

She was not alone in seeing it, however. Her neighbors could see it too. It was not something they intended to allow.

Thus, in order to prevent the further disaster that such a loss would inflict upon the already devastated family, Eddie Chance issued a call for experienced hoe hands to help clear the grass that had begun to strangle the wide peanut fields that spread out over the Alday farm. Because of the time that had passed between the initial planting and the murders, Chance estimated that thirty to forty people were now needed to make up for the work that would have been done by the murdered men and could not be done by the women in their stead.

At just after daylight on the morning of June 9, the people of Seminole County responded to Chance's call, gathering by the scores to weed the crops, working throughout the day until the fields were clear.

In response to such acts of kindness and generosity, Ernestine and her children published a letter to the community in the *Donalsonville News,* the first and most sweeping public acknowledgment of all that had been done for them since the murders:

> We, the members of the Alday family, have chosen this method (inadequate though it may be) to express our sincere appreciation to each of you who have been so thoughtful during our tragic grief.
>
> The number of you who have responded to our situation is of such tremendous magnitude we are lacking the physical and mental strength to reply to each of you individually, and we certainly would want to omit no one.
>
> The cards, letters, telegrams, phone calls, visits, flowers, food and memorial gifts to our church continue to arrive and the number of these wonderful remembrances staggers our imagination.
>
> We lack words to truly express our humble appreciation to each of you for your thoughtfulness.

Your concern and your prayers have insured the sufficiency in God's grace in sustaining us in these perilous times.

The Alday Family

On May 24, the day of the arraignment, in its final salute to the Alday family, the *Donalsonville News* published its last photographs of those who had been murdered.

In pictures that could only be seen as expressive of lives wholly different from those of the defendants, it showed Jerry and Mary both dressed in their Sunday best as they posed proudly before the curtained window of their trailer.

Ned sat casually in work clothes, grinning happily from his front porch, his hat cocked raffishly to one side.

Shuggie stood in pants and white short-sleeved shirt under the pine trees of the farm, the paper declared, "that he and his family loved so well and worked together."

Last was Jimmy, a young bachelor in jeans and short-sleeved sport shirt, as he worked with the pigs on the Alday farm.

In sum, the paper concluded, these were pictures that stood "in simple testimony of the kind of life the hardworking, close-knit family lived until violence struck late Monday afternoon."

In stark contrast, on the opposite side of the same front page, the paper displayed large photos of the six Alday caskets as they rested on the cemetery grounds immediately before burial at the Spring Creek Cemetery. Laid side by side, and decked all around with enormous sprays of flowers, they gave off a powerful sense of the profound loss, both in number and in quality, that had been suffered by Ernestine and her children. Here, in the dark coffins, lay a farm family's essential strength and sustenance, a father, three brothers, an uncle, and a wife.

It was the last time the people of Seminole County would see pictures of the family members whose deaths would preoccupy them for the next seventeen years, and whose last dreadful moments had not yet been fully revealed by the testimony that would soon be given in open court. Had they known the manner in which Ned, Aubrey, Shuggie, Jerry, Jimmy, and Mary Alday had died, what had been done and said to them before their deaths—particularly the full degree of Mary's long agony—then they might well have been seized by a fury they could not control, and the mythical lynching might actually have taken place. If so, it would have been the only action they could have taken that would have violated them even more, heaped upon them more scorn, and in the end brought upon them a greater damage than the one they had already suffered.

It was finally Ernestine and her daughters who moved the community to an abiding calm in the way they calmed themselves, in their generosity, their silence, their restraint. It was as if she and her children already knew that there was a tragic opposite to the ancient legal premise that some injuries are too slight to find a remedy in law, knew profoundly and from the very beginning of their long ordeal that there were also injuries too great for justice ever to be done, that in the end, with the legal process now in motion, there was nothing for them to do but wait until it could run its course.

Chapter Sixteen

Ernestine and her daughters were not the only family members suffering because of what had happened on River Road. Hundreds of miles away, Riley Miller was still looking for his vanished son.

Thus, although Georgia was moving toward a conclusion of the investigative stage of the Alday murders, in Pennsylvania, the fate and whereabouts of Richard Wayne Miller remained unknown, despite a search that had been going on since the day of Miller's disappearance.

Not long after placing a Missing Person over the NCIC teletype, as well as a description of the car with Maryland plates that had been abandoned a few yards from Schooley's truck, Trooper Good had been contacted by Maryland authorities. They had notified him that the general descriptions of the men Deborah Poole and Norman Strait had seen near Lawrence Schooley's truck fit those of the three men who had escaped from the Poplar Hill Correctional Institute only days before.

Since those initial identifications, however, little had developed on the case as Good and other Pennsylvania authorities concentrated their efforts on locating Miller.

For days after the disappearance, extensive ground searches of every conceivable area in and around McConnellsburg had been conducted. Dozens of foot and road patrols had combed the largely rural areas of Jefferson County, while other authorities had followed up on the scores of leads and possible sightings that had been flowing into the Pennsylvania State Police barracks north of McConnellsburg.

As the days passed and the trail grew steadily cooler, police officials grew willing to follow almost any suggestion in their frustrated efforts to find Richard Miller.

"We had done grid searches, called in every local fire department and police force we could think of to help us," Good recalled, "but nothing had broken. At a certain point, we were willing to try anything."

Consequently, one afternoon several days after Miller's disappearance, when two local psychics appeared in Good's office, he listened quietly to their claims.

Beulah Johnson and a gentleman companion known only as Mr. Frantz told Good that they had long worked as psychics, and that they had developed a method for finding people who'd disappeared. They'd heard of Miller's disappearance and had come in order to assist the police in their search for his whereabouts.

Good leaned back in his chair. "Assist how?" he asked.

Johnson and Frantz explained that they were able to pick up "vibrations" of disappeared persons, and by following those vibrations, moving in the direction where they felt them most strongly, they were able to home in on a missing individual, as if closing in on a radio signal emitted from his body.

Good, his search at a dead end in all other areas, decided to pursue the issue a moment longer. "How do you start?" he asked.

"We're members of the American Map Society," Johnson told him. "We use a map."

"What kind of map?"

"One of the area where the person was last seen," Frantz answered.

Good nodded, then took a map of the general area around McConnellsburg, one that included northern Maryland, and spread it out on his desk. "Okay," he said, "let's see what you can do."

"I need a picture of Richard Miller," Johnson said, "a picture or something that belonged to him. I need to think about him while I look at the map."

Good gave her a photograph of Miller, and watched doubtfully as she held the photograph in her hand for a moment. A few seconds later, Johnson produced a pendulum that she then swung gently over the map, while continuing to hold onto Miller's picture. Frantz watched the pendulum as it drifted back and forth over the map, his eyes focused on its movements as if he were reading a complicated text.

"That direction," he said, pointing to the general area of farmland east of McConnellsburg. "He's over that way."

For the next three days, Good, Johnson, and Frantz roamed the

The Alday funeral. The Spring Creek Baptist Church could not accommodate the six caskets that held the murder victims.

Ned Alday with his youngest daughter, Faye, on the porch of the family homestead.

Mary Alday behind her desk at the Seminole County Department of Family and Children Services.

Aubrey Alday one year before his murder.

Shugie Alday and his wife, Barbara, at home.

Jimmy Alday in his Future Farmers of America jacket.

Jerry and Mary Alday on the Easter Sunday a month before their deaths.

Billy Isaacs, the state's
star witness.

Carl Isaacs, by all accounts the
gang's unchallenged leader.

Wayne Coleman arrives
at the Seminole County
Courthouse.

George Dungee shortly after
his capture in West Virginia.

Clockwise: Wayne Coleman, Billy Isaacs, and Carl Isaacs at the time of the retrials.

Ernestine, Nancy, and Patricia today.

woods and remote roads and farmland of southeastern Pennsylvania in an effort to find Richard Miller. In stop after stop, Good, growing more skeptical with each passing second, would watch beside the patrol car while Frantz and Johnson tried to work their wonders, repeating the same procedure again and again.

"We'd stop at some place where they'd picked up a vibration," Good remembered, "and either Beulah or Frantz would get out and start to work."

Frantz worked alone, with no equipment, simply stretching his two arms out in midair then letting them drift left or right until they began to quiver slightly, then more violently, then so fiercely that his whole body would shake convulsively. When the shaking reached its point of greatest violence, Frantz would suddenly grow rigid, point in a particular direction, then declare that Miller's body lay in the exact direction his outstretched arms indicated.

Unlike her psychic coworker, however, Beulah Johnson came to the search armed with the latest in psychic technology, two metal clothes hangers which had been bent into L-shapes. While Good and Frantz stood by, Johnson would hold each hanger at its shorter end while keeping Miller's picture folded in one of her hands. With arms outstretched, she would then lift the hangers into the air and wait.

What happened next astonished even the dubious Good. Within seconds, one of the hangers would begin to move, turning in a complete 360-degree circle before slowly drifting toward the other. When the two crossed, Beulah would nod confidently, as if she'd just sighted her prey between the cross-hairs of a rifle scope.

It was a procedure Johnson tried again and again over a period of three days, until finally, exasperated, Good decided to try it himself.

"If this thing whips around in my hand," he told Johnson as he drew the two hangers from her hand, "I'll jump right out of my boots."

Johnson stared at him solemnly. "You must believe," she said.

Good immediately repeated the movements he'd by then seen Johnson go through dozens of time. The response was immediate. "The end of one hanger did that same weird rotation," Good remembered, "rotating in midair without me doing a thing to turn it. Then it drifted over and crossed the other hanger just as it had done when Beulah held it."

"You have the power," Johnson cried.

Good shook his head determinedly. "These hangers may turn in my hands," he told her, "but they sure don't tell me anything." Then he returned the oddly quivering hangers to Beulah Johnson's care, abandoning all hope for an extrasensory solution to the fate of Richard Miller, and now utterly dependent upon those more difficult and tedious efforts which, though less intriguing, it seemed to him, still had their feet planted firmly on the ground.

That less dramatic solution first presented itself on the morning of May 18 when West Virginia State Trooper Frank Thomas released a volley of automatic rifle fire over the heads of Carl and Billy Isaacs, Wayne Coleman, and George Dungee.

Within hours of their arrest, Good had made contact with the Georgia authorities, who had by then returned their prisoners to the state. Now convinced that Richard Miller was dead, Good's efforts were dedicated to finding his body as the first step in the murder investigation that was sure to follow.

After several hours of negotiation, Wayne Coleman agreed to return to Pennsylvania in an effort to recover Miller's body.

Cocky and nonchalant, Coleman arrived by plane in Hagarstown, Maryland, shortly after his arraignment on May 24. Already given a guarantee that nothing he said or did during his time in Pennsylvania could be used against him, Coleman made no effort to conceal his involvement in the murder, even laughingly telling officials that he'd pulled the trigger himself because he "didn't want the others to have all the fun."

Coleman was cooperative and forthcoming regarding the details of Richard Miller's death, but he was less helpful when it came to locating his body. For nearly three days, Good, along with several heavily armed officers, escorted Coleman from place to place along the Pennsylvania-Maryland border. Repeatedly, Coleman claimed to recognize geographical and commercial landmarks, highways, side roads, and meandering streams in a random, discursive order that tied accompanying officials in knots, drew them back and forth in a series of zigzag patterns, and finally convinced them that Coleman had no idea where he had been either directly before or at the time of Richard Miller's murder.

"Wayne Coleman absolutely did not know where he was at any given time," Good remembered. "At one point he was even recognizing little roads around Mercersburg, Pennsylvania, a little town that was completely in the opposite direction from where he'd gone after taking Richard Miller."

Fed up after two days of following one wild-goose chase after another,

Good finally faced the disappointing fact that in all likelihood Coleman would not have been able to render any real assistance in finding Miller's body even if he had wanted to. Consequently, he reluctantly returned Coleman to Georgia custody.

It was only after Coleman's failure to locate Miller's body that authorities turned their attention to the remaining Alday defendants, and to their surprise found Carl Isaacs willing to come to their assistance.

Once in Pennsylvania, Carl presented a demeanor that was less flippant than that of his half-brother, though no less devoid of any sign of remorse.

In his knowledge of the area, Carl proved himself far superior to Coleman. Where Coleman's sense of place had appeared as little more than a rolling fog of disconnected impressions, Carl's gave every indication of being as thorough as it was precise. After being taken to where Lawrence Schooley's truck had been abandoned, he directed officers unerringly westward through a tangle of small towns and a broad swath of nondescript landscape that had utterly baffled Coleman only a short time before.

"There was not one tiny detail of that area he didn't remember," Good recalled years later. "And once, he told us that they'd all come to a T-shaped intersection, and that they'd been traveling so fast that they'd skidded across it into a parking lot. Well, when we got to that intersection, we drifted on across it into that parking lot, and as we were driving, we glanced over, and there they were, still on the pavement, the skid marks they'd left nearly six weeks before."

At that moment, Larry Good knew that finally, after so much work and so many false leads and blind alleys, he was about to find the body of Richard Wayne Miller.

However, about forty miles southwest of McConnellsburg, at Harry's Truck Stop in Pratt, Maryland, Carl momentarily appeared to lose his bearings. To jog his memory, Pennsylvania authorities summoned Maryland State Police Officer John McPharland, a man well known for his thorough command of the region's many obscure roads.

Standing six feet eight inches tall and weighing nearly three hundred pounds, McPharland practically filled the back seat of the car as he pulled himself in beside Carl Isaacs.

"He was very calm," McPharland remembered, "very matter-of-fact when he talked to me."

For a few minutes, Isaacs described in general terms the route he thought he had taken from Harry's Truck Stop. As he listened, McPharland traced the route in his mind, moving down U.S. 40, following Isaacs' narrative in his head, until he was sure he knew the area Isaacs had described.

Still in the back seat with Isaacs, McPharland continued to listen as the car headed west along Route 40 toward the small town of Flintstone, Maryland. At times, Isaacs would grow silent, then suddenly indicate some local landmark that he said he'd passed along the route that had taken Richard Miller to his death.

Once near Flintstone, Isaacs began to recognize the area in every detail. He directed McPharland to turn left onto Williams Road where, he said, he'd encountered a police car and made a quick dash up a small incline that McPharland recognized as Wallizer Hill.

"Isaacs said they'd waited on the hill for the car to pass," McPharland recalled, "then headed back down to Route 40 again, turned right, and driven on across Polish Mountain."

Once beyond the mountain, Isaacs suddenly recognized another road where, he said, he'd turned left and headed south for a distance of four or five miles.

The road was Murley Branch Road, and not far beyond the little village of Twiggtown, Isaacs began to tense slightly as the patrol car neared a second road, one that turned off to the left and was known locally as Brice Hollow.

"Turn here," Isaacs said.

About a half mile up Brice Hollow, Isaacs recognized an old logging road and turned to McPharland. "We went up that way," he said. For the next few minutes, Isaacs described the route he had taken up the road, pointing out various landmarks by which officers would be able to locate Miller's body.

"Isaacs didn't want to go up there with us," McPharland remembered, "but he said that up the logging road we'd come to a trash dump, and that we should go off to the left at that point, and that we would find Richard Miller's body not far away."

McPharland, Good, and several other officers proceeded up the logging road. A few minutes later they spotted the unsightly, debris-strewn dumping area Isaacs had described, then turned left onto a trail that led jaggedly through the brush. They'd only gone down it for a few yards before the long search for Richard Miller came abruptly to an end.

"He was lying facedown so I couldn't see his face," Good remembered, "but his father had told me he wore dingo boots, and I could see them very clearly in the grass even before I got close to the body, so I knew that it was Richard."

Once Miller's body had been located, investigators turned to the questions of how and why he had been murdered. Here, once again, Carl Isaacs was more than willing to oblige them. It was a question of getting away, he told investigators matter-of-factly, of making sure that there would be no witnesses. From the moment Richard Miller had approached them, Isaacs said, he was a dead man.

The only question had been where the murder should be carried out and which of the four would be the one to do it. The obscure logging road had provided the answer as to location, Isaacs said, but not as to who would do the killing. Thus, with Richard Miller on his knees before them, they had openly discussed who would kill him, arguing back and forth for several agonizing minutes while Miller pleaded for his life. "That was the worst part of it for me," Maryland District Attorney Investigator Bill Baker recalled, "just thinking about Richard's last few minutes. No one should have to die like that."

Indeed not, according to Ronnie Angel, who'd accompanied both Coleman and Isaacs to Pennsylvania, and had been at Good and McPharland's side when the body was discovered. "It was really bad, the way he looked," he said years later, "and the way they'd just laid him down and shot him, a young boy, only nineteen years old. I was determined that somebody was going to pay for killing him, no matter what happened to the Isaacs brothers and Coleman and Dungee in Georgia."

By then the fate of the Alday defendants was in the hands of the courts, and Angel knew that those who would eventually prosecute them would want the strongest imaginable case. The problem was that although the physical evidence was steadily accumulating, there was, as yet, no entirely credible witness to the murders other than the four men who had committed them, men whose statements, to the extent that they had given them, were full of conflicts and contradictions. Because of that, Angel suspected that a deal of some kind would have to be struck with one of the four defendants if the truth were ever going to be known about what happened inside the trailer on River Road or in the isolated woods six miles away.

The question was, which one?

Chapter Seventeen

The ultimate decision as to "which one" fell to Peter Zack Geer, the fifty-three-year-old former state attorney general who was widely reported to have been hired by the Aldays as their special prosecutor in the case. In fact Geer had never been hired, but had telephoned Ernestine and volunteered his services in the case shortly after the capture in West Virginia.

At the time of the murders, Geer had known Ned, Bud, and other of the Alday men for several years. He had fished with them on Lake Seminole, and occasionally been a guest in their homes. He had found Ned a happy, joyful man, and had enjoyed spending time with him. As to the murdered sons, they'd struck Geer as perfect representatives of the family life they'd enjoyed, modest, upright, and good-humored. Prosecuting the men who'd murdered them was something he could hardly have been more eager to carry out.

Ernestine accepted Geer's services with the same deference with which she'd accepted the aid of other, less notable, family friends. More important, however, was her need to avoid the agony of remembrance. Often breaking down in tears, her long self-control at times crumbling without warning, she wanted to distance herself from the trials. She knew what the testimony would be like, how graphic it would have to be, and she did not want to hear it. She had already decided that she could not bear to attend the trials. Turning the case over to Geer provided another way of pulling back from the trailer on River Road, of managing not to cross its tragic threshold.

With Geer's appointment, the prosecutorial process shifted into the fast lane of statewide notoriety. At six feet six inches and 280 pounds,

Geer would have been an imposing figure almost anywhere, but within the spare reaches of Donalsonville and its environs, his was a starry presence indeed. Long one of Georgia's best-known and most colorful political personalities, Geer was a media bonanza, a natural for its incessantly shifting spotlight.

Nor was Geer unaware of the extreme public interest in the case. Without doubt, these trials would be the most famous in the history of the state. They would be accompanied by a media blitz.

But if the Alday case was ripe for publicity, it was also fraught with dangers. Having taken on the prosecution of the Alday defendants, the pressure to bring those prosecutions to an acceptable conclusion—one the public had already defined as including convictions and death sentences—was enormous. To fail in either case was unacceptable.

What Geer wanted, of course, was an airtight case, one in which every element necessary for an entirely successful prosecution was in place. Highly intelligent and fully experienced, Geer knew exactly what those elements were. He also knew that from the very beginning of his prosecutorial efforts, he had all of them but one.

First, both the motive and the opportunity to commit the murders were obvious and demonstrable. Without doubt, all the murdered Aldays had been robbed and Jerry and Mary Alday's trailer burglarized. At various stages of the investigation, a large number of their possessions, such as Mary Alday's Timex watch, had been found in the possession of the defendants. Thus, the murders could be tied to the burglary of Jerry Alday's trailer, the subsequent arrival of the Aldays, and the defendants' decision to leave no witnesses to their crimes. Consequently, the motive could not only be easily established, but once proven, it would serve to demonstrate that the murders themselves had been committed during the commission of a felony, a crime for which Georgia's new, and as yet untested, capital punishment statute called for the imposition of the death penalty.

As to the question of the defendants' opportunity to commit the crimes, numerous witnesses, such as Jerry Godby, could place them in the area of the Alday trailer at the time of the murders.

In addition to demonstrating motive and opportunity, Geer could easily establish that, beyond the question of the murders being committed during the commission of a felony, they were also multiple, with no less than six victims, and had been gravely and wantonly aggravated by the rape and kidnapping of Mary Alday, two other elements that fit the state's capital punishment statute.

Once the gravity of the crimes, along with the defendants' motive in and opportunity for committing them, were established, Geer knew he could go on to present the physical evidence, of which, it seemed to him, there was an overwhelming abundance, everything from an assortment of fingerprints found in the trailer and in various automobiles and on numerous articles used by the defendants, to ballistics tests that tied their weapons to the murders, to a vast array of items associated with the Aldays and found in the possession of the defendants at the time of their arrest in West Virginia or previously dumped by them in Sumter County, Alabama.

Both in general matters such as motive and opportunity as well as in such specifics as fingerprints and ballistics—and without the slightest doubt in either case—it was clear to Geer that the preponderance of the evidence would conclusively argue for the guilt of the defendants. But he also knew that sound physical evidence and eyewitness testimony from outside the trailer still left out that element which every prosecutor ultimately required in order to make his case so utterly airtight as to put to rest the reasonable doubt of even the most wily, suspicious, merciful, and, as it were, unreasonable of jurors.

What Geer needed was another set of eyes. Not Jerry Godby's, who'd seen two cars pass from a distance of many yards as he poured insecticide into a peanut sprayer, but another set entirely, one that had been inside the trailer at the time of the murders, and had then moved out of it, following along as Mary Alday was transported six miles down River Road, taken from a car, led off into the woods, and shot two times in the back.

A casual glance at the defendants' birthdays, along with the most cursory reading of the statements Coleman and Dungee had already given various officials in Georgia and West Virginia, made it clear that the eyes Geer needed were in Billy Isaacs' head.

Not one of the defendants had sought to link Billy to the actual murder of any of the Aldays, or even to lay his body on top of an anguished Mary Alday during the final hours of her life. In addition, even if he should be tied to such actions, his age alone would keep him from the electric chair.

For Geer's purposes, the younger Isaacs was clearly the perfect candidate for the eyewitness he needed to conclude his case. Billy was probably the least culpable of the four defendants. Certainly he was the youngest, and thus well beyond the reach of death. And yet, he had seen each and every outrage that had been committed between 4:30 and 6:00

P.M. on May 14, 1973. Thus, for Geer, the only question that remained was how much Billy Isaacs would be willing to tell of the horrible scenes he had witnessed, how steady and untrembling his finger would remain when he was called upon to point it at his brothers.

By the end of May, Judge Walter Geer—the special prosecutor's uncle, a kinship defense attorneys would raise many times in the coming years—had appointed eight lawyers to defend the four defendants in four entirely separate trials.

As already noted, however, within days of their appointments, shifts began occurring within the shaky ranks of the defense. Most notably, Bobby Lee Hill and Fletcher Farrington of Savannah took over the defense of Carl Isaacs in a move that Isaacs heartily approved. In the first of what would become many public pronouncements, Carl declared that he was aware that "Bobby L. Hill was on the counsel that overturned Georgia's last death penalty law." Because of that, Carl went on, "I know that these men are irrevocably, unalterably opposed to the death penalty, and that they will do everything within their talents and abilities to help me."

He was right. Bobby Lee Hill had for many years worked tirelessly to rid the state of Georgia of what he considered the unspeakable barbarity of capital punishment. For Hill, the heinousness of the Alday murders was not in question. In a sense, that very heinousness made his defense of Carl Isaacs even more critical. For surely if any crime deserved the imposition of the death penalty, it was the series of outrages that had occurred in and around River Road on May 14. But for Hill, that was just the point. Capital punishment was never appropriate, no matter what the crime. It was itself a form of murder, and simply because it was imposed upon those who had, themselves, committed murder, made it no more justifiable than the original offense.

Thus, for Hill, Carl Isaacs was the perfect candidate to test Georgia's new death penalty statute. As a court case it could serve to topple the new law from the lofty perch upon which the state legislature had placed it only a few months before, and he fully intended to use it to do just that.

As for Ernestine and her daughters, they could do no more than watch from their self-imposed silence as Hill assumed control of the case. As a lively media figure, he would bring it almost as much public attention as their own special prosecutor.

In addition, as Nancy and Patricia were beginning to understand, he would also shift the focus of the trial away from what had happened on River Road to the diminutive, nineteen-year-old man who was now on trial for doing it. Increasingly they had begun to notice that the names of the Alday dead were no longer mentioned, that they were lumped together in a faceless mass, that their pictures were no longer displayed in articles about the case. The complexity of their lives, it seemed to the Alday sisters, had been reduced to a one-word description of their economic function: farmers.

Ironically, just as Ned, Aubrey, Shuggie, Jerry, Jimmy, and Mary were fading into mist, the images of their murderers, particularly Carl Isaacs, were being drawn with greater and greater detail. With the arrival of each new magazine or newspaper, Nancy and Patricia saw pictures of Carl, or read his latest comments. "We could tell that our family was being killed off again," Nancy recalled years later, "that it would be Carl who'd be remembered from now on, his whole life, every little thing that had ever happened to him, and that my father and my brothers and my uncle and Mary would be these dead people he was associated with. Dead farmers. That's all."

To Nancy, Patricia, and others of the Alday children, the "dead farmers" remained what they had always been, the heart and soul of their once extended family, people whose sudden absences left enormous empty spaces. By then Faye had graduated from Seminole County High School, but with few relatives in the stadium to see it. With all but one of her brothers dead, her father dead, her uncle dead, it had been an affair of mournful women. From their seats in the old wooden bleachers, the surviving Alday women had watched Faye's graduation in a stony silence, their blue eyes glistening in the summer sun. "That was the first day that it really seemed like they were all missing at once," Patricia remembered. "Normally we would have filled the stands, but no more."

Immediately upon assuming control of Carl Isaacs' defense, Bobby Hill made a series of pretrial motions, the first of which was a motion for a closed committal hearing in which Hill declared that Carl would plead innocent to all charges. Quickly following Hill's lead, lawyers for the remaining three defendants also asked for speedy committal hearings and stated that their clients would plead innocent to all charges.

Closed hearings were subsequently granted, thus banning all prospective jurors from attendance. Hearings were held on August 9, at which time all four defendants were bound over to the grand jury.

Only a few days later, the September issue of *Front Page Detective* arrived at the newsstands of Seminole County. Inside its tawdry pages, the Alday family was treated to its first dose of blatantly exploitive media coverage of the tragedy they had suffered nearly four months before. In an article entitled "Too Evil to Be Called Animals," the magazine related in typically lurid and perfervid language the last unspeakable hours of the "sexually assaulted and slaughtered pretty Mary Alday," who, according to the author, "had been repeatedly raped and subjected to a hideous ordeal of sexual torture." Even after her death, the article went on, "the killer had continued to violate the young woman's body."

For Ernestine, this first exposure was unbearably painful. She refused to read it. But neither Nancy nor Patricia could stop themselves. The effect was jolting. "It was hard to imagine that people would write things like that, knowing that we would read them, or at least hear about them," Nancy remembered. "But, at least, we thought that would be the end of it, just this one disgusting little article, and after that, we would be left alone."

Instead, as later events would demonstrate, it was just the beginning.

At approximately 6:00 P.M. on September 4, the Seminole County grand jury indicted Carl Junior Isaacs, Wayne Carl Coleman, William Carroll Isaacs, and George Elder Dungee for a total of nineteen charges in the Alday case, including a full six counts of murder for each defendant.

Although eight of the twenty-one members of the Seminole County grand jury were black, Hill and Farrington filed a motion declaring that the method of securing grand jury members was discriminatory in that it tended to exclude blacks from service.

Meanwhile, on September 13, attorneys for Billy Isaacs asked that his case be remanded to juvenile court, a motion that was later denied.

Two days later, on September 15, Hill and Farrington were once again before Judge Geer, this time filing for a change of venue for Carl Isaacs' trial, a motion which, if granted, would have removed the trial from Seminole County.

Attorneys for Coleman and Dungee immediately filed similar motions.

A hearing on the motion for change of venue was conducted twelve days later, on September 27. During the hearing, Hill and other members of the defense team introduced a great deal of evidence to support their contention that the pretrial atmosphere in Seminole County had reached such a level of public outrage that Isaacs could not possibly receive a fair trial.

To support his argument, Hill introduced scores of clippings from the *Donalsonville News*, along with other newspaper clippings from such neighboring communities as Bainbridge, Georgia, and Dothan, Alabama, both approximately forty miles away. In addition to these newspapers, Hill presented evidence that 300 to 450 copies of the September issue of *Front Page Detective*, with its title reference to the Alday defendants as "Too Evil to Be Called Animals," had been purchased in Seminole County.

As a result of the pervasive and inflammatory nature of such media coverage, Hill requested a change of venue, which would allow the trial to take place in a less prejudicial location, and went on to suggest certain more appropriate sites, beginning with various Georgia counties, but ranging even farther, to such places as Cook County (Chicago), Illinois; Kings County (Brooklyn), New York; and Washington, D.C.

Geer, however, vigorously opposed the removal of the trial from Seminole County, arguing forcefully that it was the county's right to try those who had offended it, and that to suggest its inability to do so was nothing less than an insult and an affront to its citizens.

Nearly two weeks later, on October 9, Judge Geer denied all motions for change of venue and set Carl Isaacs' trial to begin on December 31, 1973.

Three weeks after Judge Geer's decision, a second sensationalistic account of the Alday murders arrived on the newsstands frequented by the surviving Aldays. It was the November issue of *Detective Files,* and its cover was captioned in bold letters "Sex Ghouls in Georgia, 'Six for the Grave . . . One for Us.'" Inside, under a display of mug shots of the Alday defendants, the magazine declared in bold type that "in an effort to satisfy their depraved lust, the foursome didn't shrink from wantonly disposing of anyone who happened to get in their way." Thus, according to the article, "six members of a farm family were obliterated . . . by that breed which cares nothing for anything except its own brutal needs," and whose "grinning, hard-faced intentness is known by instinct to all females."

Although quite a few local residents of Seminole County were able to acquire the September issue of *Front Page Detective,* the accessibility of the *Detective Files* November issue was less uncontrolled. Now alerted to the possibility of such painful accounts of the murders, local merchants had since September been carefully scrutinizing the various police and detective magazines which, before then, they had routinely placed on their shelves. Consequently, they were ready for *Detective Files* when it showed up, and deeming it, in their own words, "gross" and "misleading," they quietly removed it from their shelves.

For Ernestine and her daughters, the months during which the defense and prosecution teams prepared their case in the upcoming trial of Carl Isaacs were uniquely dark and painful. The first family Thanksgiving since the murders took place at the enormous dining room table, with Ernestine serving turkey with all the trimmings to her monstrously diminished family. Nancy and Patricia were there, of course, along with Elizabeth and Faye, but the old boisterousness was gone. "It was so quiet," Patricia remembered, "and we were never a quiet family."

Only a few days later, a further diminishment occurred. By then, Ernestine had come to face one of the harshest and most inevitable consequences of the grave loss that had been inflicted upon them on the afternoon of May 14. Without the men, the family simply could not continue its most basic economic activity.

"As far as farming went, it was just impossible to carry on with it," Nancy recalled. "And we just couldn't sit there and let everything go to rust. We had to get what we could out of it."

Consequently, on the morning of December 14, approximately two weeks before Carl Isaacs' trial was to begin, an auction of the Alday farm's equipment and supplies was held on the grounds of the family homestead on River Road. By then the farm had been bereft for months of the men required to carry out its strenuous labors. As a result, Ernestine had finally acceded to the wishes of the Campbell family, who were Mary Alday's heirs, and Shuggie's wife, Barbara, to auction off the estate's heavy equipment and supplies, all of which had remained idle for the preceding six months.

"I got up and baked a bunch of cookies for the people who came to the house that morning," Patricia remembered. "It was cold, and we served them cookies and coffee while they looked over all the stuff that was for sale."

Then the auction began, and, wrapped in a long coat against the winter chill, Ernestine stood silently and watched as the auctioneer moved from jeep to rotary tiller to peanut planter. With each passing hour, the family saw their farm shrink as one piece of machinery after another was offered for sale, bought and then driven away from the home.

"We didn't go much," Ernestine told Charles Postell, the *Albany Herald* reporter who covered the auction and about whom the Alday family would hear a great deal more in the coming years. "We didn't take much time off for the pleasurable things . . . just stayed home and worked and went to church."

At the end of the day, the auction had netted the family nearly thirty-three thousand dollars, a sum of money that was then added to an overall family estate whose legal complications were only beginning to be guessed, and whose painful outcome neither Ernestine nor her daughters could possible imagine.

Christmas followed the auction by only eleven days, and once again the family gathered at the homestead. Ernestine and Faye had put up a tree, and brightly wrapped gifts were spread out all around it. In Christmases past, Ned had always been the last to open his presents, but on this Christmas it was Ernestine. "It didn't feel right," she would say many years later.

For the daughters, Ned's absence was particularly painful. "He loved chocolate-covered cherries," Nancy remembered. "And every Christmas, each of the kids would buy him a box. But that Christmas, no one bought any. No chocolate-covered cherries, that's what I remember most."

Six days later, on the night of December 30, 1973, Ernestine was once again surrounded by her children in the house on River Road. The trial of Carl Isaacs had been set to begin the next day, and in the hours before it began, each of the sisters made her way to Ernestine's side.

"I don't know why we came that night," Patricia said years later, "but we all ended up there, every one of us. We knew that we were going to hear terrible things over the next few days, and I guess we sort of wanted to be together one more time before that started."

Chapter Eighteen

While the weeks passed slowly along bleak stretches of River Road, the green crops of summer drying to a crackling brown, Geer and Hill continued to work on their cases.

For Hill, the essential task would be to dispute as much as possible any attempt to put a specific gun in Carl Isaacs' hand at any specific moment. The forensic evidence, particularly fingerprints, indisputably placed Carl Isaacs in the Alday trailer, but none of it could be used to demonstrate that while there he had actually committed murder.

Thus, for Hill, the main thrust of the defense would be to impeach the testimony of Billy Isaacs, to impugn him as a self-serving family traitor who had sold out his brother in order to save his own skin.

It was Geer's task to make sure that didn't happen, but also to arrange and present the evidence necessary to re-create the murders as vividly as possible, then the physical evidence that linked Carl Isaacs to the crimes, and finally to call Billy to the stand to give eyewitness testimony that Carl Isaacs had willfully participated in the cold-blooded murder of all six of the Alday victims.

By December 30, 1973, both he and Hill were prepared to present their cases.

Although indisputably the town's most impressive building, the Seminole County Courthouse in Donalsonville, Georgia, nonetheless suggested the pinched economic life that surrounded it. A two-story red-brick building with a short span of unpainted concrete steps, it rested at the head of what amounted to the town's central thoroughfare,

Second Street, a wide, slightly curving avenue of feed stores, auto parts outlets, and a scattering of those other perennial establishments of rural America, farm finance-and-loan companies.

Set on a rectangular lot adorned only by a few short palm trees and a smattering of squat war memorials and trophy cases, the courthouse had long been the judicial and administrative center of Seminole County. As such, it housed not only the court and adjoining jury rooms but an assortment of county offices, including the sheriff's office with its tiny jail and the offices of the county clerk and tax assessors.

In a building of small, cluttered offices where every inch seemed to be used to its full potential, the courtroom stood as the most spacious and imposing, though it, too, was anything but grand. Its bare, light-green walls enclosed a spartan gathering of wooden furniture, and its large windows rattled loudly in the wintry winds that blew in from the fields. In summer it was ventilated by two overhead fans that gave the entire room a sense of being antiquated, a place where old men had once lounged in open shirts and suspenders and discussed their exploits at Antietam or Bull Run.

In its overall affect, then, Judge Walter Geer's courtroom was stereotypically small-town southern. Or so it must certainly have seemed to the four men from Baltimore who were now destined to be tried within its walls.

The first of them, according to the docket set by Judge Geer on October 9, was to be Carl Junior Isaacs, the man who by then most investigators believed to have been, despite his youth, the malignant moving spirit behind the horrors that had occurred on River Road.

The preliminary proceedings in the trial of Carl Isaacs for the murder of six members of the Alday family began at 9:30 A.M. on December 31, 1973. Almost immediately, during the extraordinarily brief voir dire questioning of prospective jurors, it became obvious that many of the jurors were extremely familiar with the details of the case. They had read newspaper accounts published not only in the *Donalsonville News,* but in numerous other dailies from Dothan, Alabama, to Atlanta. In addition, many of the prospective jurors had also known at least one of the victims, and had even attended the Alday funeral at the Spring Creek Baptist Church five months earlier.

Nevertheless, within a single day, the voir dire had been completed, and a jury for Carl Isaacs' trial had been assembled entirely from among residents of Seminole County or its vicinity.

Thus at 9:00 A.M. on New Year's Day, January 1, 1974, Geer began the courtroom phase of his prosecution, calling with lightning speed witness after witness in a parade of testimony that whisked the jury from the initial discovery of the murder victims through the various stages of the investigation into their deaths, and finally ending with the dramatic capture of the Maryland escapees in the hills of West Virginia.

He began with Bud Alday, who swiftly recounted a series of events by then familiar not only to the community but to the United States and even several European countries in which stories of the murders had appeared.

Farrington's brief cross-examination disputed none of the facts of Bud's testimony, and succeeded only in having him state the obvious fact that although he'd seen the dead bodies in the trailer, he had not seen Carl Isaacs in the vicinity of the trailer at any time.

Next, Geer called Sheriff White, who took the jury back to the trailer and retraced his journey through it, along with the subsequent arrival of other law enforcement officials, culminating in the discovery of Mary Alday's body some six miles from the trailer.

Jerry Godby took the stand after White, providing the first eyewitness testimony that could place Isaacs in the vicinity of the trailer at the time of the murders. Under Geer's direct examination, Godby stated that he'd been working in front of Jewell Easom's house when he'd seen a green Chevrolet Super Sport pass by. He'd been high in the air, at the time, working on a "spray outfit" that was hooked to the back of a tractor when the car had passed at a distance of between twenty-five and thirty-five feet. The tractor had not been moving, he said, and he'd been sitting on the lid of the tank, from which vantage point he'd seen the car pass at a speed he estimated at approximately forty to forty-five miles per hour.

He'd also seen the driver of the car, he told the jury. It was a young white man in a dark shirt with long, shoulder-length hair, and he'd nodded to him as he passed. Another man had sat in the passenger seat, while other men had followed behind in a second car, a blue and white Chevrolet Impala.

In a final, crucial detail, Godby said that the driver of the Super Sport had waved to him as he passed so that his attention had been drawn to the driver sufficiently for him to take a careful look at his face. Then he positively identified Carl Isaacs as the man behind the wheel.

In his cross-examination, Hill labored to establish that Godby had been wearing a cap at the time, and that it might have obscured his vision, a speculation Geer laughed at in his immediate redirect.

"Can you see pretty good when you're hunting with that cap on?" Geer asked.

Godby smiled. "Better than I can shoot," he said, then leaned back and waited as laughter rippled through the crowd of spectators in the room.

In the afternoon session, the pace continued with the same breathless rapidity Geer had established during the morning session. "There was practically no cross-examination," Geer recalled, "because there really wasn't anything to cross-examine about, since the evidence itself was so absolutely overwhelming."

Overwhelming or not, it still had to be presented, and during the afternoon session, Geer began to establish it conclusively.

Max Trawick described the discovery of Mary Alday's body, while later, Joyce Hinds, one of Mary's coworkers at the Department of Family and Children Services, identified the Timex watch with the Roman numerals on its face that she'd seen Mary wearing when she'd left work on the afternoon of her death. Barbara Alday, Shuggie's wife, followed Hinds to the stand and also identified Mary's watch, along with her husband's wallet, one of the many items that had been recovered in the woods of the Boyd Cutoff in Livingston, Alabama.

Later in the afternoon, Ronnie Angel returned to Donalsonville to testify about his part in the investigation, particularly as to the various weapons he had either recovered himself or received from other investigators. The inventory was impressive: a Smith and Wesson .32-caliber revolver, a High Standard .22-caliber revolver, a .380-caliber automatic pistol, a Stevens model 8722-caliber semiautomatic rifle, a Remington mode 572 slide-action .22-caliber rifle, and a Marlin .22-caliber automatic rifle.

He had brought most of these weapons back to Georgia after finding them in West Virginia, Angel told Geer in the final moments of his testimony.

"Did you bring any people back to Georgia with you?" Geer asked.

"Yes, sir, I did."

"Who did you bring back?"

"I brought back Billy Carroll Isaacs," Angel said, his eyes drifting over to where Nancy and Patricia Alday sat watching him from across the courtroom. "I brought back George Elder Dungee." He could see their eyes trained on him silently and respectfully. "I brought back

Wayne Carl Colemen." More than respect, a terrible and wondrous gratitude. "I brought back Carl Junior Isaacs."

"Do you see Carl Isaacs in the courtroom?"

Angel returned his attention to Geer. "Yes, sir, I do."

"Would you point him out for the record?"

Angel directed his gaze to Isaacs. "He's the man sitting there with the long brown hair and dark blue shirt," he said, then watched as Isaacs returned a cold, hard stare.

With his eighth witness, Geer began to introduce the first of the forensic evidence he would put forward for the prosecution, though in this first instance, dwelling on it very briefly.

Under his direct examination, Dr. Larry Howard discussed the autopsies, going into the necessary technical detail as to the positions of the wounds as well as the calibers of the various weapons used to inflict them. Collectively, Howard said, the Aldays had been shot a total of fourteen times with no fewer than four different weapons. Of the six, Ned had been fired upon the most, six times with three different weapons, in a barrage that had nearly pulverized the contents of his skull.

Sitting in the courtroom, it was hard for Patricia to understand why her father had been subjected to such a horrendous hail of gunfire. "Then the next day Billy Isaacs testified about how Daddy died," she would say years later, "and I thought, 'Yes, that was my daddy, that was what they'd had to have done to him.'"

On the following morning, Geer opened the second day of his prosecution by calling Nick Campbell to the stand.

Though only twenty-five years old, Campbell had been working in fingerprint identification for nearly seven years, and had worked directly under Ronnie Angel during the investigation of the murders.

On May 15, he had arrived in Donalsonville and gone directly to the trailer on River Road.

"Did you lift any fingerprints from the interior of that trailer?" Geer asked.

"Yes, sir, I did," Campbell said. "From several locations from the front bedroom to the rear bedroom."

In total, he told Geer, he had lifted twenty latent fingerprints from the trailer's interior. Of the twenty prints, most had proven negative with regard to the four Alday defendants.

Most, but not all.

In the south bedroom, he'd found on a small cabinet drawer a print that he identified as the left thumb of Carl Isaacs. He'd also found a fingerprint on a Pabst Blue Ribbon beer can, the very one that had so horrified Bud Alday five months before as he'd glimpsed its eerie aluminum sheen in the shadowy light of Jerry Alday's trailer. It was the left thumb of Wayne Coleman. Another beer can had borne the right thumbprint of George Dungee.

"All right, sir," Geer said, and with no follow-up questions, Campbell proceeded to his next fingerprint findings: the right little finger of Billy Isaacs on a Kodak camera box found in the north bedroom of the Alday trailer, the right middle finger of Carl Isaacs lifted from the inside rearview mirror of the Chevelle found in the woods near Mary Alday's body, along with two others of Isaacs' thumb taken from the chrome strip between the left door and vent windows.

But that was not all.

During his search of the floorboard of the abandoned Super Sport, Campbell testified that he had found a road map entitled "All About U.S. 15 and 17," a reference work which, as it turned out, Carl Isaacs had fingered to the bone, in the process leaving fully identifiable impressions of his left index, left middle, and left ring fingers.

And there was more, Campbell went on. On May 17 he had processed Mary Alday's blue and white Chevrolet Impala and found the left thumbprint of Carl Isaacs on wood-grain paneling inside the car's left door.

"All right," Geer said. "Did you recover any other items in Alabama near the Mary Alday car?"

"Yes, sir," Campbell answered, then listed a damning assortment found inside an old black suitcase the Alday defendants had discarded in their flight from Mary Alday's car: Shuggie's driver's license application, fishing license, hunting license, dental appointment cards, and his wife, Barbara's, fishing license.

"Now where did you find these items?" Geer asked.

"In a wooded area at the location of the Alday automobile in Alabama."

From a few feet away, Nancy listened as Campbell described the various personal articles he'd found in the woods of Sumter County. In her mind she could see her brother's old black suitcase as it must have appeared to Campbell, battered and discarded, empty except for the things he'd found inside, items that were meaningless to him except as evidence, but which to her were powerfully evocative of the life her father, uncle, and brothers had lived, their long days of fishing on the lake or stalking through its adjoining woods in search of quail or rabbits. "You began to see what you were going to miss," she recalled in 1990. "Not just the people, but all the things they did and enjoyed. Not just their lives, you might say, physically, but how much they enjoyed being alive, all the things they'd liked to do, but wouldn't be able to ever do again."

Chapter Nineteen

O n the third day of the trial, Geer presented the preponderance of his physical evidence in the form of Kelly Fite, the chief criminalist for the Georgia Crime Lab.

Geer knew that Fite's testimony would be protracted and that certain aspects would inevitably be tedious, but he hoped that its sheer volume and conclusiveness would set the stage for the far more dramatic testimony of Billy Isaacs which he'd already scheduled to follow Fite's.

As to Fite's testimony, Geer proceeded through it as rapidly as possible, building cumulatively at each stage of his presentation. He began his discussion with the question of guns.

Fite testified that he had fired and compared some three or four thousand guns, among them State's Exhibit 33, a .32-caliber pistol with the serial number 67997 that had been given to him by GBI agents involved in the investigation of the Alday murders.

"All right, sir," Geer said. "Now I ask you whether or not on May 15 you were delivered any bullets that had been extracted from the bodies of the Alday family."

"Yes, sir, I was," Fite said. "I was handed three .32-caliber bullets at the Evans Funeral Home, and extracted two others, myself."

"Did you make any test firing with the weapon you have identified with these bullets?"

"Yes, sir. I did."

"What were your findings?"

"I found the test bullet from the .32-caliber revolver to be identical with the three .32-caliber bullets taken from the head of Ned Alday."

Geer then showed Fite State's Exhibit 35, a .22-caliber revolver, serial number 1967864.

"And on the 15th of May, 1973, you received several .22-caliber bullets from Dr. Larry Howard at the Evans Funeral Home?" he asked.

"Yes, sir."

"All right, did you make some test firing with this .22-caliber pistol?"

"Yes, sir, I did test fire this gun, and compared my test bullets with the .22-caliber bullets Dr. Howard extracted from the head of Jerry Alday."

"And what did you find?"

"I found that my test bullets and the evidence bullets were identical with respect to land and groove structures," Fite answered.

The bullets had been much too mutilated during their destructive passage through Alday's skull for Fite to be certain that they had unquestionably been fired from the .22 that had been recovered in the hills of West Virginia.

"Were you handed any other .22-caliber bullets by Dr. Howard on May 15?" Geer asked.

"Yes, sir, I was," Fite replied. "I was handed one at the Alday house trailer."

"Where did this bullet come from?"

"Underneath the head of Jerry Alday."

"Was this bullet in a better condition than the other .22-caliber bullets you testified about?"

"Yes, sir."

"Now, have you made any test comparison with that bullet and that .22-caliber pistol, State's Exhibit 35?"

"I found that this bullet is identical with test bullets fired from that Exhibit."

Geer then handed Fite yet another pistol, this time a Husqvarna .380 automatic, commonly known as a nine-millimeter short, with the serial number 53219. Fite identified the weapon, then waited for the inevitable question.

"Now, were you handed any .380 bullets from Seminole County on May 15, 1973?"

"Yes, sir, I was. It came from a towel which was wrapped around the head of Shuggie Alday."

"Have you compared that bullet with the test firing from the automatic weapon we have under consideration?"

"Yes, sir," Fite answered. "I found that the bullet from the towel was identical with respect to land and groove structure and gross and microscopic similarities."

In other words, according to Fite, the bullet that had slammed through Shuggie Alday's skull had been fired by the same nine-millimeter short that had been recovered in West Virginia by Frank Thomas the day of Isaacs' capture.

From ballistic evidence, Geer then moved on to evidence that linked Mary Alday's Impala with Richard Miller's Chevrolet Super Sport, the car the Maryland escapees had stolen in McConnellsburg, Pennsylvania, before driving south to Florida.

According to Fite, GBI agents had delivered a mysteriously battered portion of the hood of the Impala on June 5, and asked if its injuries could be matched with an equally mysterious injury that had been suffered by the taillight assembly of the Super Sport, a portion of which they had delivered to him two weeks earlier.

"The agents requested that I examine these scratch marks," Fite told the jury, "and, if possible, determine if the taillight of the Super Sport had been in contact with the hood of the Impala."

"Did you make such an examination?" Geer asked.

Yes, Fite answered, he had. Over the next several days, as he explained to the jury, he had gone through several stages of his own scientific investigation, first cutting the tool marks out of the hood of Mary Alday's car, a procedure that reduced the cumbersome assembly to a small rectangle of only a few square inches. Under a comparison microscope, Fite was able to see numerous microscopic striations within the dented area. Along these striations, Fite could see flecks of green paint. The same process applied to the taillight assembly of the Super Sport revealed the presence of blue paint. A comparison of this paint, Fite said, with samples taken from Mary Alday's car revealed that they were identical with respect to color, texture, and other less obvious properties. Repeating the process on the green paint taken from the Alday car and the Super Sport, Fite found a similar identity. In addition, the striations on the two cars were identical.

The obvious conclusion was that the two cars had been in close and violent contact, a circumstance, as Geer well knew, that Billy Isaacs would soon be able to explain.

On the afternoon of January 4, the normally peaceful streets around the courthouse square in Donalsonville bustled with excitement and anticipation. Within a few minutes, the somewhat formal and tedious testimony in the trial of Carl Isaacs would be over. From then on, there would be no more talk of ballistics, test firings, and microscopic comparisons. The pistols before the community's consideration would no longer be fired into tanks of water, but into the heads and backs of six of their own. There would be no more discussion of postmortems. Now the talk would deal with the murder of living human beings rather than the minute examination of their lifeless flesh, and for the first time, the full story of what had happened along River Road between 4:00 and 6:00 P.M. on May 14, 1973, would be known. Finally, after many months of speculation, the community would be allowed to hear in all its dreadful detail precisely how, why, and with what level of cruelty Ned, Shuggie, Jerry, Jimmy, Aubrey, and Mary Alday had lost their lives. Up until then, they had heard only bits and pieces of the story; now they would receive a firsthand, eyewitness account of the six murders with which they had been preoccupied for nearly seven months.

"You could really feel the tension in the air the day Billy Isaacs took the stand," Bo McLeod would later say of that fateful afternoon. "Everybody knew that he was the one person in that courtroom, besides Carl, of course, who'd actually seen everything that happened in the trailer, and then in the woods a few miles down the road."

Nor was the drama centered around him lost on Billy Isaacs. "I knew they were all waiting to hear what I would say about Carl and the Aldays," he remembered in July of 1990, "but the only thing I can think of now is what a scared little kid I must have been the day I took the stand in front of all those people."

Some of those people were seated only a few short yards from the witness stand, their eyes leveled silently upon him as he took his seat in the witness stand. Nancy and Patricia were there, along with Norman, their only surviving brother, and Fay, their youngest sister, all of them even more apprehensive on this third day of testimony than they had been at the first day of the trial. For the testimony of Billy Isaacs would necessarily be the most difficult to bear, and all the Alday children found themselves drawing together to receive it, dreading every word, but absolutely determined to hear it.

From the beginning, Ernestine had absented herself from the proceedings. But for her children, attendance at the trial had been thought of as a solemn duty, a final act of love and devotion to their slaughtered kin, and as a way of making it clear that the men and woman who had been shot to death on May 14 had been real human beings. "They weren't just bodies bullets had gone through," Nancy later said. "They were not just little outlines on a chart, and we wanted everybody to remember, especially the murderers, that other people had loved the people they killed and would never let them be forgotten."

As his testimony was about to demonstrate, Billy Isaacs had certainly not forgotten them.

Chapter Twenty

Sixteen-year-old William Carroll Isaacs took the stand in the presence of his counsel and cocounsel, D'albert Bowen and John Irwin, with the understanding that their client would speak only on those events which pertained to the murders on River Road, that nothing about the death of Richard Wayne Miller would be discussed during his testimony, that no murder charges would be filed against him in Georgia, that instead he would be charged only with the considerably lesser offenses of burglary and car theft, but that for these crimes he would receive the maximum allowable sentences of twenty years each, to be served consecutively.

Now, at sixteen years of age, Billy Isaacs faced an absolute minimum of twenty years of incarceration. Under even the best of conditions, he would enter prison as a boy and come out as a man already at the edge of middle age.

It was by no means a sweetheart deal, but with six murder charges, along with kidnapping, as possible elements within a bill of indictment, Isaacs had hardly been in a strong negotiating position.

Thus, early in September, Isaacs had agreed to testify against the other three defendants, and on the twenty-first of that same month had been interviewed by Geer in the offices of the Randolph County Sheriff's Department in Cuthbert, Georgia, a small community approximately fifty miles from Donalsonville.

Since that single meeting, however, they had not seen each other, and as Isaacs made his way to the stand, Geer wondered if such a boy, only a few years beyond childhood, would be able to go through what now lay before him, in the presence not only of a large contingent of the Alday family, but, perhaps more important, of his revered older brother, Carl.

If Geer had had any doubts about either Billy Isaacs' willingness or his ability to testify against his brother, they were quickly resolved when, in answer to one of Geer's first questions, he coolly pointed Carl out as the man "in the orange-colored shirt" who sat little more than twenty feet away.

"Is he your brother?" Geer asked.

"Yes, sir."

"Do you know George Dungee?"

"Yes, sir."

"Do you know Wayne Carl Coleman?"

"Yes, sir, he's my half-brother."

"Where did you get in the presence of these individuals you have named?"

"Baltimore County, Maryland."

"Do you know where Carl Isaacs had been before he came and picked you up?"

"In a prison camp," Billy said. "He told me he had escaped."

Billy Isaacs then related the tortuous route from Maryland to Pennsylvania back to Maryland which had directly preceded the precipitous drive southward through West Virginia, North Carolina, South Carolina, Georgia, and across the state line into Florida. It was there, in a motel near Jacksonville, Isaacs said, that the four had remained for two days before making that fateful decision to head north again, finally crossing back into Georgia.

"Did you have an occasion to visit a mobile home in Seminole County, Georgia?" Geer asked.

"Yes, sir."

Geer then asked Isaacs to look at a photograph, State's Exhibit Number 1.

"Do you recognize that?" he asked.

"Yes, sir."

"What is it a picture of?"

"The Alday trailer home," Isaacs answered.

"And that's the place you visited with whom?"

"With Carl Isaacs, Wayne Carl Coleman, and George Dungee," Billy answered.

"Approximately what time did you get to this mobile home?"

William Carroll ("Billy") Isaacs drew in a long, apprehensive breath as he began to move inevitably toward the single most horrendous experience of his life.

"It was in the evening," he began, "around a quarter after four or four-thirty . . . "

Only a few feet away, staring evenly into Billy Isaacs' soft brown eyes, Nancy and Patricia sat silently and waited. "No one can ever imagine what it's like to sit and know that you're going to hear things that you'll never be able to get out of your mind," Nancy would say nearly seventeen years later.

Still, for the next two hours, the two sisters did just that, lived through an unprecedented slaughter, an assault upon the bodies of the closest kin that had by then become a further assault upon their land and livelihood and dignity, moving through the terrible hours slowly, as if it were a motion picture playing in their heads, bearing them onward toward unimaginable cruelties one excruciating frame at a time.

"It was in the evening," Billy Isaacs said, "about a quarter after four or four-thirty."

Richard Miller's green Super Sport was acting up, its carburetor shot, pumping gas incessantly, eating up their money. At first they'd looked for an isolated gas tank somewhere, but the only one they'd found was filled with diesel fuel.

So they'd continued on down a small, paved back road, through wide, flat fields, looking for a mark, a quick hit good enough to buy them a little more gas, a few more beers, maybe a night in some motel that had a television and a hot shower.

But the fields seemed to stretch out forever, featureless and vague, so that for the longest time, while the engine guzzled ceaselessly, they saw nothing but the gently undulating furrows and the small seedling plants that had just begun to sprout within them, saw nothing but a few isolated sodbusters crouched over the wheels of their tractors, saw nothing but empty land and empty sky, saw nothing until, at last, a likely mark swam into view.

"The Alday trailer home," Billy Isaacs said.

"And when you got to this mobile home," Geer asked, "did anyone go in?"

"Yes, sir."

"Who went in?"

"Wayne Carl Coleman," Billy Isaacs answered matter-of-factly, ticking off their full names. "Carl Junior Isaacs."

He'd been able to see them from his place in the back seat. Dungee had taken Carl's place behind the wheel so that he could press his foot on the accelerator to keep the engine from shutting down. This had left Billy alone in the back seat, from which position he had been able to keep Carl and Wayne in plain sight as they moved toward the trailer's back door, then turned its gray aluminum knob effortlessly.

"It was unlocked," Billy Isaacs said.

"Did you see them go in?"

"Yes, sir."

He saw them disappear into the trailer's shadowy interior. For a time he waited, still sitting silently in the back seat while Dungee continued to keep his foot on the accelerator, racing the engine slightly from time to time to make sure it didn't gutter out.

"Did you, yourself, later go in the trailer?" Geer asked.

"Yes, sir," Billy Isaacs said.

They were burglarizing the inside of the trailer, stumbling around in it, checking out drawers and cabinets, moving in their usual disorderly fashion from one room to the next. They had done it many times before, countless times, more than anyone could remember. Nothing had ever gone wrong before.

"Did someone arrive?" Geer asked.

"Two men in a jeep," Billy Isaacs said.

From twenty feet away, Patricia listened intently, her eyes trained on Billy Isaacs. Even without him saying it, she knew the jeep was blue, but more than that, she knew the men inside it, the "two men," as Isaacs had described them in the most minimal of terms. Ned Alday, her father. Jerry Alday, her brother. She had worked with them, played with them, laughed and cried and argued with them. Theirs were among the first hands she had ever touched, the first voices she had ever heard. Now they were moving into a driveway, and someone was watching them from behind the lacy curtains of Mary Alday's kitchen window, watching silently as their bodies jolted forward slightly when the jeep came to a halt in the bare, unpaved driveway of her brother's trailer.

*　*　*

"Two men in a jeep," Billy Isaacs said.

"What happened?" Geer asked.

An instantaneous decision, little more than a sudden reflex. Carl and Wayne had bolted out of the trailer and swept around the blue jeep. Carl drew his pistol and Wayne drew his pistol.

"And I pulled mine out," Billy Isaacs said.

Over the barrel of his own .22 pistol, he could see Ned and Jerry Alday as they were led back into the trailer. It was still dark inside, and they peered around briefly as they were directed to the kitchen table and told to sit down. To his right, he could see Carl watching them, his hand wrapped around the gleaming pearl handle of a second .22 he'd found inside the trailer.

For a moment, a small, barely human communication took place between Carl and the younger of the "two men."

"You live here?" Carl asked.

Jerry answered that he did, and Carl asked nothing else within Billy Isaacs' hearing because he and Coleman had left the kitchen by then to search the trailer again.

"What were you looking for?" Geer asked.

"For money," Billy Isaacs said. "For guns or clothing or something like that."

But they'd had very little luck in finding anything of value, so once back in the kitchen, they'd robbed the two men, and gotten the comparatively big haul of a penknife, a cigarette lighter, a wallet, and some change.

Then there was more talk.

"You married?" Carl asked Jerry Alday.

Jerry said he was, then added that his wife would be home soon. But there was no reason for him to wait for her, he told Carl, since his wife never carried any money beyond the few dollars she needed to take with her to work.

Perhaps in that instant, Jerry Alday caught something in Carl Isaacs' eyes that made him realize he'd made a terrible mistake. One he tried desperately to correct.

"He told Carl please not to hurt her," Billy Isaacs said.

"And after this was done, what took place?" Geer asked.

"Carl took the younger of the two men into the south bedroom," Billy Isaacs said, "and Wayne took the older man into the bedroom on the north side."

"Go ahead."

"There were shots from the south bedroom and from the north bedroom," Billy Isaacs said.

Listening mutely from behind the front rail of the courtroom, Nancy could hear more than Billy Isaacs' voice. She could hear the hail of gunfire that must have rained down upon her father and brother a few seconds after they'd been led to the opposite bedrooms of the trailer. Particularly on her father as he tried again and again to rise from the bed he'd been forced to lie down on, lifting himself repeatedly as Carl Isaacs and Wayne Coleman continued to fire at him at point-blank range. She could see the blue smoke that must have wafted from the two tiny rooms after the last reverberations from the pistols had finally died away.

Within minutes, her father and brother were dead. But even then it wasn't over.

In a sense, it had just begun.

"A middle-aged man pulled up on a green John Deere tractor," Billy Isaacs said.

Jimmy Alday slid out of the trailer seat, walked up to the back door of the trailer, and politely knocked, fully expecting Jerry to open it and, as he always had, cordially invite him in. What he saw was another visage entirely, of course, meaner, coarser, and in its grim aspect, unimaginably different from any face he had ever seen.

"Wayne Carl Coleman opened the door and told him to come inside," Billy Isaacs said.

"Did he put a gun on him?"

"Yes, sir."

"What happened then?"

As if caught in the black grooves of a warped phonograph record, the same actions were repeated in almost the same order, first robbery, this time the limited take of a hat, a pair of sunglasses, and a nearly empty wallet, then a short, dreadfully clipped exchange.

"Carl asked the man why he came up to the trailer," Billy Isaacs said.

"To see my brother," Jimmy replied.

"No, you didn't," Carl said. "You heard gunshots, didn't you?"

Jimmy shook his head. He had heard no gunshots, he told Carl. But in that instant, he must have realized that they had been fired outside

his hearing, that someone had been shot, that it was probably his
brother. He did not have time to ask.

"Carl took the man into the living room and shot him once behind
the back of the head," Billy Isaacs said.

Three men were now dead, a body in almost every room, the dark
air inside the small trailer choked with a thick bluish smoke, the smell
of gunpowder everywhere, and still they did not leave.

"Carl went outside to move the tractor and told George Dungee to
come into the trailer and watch out for Mary Alday when she came
home," Billy Isaacs said.

"Was Mary Alday the next person to come to the mobile home?"

"Yes, she was."

"And when she arrived, tell us what happened."

She'd pulled into the driveway almost immediately, but Dungee, his
mind forever inattentive and unfocused, had not seen her.

"I cussed at George and told him he should have been looking out
the window," Billy Isaacs said.

So it was Carl who'd first spotted Mary as she made the gentle curve
into the now crowded driveway and brought her blue and white Chevrolet Impala to a stop.

"She hopped out of her car," Billy Isaacs said.

And Carl hopped off the tractor.

"Carl came up behind her with a pistol in his hand and brought her
on into the trailer," Billy Isaacs said.

"What happened then?"

"She had a grocery bag in her arms and Carl knocked it out of her
hands," Billy Isaacs said.

Seated with her sisters in the first row of benches behind the courtroom rail, Patricia closed her eyes slowly, sensing as everyone in the
community already had, that of all those who had suffered so much on
the afternoon of May 14, Mary had surely suffered the most. There was
even something in this first petty act of violence against her, the knock-
ing of a bag of groceries from her defenseless hands, that had seemed
to send a jolt through those who sat in the hushed but crowded courtroom. How pointlessly humiliating a thing to do, how impossible it must
have been for Mary to comprehend it, and how it must have signaled
to her even at this first moment that as a human being, at least in the
minds of the men around her, she had already ceased to be.

The warped record spun again, and Mary Alday, just as Ned, Jerry, and Jimmy before her, was robbed of the few personal possessions she had.

"Carl took the pocketbook from her, opened it up and dumped it onto the table, and perfume and a wallet and car keys fell out of it," Billy Isaacs said.

"Any money?"

"There was a dollar bill inside."

"What happened after that?"

Nothing less than the utterly inconceivable.

"Two men pulled up in a bluish-green pickup truck," Billy Isaacs said.

For a moment, the four men stared unbelievingly out the small square windows of the trailer. The only sound within it was Mary Alday's crying.

"Carl told her to shut up," Billy Isaacs said.

But she didn't.

So he hit her.

Outside, however, the men, Shuggie and Aubrey Alday, were laughing, and after a moment, when they continued to sit in the bluish-green truck, making no effort to get out, Carl decided to go out and get them.

"He told me to come along with him, so we went out the front door of the trailer," Billy Isaacs said.

Armed with a .22 and a .38, they silently slunk around the side of the trailer, then fanned out around the truck, one at each door.

"Carl stuck his pistol up in the driver's face and told them to get out and me and Carl took them inside the trailer," Billy Isaacs said.

The laughter had stopped by then, but Carl continued to dwell upon it. "You think it's funny?" he demanded. "You laughing at me?"

No, the men told him, they'd been laughing at having just missed a black flowerpot as they'd turned into the driveway.

The laughing had stopped, but the crying had not. Mary had begun to whimper uncontrollably again. By then, she'd glimpsed Jimmy's body as it lay facedown on the living room sofa no more than ten feet away. "He looks like he's been hurt," she said to Shuggie and Aubrey as they sat where Carl had put them, carefully out of sight of Jimmy's body, crouched together on the kitchen floor.

Then, just as before, the next cog in the disordered machinery that now controlled everything that happened within the trailer clicked into place.

"Carl and Wayne was whispering to each other and Wayne took

some towels off from the kitchen table and went into the bedroom on the north side of the trailer," Billy Isaacs said.

But this time, additional preparation was required.

"Carl and George Dungee took Mary Alday into the bathroom," Billy Isaacs said.

Then he returned, leaving Mary with George, and took one of the men into the south bedroom while Coleman took the other one into the north bedroom.

"There were several shots from the bedroom Wayne had took the man into," Billy Isaacs said, but from the other bedroom, the one to the north, he heard only "clicks."

During the afternoon of killing, Carl's .22 had emptied.

"And so he came out of the bedroom real fast and grabbed ahold of my pistol and went back in the bedroom and there was one or two shots," Billy Isaacs said.

When Carl came out again, he was laughing. "That damned bastard begged for mercy," he said.

"That damned bastard" was Nancy's brother, and with his death, the last of her blood relations, the last of those male Aldays who had sustained the family farm for two generations, who'd fed its hungry hogs and grown its peanuts and hunted its covey of small, brown quail across every inch of the five hundred acres of their own land, was gone.

Now all that remained was Mary.

"She was still in the bathroom," Billy Isaacs said.

But once the last of the men lay dead, she was brought back into the kitchen and made to stand by the table. She was still crying, and Carl was still screaming at her to shut up while his eyes darted about the scattered contents of her pocketbook. He was looking for her car keys, and when he found them, he snatched them up.

"Then Carl and Wayne went outside and opened up the trunks of the cars outside, and Carl came back in and he told me to go out and help Wayne transfer the items from our car over to her car," Billy Isaacs said.

Billy had obeyed without question, and while he and Wayne continued to move their supplies from the Super Sport to the Impala, Carl began to paw at Mary Alday's breasts. For a time she resisted him, but he hit her again and again, so that by the time Billy returned to the trailer, she had given up.

"I opened the trailer door a few inches and Mary Alday was laying on the floor," Billy Isaacs said.

He could see Mary Alday on her back beneath the table, her white panties already stripped from her and flung to the side. The top part of her pants suit had been pulled up around her neck, revealing the two white breasts Carl had groped for, then seized by force, and now, for a time, appeared to be finished with.

"Carl Isaacs was standing by the kitchen table with his pants down," Billy Isaacs said. "George Dungee was standing behind Carl Isaacs."

As if, perhaps, he were the next in line.

But he was not.

"I closed the door of the trailer and went out and told Wayne that Carl was messing around with Mary Alday and Wayne Coleman said that he was going to go in," Billy Isaacs said.

And so he did, disappearing into the trailer's tiny, crowded kitchen, while Billy remained outside as the minutes crawled by one after another until he couldn't take it anymore and returned once again to the trailer door, opened it a few inches, and peered in.

"Wayne Coleman was on top of Mary Alday," Billy Isaacs said.

"What happened after that?"

"I told Carl to come on, that everything was ready."

"What took place then?"

"I closed the trailer door and went out and stood by the 396 Chevy, and a few minutes passed and the trailer door opened."

And out they came.

Carl Isaacs.

Wayne Coleman.

George Dungee.

And . . .

"Mary Alday had a red handkerchief tied around her eyes and had her hands tied behind her back and had a handkerchief tied around her mouth," Billy Isaacs said.

In that condition, she was placed in the back floorboard of her own car, with Dungee there to guard her, while Carl sat alone in the front seat behind the wheel.

At last, they were ready to go, but then, for the first time, their luck began fitfully to run out.

The Super Sport wouldn't crank.

"So Carl took the front of Mary Alday's car and pushed it out on the paved road until it finally started," Billy Isaacs said.

And again, as they moved northward down River Road, past Jerry Godby on his tractor and Mrs. Eddie Chance in her garden, and little Michael Jackson in his yard, their luck sputtered out briefly once again.

"Wayne had lost his wallet and he thought it was back in the trailer," Billy Isaacs said.

After returning to it, they headed out again, still moving northward down River Road until they came to a break in the forest which bordered it.

"We went across the field and zigzagged through the woods until we came to a little clearing in amongst the woods," Billy Isaacs said.

And there the Impala halted.

"Carl got out of the car and told me and Wayne to take the Super Sport on down in the woods as far as we could and wipe down the fingerprints," Billy Isaacs said.

Which, as always, they obediently did, but also as always, poorly did, shoddily and hastily did, leaving prints everywhere for Dr. Larry Howard to find and tell the world about.

Then they returned to the Impala.

"What, if anything, did you see?" Geer asked.

"Mary Alday was fully undressed," Billy Isaacs said.

She was nude, and leaning against the hood of the car. Carl was standing beside her until he saw the two other men approach. Then he suddenly stepped away and grabbed her by her wrist and threw her on the ground.

"What happened then?"

"Carl asked me and Wayne if we wanted any," Billy Isaacs said.

But Coleman had already had his, and Billy didn't want "any." Only George Dungee remained.

"George Dungee said he wanted to have sexual intercourse with her," Billy Isaacs said, using a pristine, clinical language that Dungee would not have known.

But Carl, as always, was the first in line.

"Carl said wait a minute because he wanted to have it first," Billy Isaacs said.

"What happened then?"

"He had sexual intercourse with her and then got up."

Now, at last, George could have his.

"And George Dungee had sexual intercourse with her," Billy Isaacs said.

Even then, however, it was not over.

"When Dungee got finished he got up and Carl asked me if I was sure that I didn't want any and I said no, that I did not. So Carl said that he wanted to have some peanut butter," Billy Isaacs said.

"Some what?"

"Some peanut butter."

"Go ahead."

"So he laughed at me and George and Wayne. And he turned her over on her stomach and he had sexual intercourse with her rectum."

"What happened then?"

"He got up and was laughing and before he had sexual intercourse in the rectum with her he had tried to get Mary Alday to have sexual intercourse in the mouth, but she refused, so Carl hit her upside of the head with his fist and he knocked her unconscious."

"How long did she remain unconscious?"

"Until Carl finished having sexual intercourse with her in the rectum. She came to when Carl had finished having sexual intercourse with her the second time and she sat up on the ground and asked if she could please get dressed and Carl said no."

There was no need for Mary Alday to get dressed.

She was about to die.

"We was getting ready to take Mary Alday down into the woods away from the car," Billy Isaacs said.

To kill her, of course, but murder was something George Dungee had not yet tasted . . . and wanted to.

"And so before Wayne took her down into the woods, Dungee spoke up and said, 'What about me?' " Billy Isaacs said.

To which Coleman shrugged, then handed Dungee his .22.

"And George took Mary Alday down into the woods a little ways away from the car, made her lay facedown on the ground and he shot her twice," Billy Isaacs said.

"And where did you go from there?"

"Headed toward Alabama."

"And when you got to Alabama what, if anything, happened to the Mary Alday car?"

"It was the next afternoon and we was going through a little town in Alabama and Mary Alday's car started overheating and Carl pulled off of the main road a ways and the car just blew up in one cloud of smoke."

With the Alday car now irrecoverably disabled, the four men had then proceeded to take what they needed from the abandoned car and toss the rest over a barbed wire fence and into a weedy field for Ronnie Angel and Horace Waters to find and bring back to Donalsonville.

Now on foot, they had retreated into the nearby woods, waited until nightfall, then walked into town, where they'd stolen a Chevy Caprice and headed north, finally reaching as far as West Virginia, where, for a final time, under a hail of shots from Frank Thomas's AR-15, their luck ran out completely.

It was over now, the first run through the story of May 14, and as Nancy and Patricia made their way out of the courtroom, they looked forward to hearing it only two more times, in the trials of Coleman and Dungee. After that, they would never have to hear it again.

"We felt a little relieved at the end of Billy Isaacs' testimony," Nancy Alday remembered, "like we'd gone through the worst of it."

But they had not.

Chapter Twenty-one

I n his cross-examination of Billy Isaacs, Bobby Hill, anticipating the sort of family background and mitigating circumstances that would be much more fully explored in later trials, led Billy back through his early years. In response to Hill's questions, Billy testified that he and Carl had not been raised together because when he was five, the two brothers had been placed in different foster homes because their mother could not support them.

"Did you ever know your father?" Hill asked.

"I don't verily remembered him."

But he did know his brother Carl, and on that fateful night in Baltimore, he'd been glad to see both Carl and Wayne.

"Did they ask you to go with them?"

"They asked me if I wanted to go."

"What was your answer?"

"Yes."

"Why did you want to go?"

"Just got the urge to be with my brothers."

For William Carroll ("Billy") Isaacs, it would always remain just as simple as that.

On January 2, the day following Billy's testimony, the prosecution and defense made their closing arguments in the case.

Rising to his full, imposing stature, Geer, in a deep, orotund voice, presented the situation as he saw it.

"What you do in this case," he told the jury, "is going to determine whether or not members of the Alday family can be shot and killed by a meandering band of killers."

As to Billy Isaacs' testimony, Geer was willing to admit that his star witness had not come from the most upstanding of the nation's citizens. "I can't get a Baptist preacher to be my witness," he declared. "Baptist preachers, Methodist preachers, Holiness preachers, rabbis, and Catholic priests are usually not at a mobile home where shootings are taking place. They are not usually in the woods where a woman is repeatedly raped and shot dead. Billy Carroll Isaacs was there."

In conclusion, Geer returned once again to the jury's responsibility to its community. "This community wants to know whether or not peaceful, law-abiding citizens can be shot down and killed and its wives raped and mistreated. The state of Georgia, from the mountains to the sea, wants to know what you are going to do about it."

Then, ticking off the names of the Alday dead one by one in a slow, dramatic cadence, Geer made his final plea. "Ned Alday. Jerry Alday. Chester Alday. Aubrey Alday. Jimmy Alday. Mary Alday. Their lips are sealed forever. They are dead. Carl J. Isaacs saw to that. God will tend to whether or not mercy shall be on his soul. Your duty is to say whether or not he is guilty or innocent. We ask you for a verdict of guilty."

In a very brief statement, Fletcher Farrington admitted that Carl Isaacs had been present in the Alday trailer, but he vigorously disputed the testimony of his brother Billy. Noting that some of the victims had been murdered by weapons that had been under Billy Isaacs' control, Farrington argued that Billy's testimony was entirely self-serving, meant not so much to convict Carl as to exonerate himself from any criminal responsibility for what had happened on River Road. "Billy, when he gets to Georgia and decided to be good, says, 'Carl took my gun from me.' Why is Billy not on trial? Billy figured out a way to save his skin, put it all on everybody else."

Sixty-eight minutes after Farrington had concluded his argument, the jury reached its verdict. It had found Carl Junior Isaacs guilty on all counts.

*　　*　　*

The penalty phase in the trial of Carl Isaacs began on January 7, with Geer as the first to speak.

"Now, what is your punishment to be?" he asked. "This is not an ordinary murder case. This is the most serious murder that ever happened in the history of Seminole County."

Geer then returned to the notion of the jury's duty to protect its community against the likes of Carl Isaacs. "There is only one way for you to make sure that this sort of tragic, senseless crime will not reoccur [sic] in Seminole County," he told the jury. "That's for your verdict to speak out and ring around the world that we have imposed death on Carl J. Isaacs."

It now fell to Bobby Lee Hill to make the last plea. In an argument only slightly longer than Geer's, he accepted the jury's finding of guilty under the law and assured them that he would not reargue the facts of the case as he stood before them now.

"Carl Isaacs is guilty because you said so," Hill told the jury. "I understand that for starters."

But the issue of Isaacs' guilt was not the only one the case raised, Hill contended. There was another matter at stake as well, one whose profundity could hardly be overestimated. "This whole case is about human life," Hill told the jury. "The people in that trailer who fired those guns obviously thought very little about human life. It is obvious that the guilty and the weak and the bitter think very little of human life."

The cheapening of human life had been going on relentlessly for years, Hill continued, a process that the Vietnam War and television violence had greatly accelerated. He hoped the jury would take the opposite course, hold all life infinitely dear. "Well, would you want to participate in the continuing of cheapening life? All you have to do is just come back and say that Carl Isaacs ought to be put to death over in Reidsville in a steel chair which attaches to electricity and puts him to death. So just continue that effort, and all of us will cheapen life just a little more."

Over the past few weeks, Hill said, he had come to have considerable admiration for the Alday family. "I regret all that occurred," he told the jury, "but what troubles me more is that if Carl Isaacs doesn't care about life, does that mean you don't have to care anything about life? He is guilty. He is guilty of not caring anything about human life and he thinks it's cheap. Do you have to be?"

Hill disputed Geer's notion that the death penalty had any deterrent effect on capital offenses. "The criminals are out there killing right now," he declared. "They are not out there keeping up with what Mr. Geer is saying."

As to Carl Isaacs and the other defendants, they could now be of help to society only if kept alive and studied. "Something is wrong with Billy," Hill declared. "Something is wrong with Wayne. Something is wrong with George. There is something wrong with Carl." But rather than making any attempt to discover the source of their behavior, Hill said, "all the system now asks is that you just adopt some of his notions about the cheapness of life."

In his final remarks, Hill returned to the Aldays. "They are surely one of the best, if not the best family you have here," he said, "but you can't do anything about what happened to them except adopt the same stupid, dumb, ignorant, malicious notion that the people who did it have."

Thirty-eight minutes after Hill's conclusion, and with virtually no discussion or deliberation, the jury was escorted back into Judge Geer's courtroom. They had decided that Carl Junior Isaacs should be put to death.

Nine days later, after an almost identical trial to that of Carl Issacs, and following a deliberation of only fifty-eight minutes, George Dungee was found guilty on all counts.

In his closing arguments in both the guilt/innocence and penalty phases of the trial, Geer presented nearly identical statements to the jury.

In the penalty phase, however, Dungee's attorney, Philip Sheffield, offered what Geer himself later called "the most eloquent argument against the death penalty" he had ever heard.

"I am against killing, period," Sheffield said, then launched into a brief history of the death penalty, moving through the Old Testament practice of stoning, to the Roman practice of crucifixion, to the burning of witches in England, the invention of the guillotine in France, through the rise of hanging as the standard form of legal execution in England, a method, Sheffield noted, that could be applied as the penalty for no less than 135 separate offenses.

Georgia had used the same method for many years, Sheffield told the jury, before finally switching to what appeared the more expeditious method of electrocution. "I remember when I was a teenage boy I went to the Georgia Military Academy," Sheffield said, "and I remember on too many occasions when we would sit down to the evening mess, the lights would dim and it was said that somebody was being executed in the electric chair just a few miles from us."

It was a practice that had only ended when the United States Supreme Court had declared Georgia's practice unconstitutional because it was used only on "the poor, the indigent, the half crazy, the incompetent and the black." Now, despite the new law that had just been passed by the general assembly to correct these abuses, Sheffield argued that it was about to happen again, the same punishment for the same victim. "You have got a little ole nigger man over here that doesn't weigh over 135 pounds," Sheffield said. "He is poor and he is broke. He is ignorant. I will venture to say he has an I.Q. of not over 80. This is the kind of person who has been killed for the most part in the history of capital punishment in Georgia."

Finally, Sheffield asked the jury who would be helped by Dungee's execution? Not the Aldays, he said, whose lives could never be regained, or whose grief, as expressed in the survivors, could never be assuaged.

Who would be hurt? Sheffield asked the jury, then answered for them. "I have a visceral fear that if you order the execution of this man that you may be the ones that will be hurt, that there will be a great day of judgment when you will face the authority of all the universe and when the book of life is opened to the page January 9, 1974, and your verdict which says, 'Kill him. Kill him,' is there for all to see, and you are asked just one question, 'Why? Why?', what will be your answer?"

After deliberating for less than two hours the jury returned with their answer to Sheffield's question. Unpersuaded by either the logic or the passion of his argument, they sentenced George Elder Dungee to death, a decision Dungee received, according to news accounts, entirely without emotion.

In contrast to Carl Isaacs, who'd appeared bored and indifferent to his trial proceedings, and who'd actually yawned lazily as Geer beseeched the jury for his death, Coleman seemed clearly concerned with his trial. Throughout the proceedings he wrung his hands nervously or twiddled edgily with a box of matches. Since his capture, he'd grown a wispy blond moustache and the beginnings of a light-colored beard. Only his two tattoos, the one of a heart with "MOM" written inside it on his left arm, and on his right, a slithering snake, remained to suggest the dissolute look he'd had at the time of his capture.

But if Coleman had changed his appearance, his actions on the afternoon of May 14, 1973, remained utterly unchanged in the mind of the jury. On January 24, after yet another of what the press called a "carbon copy" three-day trial of Carl Isaacs, and a jury deliberation of fifty minutes, Wayne Carl Coleman was convicted on all six counts of first-degree murder.

In the penalty phase, Geer argued along the same lines as he had successfully argued in the cases of Carl Isaacs and George Dungee, raising only one additional issue, the specter of escape, a concern that would be dramatically heightened in regard to the Aldays' killers in the years to come.

"And if he were sent off for life," Geer asked the jury, "suppose he should escape? Would you want him back in Seminole County with a .380 automatic in his hand? Would you want him anywhere in America with any kind of gun in his hand, if you sent him off for life, and he escaped?"

In his closing argument for the defense, Harold Lambert made a few brief references to Coleman's deprived background, the foster homes he'd lived in, the lack of religious training that had been extended to him, then buttressed his arguments with a host of biblical references. "Adam and Eve had two sons whose names were Cain and Abel," he told the jury. "And Cain took revenge out on his brother Abel, and Cain killed Abel." This, Lambert said, was the first murder. What, then, was the first punishment? "What did the Lord do by way of punishment?" Lambert asked the jury. "Did he have Cain killed? No. He banished him from the country for the remainder of his life and that was his punishment." This same banishment, Lambert argued, should be Coleman's punishment as well. "Justice will be done in this case if you impose six life sentences," he said, "and maybe he can serve as a human guinea pig to find out how minds such as his work, so that society can prevent tragedies such as this from ever occurring again."

It was not an argument to which the jury devoted much attention. Less than fifty minutes after its completion, they had rejected it entirely and sentenced Wayne Carl Coleman to death.

Standing beside his attorney, Coleman's nervousness had by then dissipated considerably. He listened in silence as Judge Geer pronounced sentence, then smiled broadly. "Thanks, Judge," he said.

With the three trials concluded, the entire process taking fewer than three weeks, Judge Geer could now pronounce his selection of a date of execution for the last of the Alday defendants. He'd decided that since each of the three was equally guilty the three should die as the Aldays had, together, all of them in one day, February 15, almost seven months to the day from the afternoon of the murders.

Although, as the *Donalsonville News* reported, this date was merely a formality and would certainly be changed as the mandatory and automatic appeals were made to the Georgia Supreme Court, the wheels at least had been set in motion, wheels that were expected within perhaps two years, inexorably and at a reasonable speed, to carry the Alday killers to their deaths.

"Relief, that's what we felt," Patricia Alday said many years later from her office at the Seminole County Department of Children Services. "Relief was about all."

If it was the relief of closure that Patricia, Nancy, Elizabeth and the other surviving children felt, of things finally brought to an end, a relief that might allow the remaining Aldays to begin to live again in an atmosphere unclouded by their tragedy, then it was certainly to be short-lived.

"WHAT ABOUT US?"

Chapter Twenty-two

On February 7, two weeks after the last trial ended, and only a few days after the execution dates had been set, the *Donalsonville News* reported that Bobby Lee Hill and Fletcher Farrington had appealed for a new trial on behalf of Carl Isaacs, one based upon the contention that the verdict had run "contrary to law."

Attorneys for Wayne Coleman and George Dungee immediately followed suit, beginning an appeals process, the paper noted, which "experts" believed might take as long as "a couple of years or more."

In the same issue, the paper made the first of what would in the end be dozens of mentions concerning the amounts of money the county was spending for the array of legal proceedings which had resulted from the Alday murders.

According to the *News*, the first bills had begun to come in, and by Seminole County terms they were high: $3,864 for jury pay alone, a sum considered particularly burdensome to a county whose economic condition was far from affluent, but a figure that was a mere shadow of the vast expenditures to come.

Two weeks later, on Sunday, February 26, 1974, Ernestine and her children gathered at the Spring Creek Baptist Church to break ground on the new sanctuary she had decided to help build, and which she intended to dedicate "in loving memory" to her lost family.

Over a hundred years old, the church had long been a part of her and Ned's religious life. Isaac Alday, Ned's father, had planted the first cedar on its front grounds, and over the years a host of family members

had worshiped and officiated within its spare wooden sanctuary. Four
of the five murdered Alday men had been deacons of the church. Mary
had served as its treasurer, while still other family members had occupied various positions from training union officer to song leader.

Because of the family's long commitment to the church, Ernestine
decided that those funds which had been coming to her since Mrs.
Braswell's first five-dollar bill, and which now amounted to approximately eighteen thousand dollars, would not be used for her own or any
member of the family's personal benefit. Instead it would be spent
exclusively to help erect a new brick sanctuary to replace the rapidly
deteriorating wooden one the Spring Creek Baptist Church currently
used to conduct its services.

The ground breaking was attended by the entire Alday family, as well
as more than a hundred people from the community. Surrounded by
her children and grandchildren, Ernestine, with shovel in hand, made
the first break in the red clay earth upon which the sanctuary would be
built.

Apart from the six graves which were to be bordered with imported
black marble, the sanctuary would be the single reminder of the Aldays'
lives and deaths in Seminole County.

As to the most macabre reminder of the events of May 14, the trailer
in which all but Mary Alday had died, it had already been sold and
towed away. "We don't know where it is," Bud Alday later told an
inquiring reporter, "and we don't want to know."

As the weeks passed, though, it became clear that more than the
trailer was at stake, as issues involving the disposition of the Alday estate
steadily grew more complicated. In the weeks following the murders,
a great many legal complexities had begun to emerge. Utterly overshadowed during the first weeks after the murders, these thorny questions
of inheritance and the division of property slowly began to entangle
Ernestine in legal complexities with which she was hardly equipped to
deal.

Unaccustomed to disputes of any kind, and utterly innocent of the
law's inflexible position in matters of probate, Ernestine suddenly found
herself faced with a legal reality whose consequences she could not
possibly have anticipated: the total dissolution of the family farm.

Such a possibility equally staggered her children. Having grown up
on the wide expanse of Alday land, having played in and worked its

more than five hundred and fifty acres of fields and woods, neither Nancy nor Patricia nor any of the other surviving children could imagine that, technically, it might no longer belong to them. And yet suddenly their ownership was in contention. The stretch of land which had been held in the family name for as long as any of them could remember had fallen into a legal netherworld which could not have been foreseen at the time of the murders.

More than anything, the problem had its origin in the extraordinary closeness of the Alday family ties. As Ned had gotten older, his health had noticeably deteriorated. Worsening arthritis had made it impossible for him to obtain farm financing, since his physical capacity to maintain the farm appeared in doubt. To eliminate the risk that his own poor health might put the farm in jeopardy, and in order to make the Alday lands attractive to various agricultural loans, Ned had deeded the entire farm, all its acreage, structures—everything from barns and sheds to the family home—and various tools and machinery to his sons.

It had never been a transaction intended to remove the Alday estate from Alday control. But the slaughter on River Road could hardly have been anticipated. Nor could the legally defined line of succession which resulted.

In that line, Mary Alday, by birth a Campbell, had died last. For the hour or so she had survived her husband and his family members, she had inherited the entire Alday estate. Thus, at her death it had legally passed not to any member of the Alday family, but to Mary's next of kin, her mother and father, the Campbells of nearby Colquitt.

"As far as the law was concerned, everything belonged to them," Ernestine Alday explained in 1990. "Everything. Even the house I was living in, the one Ned built and deeded to the boys."

Ned had known his sons well enough to know that they would never have dispossessed him. He had reared them to be honest, dutiful, trustworthy, and had then demonstrated his trust by deeding them everything he had. Already frail, he could not have imagined the circumstances under which he and all his farming sons would die on the same day.

But they had. And as far as the law was concerned, the farm now belonged entirely to Mary Alday's heirs.

What the Campbells would choose to do with it, and thus with all the worldly goods the Alday family had possessed on the afternoon of May 14, 1973, would take two years to decide.

*   *   *

During the coming months, while negotiations concerning the Alday estate and the construction of its memorial sanctuary at the Spring Creek Baptist Church continued, Carl Isaacs, now housed on Death Row in Reidsville State Prison, began to erect a monument of his own, one to his own lawlessness.

Not long after Carl's conviction, Charles Postell, a staff writer for the *Albany Herald*, wrote Isaacs, requesting an interview on Death Row. Carl agreed to the interview right away, and on May 14, 1974, a year to the day of the murders, Postell published the first of several articles he would write about Isaacs in the coming weeks.

Taken as a whole, the articles, as well as Postell's later book on Carl's life, amounted to a public presentation of himself that perfectly fit Carl's criminal fantasy life, murders, rapes, robberies, and assaults piling up as fast as Carl's fervid imagination could sprout them.

Simply spinning wildly exaggerated tales of his own demonic grandeur was not enough for Carl, however. He wanted to sell himself as the living embodiment of pure, unrepentant evil by laughing at his victims, offering them nothing less than the full measure of his scorn. It was a task he set about with enormous relish.

Thus, in the first of Postell's articles, Carl claimed that on the anniversary of the Alday murders, he intended to send a note to Wayne Coleman, whose own residence was just down the Death Row catwalk in Cell 8, D-4, wishing him a happy anniversary, and telling him to "Pop the champagne."

In the interview, Carl continued to claim that he'd had nothing to do with the actual murders, but that he knew who was involved. "When I die in the electric chair," he told Postell, "my brother Billy will come forward and tell the truth."

In the same interview, Carl threatened Billy in no uncertain terms. "Billy's address is unknown to me," he said, "but he'll never live to hit the streets again. This is a big family, and he shouldn't have done what he did."

As to the killings, Isaacs declared that he "didn't think" about them, although he did give a certain grudging respect to Mary Alday. "Mary was the only one that put up a fight," he told Postell, before adding disdainfully, "the rest just lay down and got shot."

His own execution was more on his mind, however, and he expected it to come relatively soon. Even so, it was not an eventuality he dreaded, since prison life was not to his liking. "You don't know the hell they've put me through," he said.

As to what he intended to do while Ernestine was conducting an anniversary commemorative service for the people he had murdered, Carl told Postell that at about that time, he would probably be watching *Gomer Pyle,* his favorite television program.

On the evening of May 14, 1974, Ernestine Alday was not watching *Gomer Pyle.* Instead, she was standing under the large trees whose branches swayed over the graves of her kindred, her mind not locked in criminal fantasies, but on the love she had felt for Ned, Aubrey, Shuggie, Jerry, Jimmy, and Mary Alday.

By then, the black marble headstone had been laid in the small cemetery of the Spring Creek Baptist Church. Impressive in its modesty and muted reverence, it read only "ALDAY FAMILY." Within the large rectangle of black stone that swept out from the central monument, the six slain Aldays lay buried beneath plain marble slabs.

Standing very still, her white hair rocked by the warm summer wind, Ernestine spoke to the few people who had gathered on the day the stones were laid. "They lived together and joined the church together and died together," she said as her eyes drifted over the six names that had been inscribed in the individual foot stones. "I don't know why this happened. I just have to say it was God's will." She heaved her shoulders gently, unable to say more, her eyes now trained on the simple inscription she had selected several months before to adorn their graves: "They steer'd the course to the same quiet shore, not parted long, and now to part no more."

At the conclusion of the ceremony, a few hymns were sung in the old Spring Creek sanctuary, and a prayer was offered for the souls of the dead and the grace of the living.

"It was very quiet and dignified," Nancy remembered. "I think my Daddy would have liked it."

Three weeks later, at 8:00 P.M. on June 7, a gospel singing program was held at the local high school to benefit the Alday memorial fund in its effort to complete the sanctuary. Tickets were sold at two dollars each, and those who came were treated to a lively program of gospel singing from such groups as the Hymn Masters of Donalsonville, the Tone Masters of Bainbridge, and the Sunny South Singers of Atlanta.

But that was not all. Later in the evening a group of young men also gave an exhibition. The group, known as Karate for Christ, performed karate exhibitions and gave religious testimony.

During the next few weeks, donations of additional monies for the sanctuary continued, primarily from residents of Seminole County, a sacrifice that served as a tribute to the standing of the Aldays in that community since, as the *Donalsonville News* reported in June 1974, under present conditions, the average young man in Seminole County could expect to earn close to $336,000 in the next forty-five years or so, an earning capacity of less than $7,500 per year.

Still, despite the marginal life that surrounded it, the new sanctuary was completed on November 4, 1974. Dedicated to "The Glory of God in Memory of the Alday Family," its initial construction costs had been borne entirely by the Alday Fund.

With this final act of commemoration, the people of Seminole County paid their last formal respects to Ned, Shuggie, Jerry, Jimmy, Aubrey, and Mary Alday. From that point on, they would steadily recede from the mind even of their own community. That Ned had whiled away the long winter days by telling tall tales at Johnson's Grocery Store; that Jerry had been so fastidious in his dress he'd often taken apart his store-bought clothes and resewed them to perfection; that Jimmy had rushed to his prized *World Book* to get the facts in any family dispute; that Aubrey had delighted in the presence of his brother's children, paying them pennies for their kisses; that Shuggie had drawn his mother beneath his arm on the last day of his life to propose a long-awaited fishing trip; that Mary had delighted in the brightly colored phlox that sprang up in such profusion the last month of her life; all of this would be lost as their individual faces melded together during the following years, becoming featureless and void, as if themselves pressed flat beneath the steadily accumulating weight of those court transcripts and appeals in which they now existed only as words upon a page, their lives remembered solely in the protracted legal consequences that clung so tenaciously to their deaths.

Chapter Twenty-three

At the same time that the faces of Ned, Shuggie, Jerry, Jimmy, Aubrey, and Mary Alday were dissolving, Carl Isaacs' profile was emerging with increasing force and fullness.

As starved for attention as ever, and increasingly intoxicated by his own infamy, Carl began a concerted campaign to keep himself prominently in the public eye.

The medium through which he spoke continued to be Charles Postell. Spurred on by Carl's performance at their first interview, Postell suggested others, and Carl, flattered by such attention, was more than willing to comply.

Thus, over a period of many weeks, Postell periodically visited Carl in Reidsville, smuggling him miniature bottles of alcohol, a tactic that was wildly successful in loosening his tongue.

Fueled by drink, Carl quickly shed the repentant, born-again Christian pose he was simultaneously using on other outside contacts, and unleashed an unprecedented attack upon the Alday family.

In an article published in the *Albany Herald* on January 16, Carl told Postell that he'd like "to get out and kill more of" the Aldays, since they represented "the type of society I don't like." The Aldays "loved the church so damn much," Carl blustered, that "they should have been killed and buried right in the church." His reason for hating the Aldays played havoc with the Protestant ethic. "Working people don't do a damn thing for me," he said.

When it came to himself, however, Carl's heart overflowed with sympathy. He declared prison an affront to his humanity, voicing what was surely one of the most unusual and alarming complaints ever made about incarceration. The problem with being locked up, he said, was that it prevented him from being out in the world "so I can do something to ease this hate."

Although Carl remained imprecise as to what "this hate" was, he was happy to reveal his preferred method of easing it. "When I kill," he told Postell with the unflinching directness of a full-blown psychopath, "I feel a release."

While Carl bemoaned the disadvantages of incarceration, he clearly enjoyed the criminal fame that accompanied it. "You take Dillinger," he said alarmingly. "He terrorized people all over. If they got in his way, he killed them. And they made a damn movie about him."

In another article, published on January 16, 1975, Carl vented his spleen once again. This time his target was not just the Aldays, but the whole state of Georgia. He'd been in Georgia so long he was "turning into a hick." These hicks, he added, had been his downfall, and his hatred for them raged on undiminished. "That's why I can't feel sorry for the people I killed down here," he said.

These remarks returned his perseverating mind to the six people he'd murdered on River Road.

It was their religiosity which most irritated him. "They should have died in church," he howled. "I just wished I could have killed them there."

On January 15, 1975, Carl spoke again, this time claiming that his personal ambition had been to murder one thousand people. His second life's goal, he added, was to be a practicing attorney, a notion he quickly dismissed. "No, no," he said regretfully, his mind connecting suddenly to the real world, "the bar would never accept me."

Carl also took the time to do a somewhat disjointed psychological analysis of himself, first declaring that homosexuality was the root of his personality disorder, then revising the first analysis with a second one somewhat more in tune with his own hazy understanding of Freudianism. In his second swing at self-knowledge, Carl stated that it was not homosexuality, but the love-hate feelings he had for his mother that had derailed his character. "Did I tell you, we stopped by the side of the road for her to go to the bathroom right in front of us," he told Postell, as if aghast at his mother's lack of modesty. This immodesty had been grounds for murdering her, Carl went on, and so on that very occasion, he and his brother had tried to run her down. She'd kept dodging the car, however, her agility making it "very hard to kill her."

But the role of family assassin was not the only one Carl claimed to have played. Proudly, he told Postell that he'd also served as the family pimp, and had often "hit the streets to help my sister make a little money, you know what I mean?"

Carl quickly moved from his sister to his brother Billy. "If I were free and he were free," he said, "Billy would be the first person I'd kill. I should have killed him. Why didn't I kill him when I had a gun in my hand?"

For now, Carl went on, his most critical concern was not so much killing someone else as keeping someone else from killing him. Prison life, he said, was fraught with peril. At present, he told Postell, it was important for him to keep close to a knife. There were two groups in the prison who wanted him dead, he claimed. One was a group of inmates who simply didn't care for what he'd done to the Aldays, he said, and because of that, they'd put a five-thousand-dollar bounty on his head.

The other group, Carl added expansively, consisted of the Black Muslims. Of course there was little love lost between him and blacks in general. "I'd kill a nigger quicker than anybody," he blustered, since, as he told Postell, it had been black prisoners who'd raped him during a riot at the Maryland State Penitentiary. "That turned me prejudiced," he said.

All the same, it was the people on River Road who still, even in their devastation, continued to inspire his hatred. "Why should I feel sorry for them?" he barked. "They should feel sorry for me. I'm the one on Death Row."

Death Row was again on Carl's mind during an interview published on July 8. The people who were demanding the death penalty, he said, should instead be demanding "that prisons not make us suffer so much before we're put to death." This indifference to the poor quality of life on Death Row struck Carl as unspeakably cruel. "I wish the public had some compassion," he moaned.

It was the cramped space that was really getting to him, Carl added. "This goddamn cell gets smaller by the day," he told Postell. "I don't think I can take it if there are a lot of hearings and postponements before they put me in the chair."

But the prospect of execution appealed to him even less. "They're going to have to beat me to death getting me there," he warned.

By the early summer of 1977, Carl was still blabbing to Postell, while his personal Boswell scribbled down every word. By then, goaded by his continuing need for the limelight, he had come up with the ultimate scheme for immortalizing himself. Rather than fighting the guards whose duty it was to lead him to the place of execution, he now claimed that he would cooperate with them so that his execution could be filmed "in living color." "I want the whole damn world to see me exit," he declared.

At the same time, Carl had some preferences as to how the filming should be handled. "I don't want none of those glamour boys from CBS or NBC lurking around my death watch," he told Postell. "I want to leave something behind in this world, and I want this filming of my execution to be a documentary style thing." The rules of taste and propriety had to be observed, Carl said, not "carried off like a goddamn sporting event like they did Gilmore." It was a serious matter, he added, and he vowed that he "would not let this thing turn into a circus."

He did want to be paid for the filming of his execution, how-ever, though he pledged a percentage of the gross for the study of psychopaths.

Still, despite such erstwhile charitable gestures, Carl continued to maintain that he felt no remorse for the Alday murders. "I really don't give a damn," he said.

On May 13, Carl lifted his voice again. By then his own psychological assessment had shifted decidedly in the direction of self-justification.

"I am what my mother made me," he said.

For her part, Isaacs' mother responded with a call for his execution. "I don't want them around if they're going to be killing people," Betty said. "Just because they came from my body don't mean I have to put up with them killing people."

To which Carl offered a quick rejoinder: "To the old woman I say, 'Happy Mother's Day.' "

During the interview, Postell noted Isaacs' running socks and asked about his newfound interest in physical fitness.

When they read it, Carl's reply sent shivers down the spines of Patricia and Nancy Alday. "I'm going to escape soon," he declared. "And the only way you'll know where I am is the bloody little trail I leave behind."

Chapter Twenty-four

While Carl reveled in the attentions of Postell, as well as those of various television and movie producers who had begun to approach him for his story, the legal process involved in the case continued at its own interminable pace.

In June 1976, over a year and a half after sentence had been pronounced on the last of the defendants, the Georgia Supreme Court affirmed the convictions and sentences of Coleman and Carl Isaacs. Two weeks later, on July 9, it did the same in the case of George Dungee.

Thus, within three years of the murders, the first round of appeals to the Georgia Supreme Court had been exhausted. The result had left both the original convictions and sentences intact. As far as the state of Georgia was concerned, Carl Isaacs, Wayne Coleman, and George Duncan had been justly tried and could be justly executed.

These same three years had worn badly upon Ernestine. Following the initial period of remarkable strength and self-control, she had broken only sporadically. But as the years of loneliness continued, she grew increasingly melancholy, and at last fell into a severe and protracted depression. "Everything my mother saw reminded her of the murders," Nancy remembered.

By that time Nancy had decided that she and her family would not return to Albany. Instead they had moved into the house on River Road, their lives now melded even more closely to Ernestine's and her surroundings. It was a world of absences and dark memento mori.

Outside, the farm's various outbuildings were empty, all the tools and farm machinery sold at auction. In spring and summer, the warm breezes off Lake Seminole swept over the family's idle boats and fishing gear. In fall and winter, colder winds tossed its brown, desolate fields, or howled in a high ghostly voice through the rafters of the empty barn.

Inside the house, the sense of devastation was even more pronounced. There were dozens of empty chairs and beds. Monthly farm magazines still arrived with the names of the dead pasted upon them. Closets remained stuffed with clothes no one would ever wear again. Everywhere, "favorite" things—Ned's pipe, Jimmy's encyclopedias—went unused.

Nowhere was the general sense of abiding loss more painful than at the noon meal, where silence and empty chairs now ringed what had once been a crowded, boisterous table.

For a time, Ernestine had even continued to cook the same huge midday meals to which she'd become accustomed, routinely setting the table with enough food for eight or nine, where now there were only two or three plates to be filled. Serving certain dishes that she knew to have been the favorites of her husband or one of her sons proved unbearably agonizing, and at times during the now deeply abbreviated noon dinner she would suddenly begin to cry.

Nor was it much better for her daughters, particularly for Nancy, who, along with her husband and small children, had abandoned their more prosperous and interesting lives in Albany. "We left good jobs and a good life in Albany," Nancy recalled, "but once Daddy and my brothers were dead and my mother was left alone, we had no choice but to come back."

Unlike Patricia, who could find some relief at her job in Donalsonville, Nancy remained intractably bound to the old homestead on River Road. Through the long afternoons, her housework completed, she sat on the front porch, staring out over the unmoving fields, watching the clouds pass over them in broad gray shadows. At times the quiet seemed almost more than she could bear, a stillness composed not only of silenced voices, but of the whole noisy hubbub of farm life, the distant rumble of tractors in the fields, the crunch of jeeps and trucks and cars moving in and out of the gravel driveway, the sounds of labor, movement . . . life. No more.

*   *   *

Soon, however, even the old homestead was gone. For within three years of the murders, the Alday estate was no more. The legal questions involving its inheritance had been settled, and in its dreadful outcome not one of the surviving children of Ned Alday had received a single square inch of Alday land.

Mary Campbell had died last, and therefore, as a matter of law, she had inherited nearly everything, save for the portion that went to Barbara Alday, Shuggie's surviving wife.

To put to rest the various conflicting claims on the Alday estate that had arisen since the murders, it was decided that everything, even Ned Alday's life insurance policy along with any income derived from the sale of the Alday homestead, would be placed in one pot, then divided into sevenths.

Although legally entitled to nothing, Ernestine Alday received three sevenths of the family's total assets. Barbara Alday received two sevenths, and the remaining two sevenths went to the Campbell family, Mary Alday's heirs.

Within a few weeks of the settlement, the now divided Alday lands were sold, with the exception of a single acre on which Ernestine decided to built a small brick house, and upon which she continued to keep, almost as a memento of her lost family, Jimmy's blue pickup.

Nothing else was now in the hands or under the control of any member of the Alday family.

"There was nothing left for the kids after it was all split up," Ernestine would say from her small living room seventeen years later, "except for some hurt feelings."

"It was amazing what happened to our farm," Nancy remembered. "It was there, and then it was gone. We couldn't quite figure out why we'd come out with nothing after all we'd already lost, but, the way it was, there was nothing we could do about it."

Thus, the legal issues now settled, Ernestine and Nancy readied the homestead for sale, sprucing it up as much as they could to make it more attractive to a prospective buyer. Having now endured years of unimaginable events, this seemed the most unimaginable of all. "It felt very strange," Nancy recalled, "but that was nothing new."

For what was normal now? The Alday name had become inseparably linked with a tragedy of unspeakable dimension. It was their sole renown, their primary connection to the world beyond the hearth. They had become the murders.

"We'd gotten to be the community oddities in a way," Nancy said. "The Aldays were not just an upstanding farm family anymore, but 'those people,' the ones something terrible had happened to."

This was particularly true in regard to strangers. For as the years passed and the murders continued to be a subject of media interest, the black marble grave site at Spring Creek Baptist Church became a curious and macabre tourist attraction.

"I'd go into a store or a service station sometimes," Nancy said in 1990, "and somebody would come in from somewhere out of the area, and right off they'd ask the person behind the counter, 'Where's the Alday grave?' And he'd tell them, and off they'd go in that direction, like they were headed for an amusement park or something."

Although the grisly taste of tourists still focused upon the people who had been murdered three years before, the appeals system was focused entirely upon their killers. Now in the machinery of the justice system, the appeals dragged on, and shortly after the latest actions of the Georgia judicial system, defense lawyers concentrated their attention on a higher authority, the United States Supreme Court. It was hoped that its nine justices would find constitutional reason to overturn either the convictions or the sentences and thus overturn the Georgia Supreme Court's earlier finding.

But the U.S. Supreme Court found no such reason, and on November 29, it denied certiorari petitions for Dungee and Isaacs, a decision which, in effect, affirmed the constitutional correctness of the initial trial in Donalsonville as well as the later Georgia Supreme Court review.

Thus denied their initial appeals to the Georgia and U.S. Supreme Courts, Isaacs and Dungee, followed by Coleman a few months later, moved on to the next predetermined rung of the appeals system by filing habeas corpus petitions in the Superior Court of Tattnall County on February 15, 1977.

Two months later, on April 12, a hearing was held on the petitions in the Superior Court of Tattnall County. On August 31, the petitions of Dungee and Isaacs were denied.

In the meantime, on May 2, the U.S. Supreme Court had denied Coleman's certiorari petition, thus affirming Coleman's conviction and death sentence.

The following year, 1978, now four years after the murders, showed no decrease in the movements of the Alday murderers within the appeals process.

On March 15, oral arguments were heard by the Georgia Supreme Court on Isaacs' and Dungee's appeals of the previous denials of habeas corpus by the Superior Court in Tattnall County.

A month later, on April 18, the Court refused the habeas corpus relief requested by Isaacs and Dungee and thereby affirmed the superior court's initial decision. Going further, the Court also refused to reconsider its 1976 decision, a ruling that had denied the defense's contention that Judge Geer's refusal to grant a change of venue in the 1974 trial had violated the rights of Isaacs and Dungee.

On October 2, the United States Supreme Court denied Isaacs' and Dungee's certiorari petitions. The petitions had sought a review of the Georgia Supreme Court's decision affirming the Superior Court of Tattnall County's refusal of their original habeas corpus appeal, and in its decision, the U.S. Supreme Court for a second time saw no reason to question the legal process by which the original convictions and sentences had been gained.

With this "final" denial of review by the United States Supreme Court, new execution dates could now be set for two of the Alday defendants. Accordingly, on May 19, 1979, nearly six years to the day of the murders, the Superior Court of Seminole County fixed June 1 as the execution date for Carl Isaacs and George Dungee.

Meanwhile, in Seminole County, Ernestine watched as work went forward on the little brick house she'd decided to build on her one remaining acre of land. When completed it was more modern than she was used to, and seemed less sturdily built than the old place she'd shared with Ned and her brood of children. Its rooms were small neat squares. There were none of those curious little touches Ned had built into the house on River Road. Outside there were no great trees, but only the weak saplings that had been planted there, which, she knew, would never give shade to anyone in her lifetime.

But by then the old homestead had come to look a good deal different too, as she noticed when she sometimes drove by it, slowing the car to catch a better look, remembering in all its fullness the life she had lived there. The new owners had painted it a brighter color, paved the drive, and installed a swimming pool and dazzling cabana where Shuggie's trailer had once rested under the broad green trees.

As for the new brick house, it was nice enough, she sometimes thought upon returning to it. Still, the dining room seemed small, the kitchen too. Everything, she had to admit finally, seemed small, reduced, with something missing. It was them, of course. All of them: Ned, Aubrey, Shuggie, Jerry, Jimmy, and Mary. And so, to bring them back a little, to fill up the space, however inadequately, that their deaths had left behind, she hung the walls with scores of pictures she'd brought from the old house. She powdered the top of the television with them, then the bookshelves after that, the mantel, the sideboard, the end tables beside the sofa, every inch of flat space covered with frames of all shapes and sizes, frames of gold, silver, plastic, her kindred frozen silently within them: Ned slouched on his workbench; Shuggie in a bright red coat; Jerry slinging feed to the chickens; Jimmy behind the wheel of his new pickup; Aubrey with his arm draped around his wife; Mary peeping out from behind the half-closed door of the Spring Creek Baptist Church. Through the months, she stared at them silently, still clinging to her faith that it had all been part of God's unfathomable plan.

Far away, now centered in metropolitan Atlanta, the appeals ground forward interminably. Only ten days after the date of execution had been set, on May 29, attorneys for Isaacs and Dungee filed habeas corpus petitions in the U.S. District Court for the Southern District of Georgia in Savannah, once again stressing their clients' failure to get a fair trial in Seminole County due to the climate of extreme prejudice that had existed against them prior to trial. According to their attorneys, Judge Geer's refusal, in the light of such prejudice, to grant the change of venue that had been requested by the defendants prior to their trials constituted a reversible error on his part. They now asked for a redress of that error in the form of entirely new trials for Isaacs and Dungee.

In response, the district court stayed the executions of both men.

On August 16, attorneys for Isaacs and Dungee filed a motion for discovery. Now concentrating on the issue of pretrial community prejudice against the Alday murderers, their lawyers asked the court for the right to determine the level of community outrage that had existed in Seminole County at the time of the 1974 trial, which, they presumed, had made a fair trial impossible in that community.

After six years of unsuccessful appeal maneuvers, this motion for discovery finally fell upon sympathetic ears. Thus, on October 26, the Southern District Court granted the motion, and on December 3, attorneys for Isaacs and Dungee began three days of taking oral depositions in Albany, Georgia, Dothan, Alabama, and Tallahassee, Florida, depositions designed to show community prejudice against their clients prior to and during the January 1974 trial in Donalsonville.

A light had broken in the solid wall of denied petitions and refused appeals that had heretofore blocked the progress of defense attorneys in their efforts on behalf of the Alday murderers.

It was the first good news Carl Isaacs had received thus far in the appeals process, and it buoyed his spirits markedly. On November 8, 1979, Postell reported that in a letter to him Carl had expressed confidence that at some time in the future he would be granted a new trial and that he would return to Donalsonville for it.

Carl's spirits could not have been raised for long, however. For almost immediately Isaacs learned that not long after the motion for discovery had been granted, the *Albany Herald* had refused either to provide documents to the defendants' attorneys or to give oral depositions.

In response to this refusal, the attorneys filed a motion to compel discovery with the U.S. District Court for the Middle District of Georgia in Macon.

A hearing on this motion was held on January 2, 1980, and at the end of the hearing, the motion was denied.

This denial led to another appeal to the Middle District Court on February 11. This time, Isaacs and Dungee had appealed in forma pauperis from the January 2 ruling.

On the same day, February 11, 1980, Coleman's habeas corpus appeal, now straggling behind the others, was finally denied by the Tattnall Superior Court.

Approximately four months later, on July 14, the United States District Court for the Southern District of Georgia conducted a routine hearing on the possible replacement of counsel for both Dungee and Isaacs. At this hearing, Carl Isaacs was present.

As he sat silently before the court officials who were hearing his case, he must have had a great deal on his mind. Still, it is unlikely that the courtroom wrangling did not strike him as both amusing and ironic.

Because, having finally put into place the last remaining elements of his plan to escape from Reidsville's Death Row, he was now waiting contentedly for the already selected moment.

   Should all go according to plan, in just four days Carl expected that he would be through with courts and lawyers and petitions forever. At that point, he would be free to do what he'd already flippantly claimed he wished to do should he ever find himself outside prison walls: kill more Aldays.

Chapter Twenty-five

On the morning of July 28, 1980, four inmates on Reidsville State Prison's Death Row escaped by simply walking out of the prison during its early morning shift change. The four escapees made their way to a car waiting for them in the prison parking lot, its gas tank filled, the ignition keys concealed above the sun visor on the driver's side.

The escape from Death Row was unprecedented in Georgia history, and it involved four singularly ruthless men.

Timothy McCorquodale's crime, as the *Atlanta Constitution* would later say, "fit the standard definition of a heinous murder." On January 17, 1974, when he was a twenty-three-year-old Marine Corps veteran, McCorquodale, while cruising a section of Atlanta known as the Peachtree Strip, a notorious hangout for prostitutes, drifters, and drug dealers, had picked up a seventeen-year-old girl named Donna Marie Dixon, a runaway from Newport News, Virginia. He had taken her to an apartment on Moreland Avenue, where he had systematically, over a period of many hours, cut her to ribbons with razor blades and scissors, strangled her with a nylon cord, and finally broken her ankles and knees in a strenuous effort to force her body into a cardboard trunk.

Although less sadistic, Troy Gregg's crime had been no less compassionless. Drifting from state to state, Gregg and a young companion had hitched a ride with two men from Florida in November 1973. Together, they had driven north along Interstate 85 until they reached Gwinnett County, an area outside Atlanta. There an argument had developed between Gregg and the two men. It had been settled only after Gregg had cold-bloodedly shot and killed them both.

The youngest of the escapees, David A. Jarrell, had been only eighteen on Christmas Eve 1973, when he set out on foot from Lawrenceville, Georgia, a small town a few miles from Atlanta. Later that night, he met Mala Ann Still, a bank teller who'd left her job for the day to do some last-minute Christmas shopping. Two days later, her tortured body was found in a wooded area along the Alcovy River. She had been shot in the head.

The last of the four, Johnny Johnson, had been with another man when the two had met two women in Savannah on July 20, 1974. According to the one woman who managed to survive what happened after that, Johnson and his associate had forced them into a car at gunpoint, tied their hands, then driven them to a remote dirt road off U.S. 17. Johnson had led his choice of the two women, Suzanne Edenfield, out into the woods, raped her, and then shot her to death.

All four had been tried, convicted, sentenced to death, and transported to Reidsville State Prison, the "Great White Elephant" as it was called, which housed the state's only Death Row.

And all four had now escaped.

Stunned and mortified by the Death Row escape by four of the most vicious men within the prison system, Georgia authorities pulled out all stops in their effort to recapture McCorquodale, Gregg, Jarrell, and Johnson. Hundreds of officers from the Georgia Bureau of Investigation, the FBI, the Tattnall County Sheriff's Office, and the Georgia State Patrol went on alert, initiating a sweep search of Georgia and South Carolina, since all four of the fugitives had relatives in the two states.

In addition to the statewide sweeps, officers began more concentrated efforts in four towns: York, South Carolina, where Gregg's sister lived; Sumpter, South Carolina, the home of Johnson's mother; Nicholls, Georgia, where McCorquodale's father resided; and Lawrenceville, Georgia, the home of Jarrell's mother.

Within hours they were also checking the telephone exchanges of Jacksonville, Florida. By that time, the GBI had been contacted by none other than Charles Postell, the peripatetic reporter who'd long been in contact with Carl Isaacs. According to Postell, one of the Death Row escapees had telephoned him at around 10:30 on the morning following the escape. At that time, Postell said, Gregg had told him that he was calling from Jacksonville. "I thought it was a hoax," Postell later told reporters. "I thought he was calling from the prison, just trying to fool me."

But it had not been a hoax, and as the hours passed, and the public outcry over the escape mounted steadily, frantic law enforcement officials continued to comb Georgia and South Carolina in search of the four escapees.

By the early morning hours of the following day, Wednesday, July 30, it had become a nationwide manhunt, but by then, only one of the escapees, Troy Gregg, was still at large. The other three had been captured in a small, four-room brick home on the shores of Lake Wylie about ten miles southwest of Charlotte, North Carolina.

At 1:15 A.M., after a siege of nearly four hours, officers of the Mecklenburg County Police had fired teargas into the home and waited as, one by one, McCorquodale, Jarrell, and Johnson had staggered out. No shots had been fired.

With three escapees now in custody, the fate of the fourth, Troy Gregg, was quickly discovered when his body was found floating in Mountain Island Lake, about twelve miles north of where the other three had been captured. The autopsy revealed that Gregg had been beaten to death with what the medical examiner called a "wide instrument, possibly a board, belt or shoe."

The grim details of Gregg's death were discovered only a day or so after his body. It was not a pretty story. According to witnesses later interviewed by North Carolina authorities, Gregg had arrived in Charlotte still in the company of the three Death Row escapees. One, Timothy McCorquodale, had reestablished contact with members of the Outlaws, the motorcycle gang to which he had belonged, and particularly with William K. ("Chains") Flamont, a member who had himself only narrowly escaped the July 4, 1979, massacre of five fellow Outlaws at their clubhouse in north Charlotte.

Flamont, at whose lakefront home they had later been captured, had welcomed McCorquodale back into the Outlaw circle.

By then, however, Gregg was already dead. Several hours before, at the Old Yellow Tavern on the Catawba River, Gregg had made a fatal mistake. Always arrogant, and something of a braggart, Gregg had made a thoughtless remark to a female patron currently attached to one Eddie Phipps, a thirty-year-old motorcyclist who was not known to suffer fools gracefully.

Phipp's reaction was swift and sure, and, cheerfully aided by Timothy McCorquodale, he promptly stomped Gregg to death behind the Old Yellow Tavern. Gregg's body was subsequently thrown into the river, where it floated downstream into Mountain Island Lake.

Within four days of the escape, all four of the Death Row inmates had been accounted for.

But the escape, itself, who had planned it and how it had been carried out, had not yet been uncovered.

After Gregg's death and the capture of the remaining three escapees in North Carolina, Georgia law enforcement officials were determined that no such escape would ever again occur within the state prison system.

Consequently, Georgia Bureau of Investigation Agent Robert Ingram was assigned to head a GBI Task Force whose duty it was to uncover the escape plan in its most minute details, and inform prison officials in such a way that they could redesign their surveillance and other programs to make certain that such an escape could not be repeated.

Only a few days after the escape, Ingram arrived at the Great White Elephant to begin his work. He went to Cell Block D-4, a row of only ten cells located on the building's fourth floor: Death Row.

To his astonishment, prison officials had already had the bars that had been sawed through in the initial stage of the escape plan rewelded, but it was easy for Ingram to determine that although four inmates had escaped, six had been involved in the plan. One of them, Tom Fitzgerald, had apparently gotten cold feet at the last minute. Another, however, had been transferred from Reidsville to the Georgia Diagnostic and Classification Center in Jackson only a few hours before the escape had occurred. The sixth escapee had been assigned to Reidsville for nearly six years. He occupied Cell 10. His inmate number was D-17622. His name was Carl Junior Isaacs.

"I knew the other escapees pretty well," Ingram said years later, "and there was no way they could have come up with such a highly detailed and intelligent plan. The minute I saw those welding marks on Cell 10, I knew the whole thing had been thought out by Carl Isaacs. None of the others had anywhere near the brains for it."

Convinced that Isaacs held the key to the escape, Ingram drove to the Jackson Diagnostic and Classification Center as soon as possible to interview him. At first, Isaacs claimed to know nothing of the escape plan, but over a period of two years and twenty interviews, as Ingram patiently and meticulously stroked Isaacs' ego, telling him that only a prisoner of his intelligence and cunning could have devised such a brilliant plan, Isaacs began to reveal the details of the plan he had developed over a period of six years, and which the four escapees had executed on the morning of November 28. In the end, Isaacs even went so far as to produce a forty-six-page narrative whose opening words could hardly have served better to demonstrate his frame of mind: "Herein lies the truthful story of one of the greatest escapes that has ever been recorded in the annuls [sic] of crime," Isaacs wrote, "perhaps it could even be the greatest."

That it was an amazing plot could not be doubted. Whether Isaacs' detailed rendering of it was truthful, however, would remain in doubt forever. His contentions would implicate a great many people, some of whom would be charged with aiding in his escape plan. Among those charged was an *Albany Herald* reporter named Charles Postell and his wife. The charges were later dropped after it became known that Isaacs had offered $15,000 to Postell in exchange for which Isaacs would change his testimony implicating Postell. The extent of Postell's actual involvement, if any, remains uncertain. Still, Isaacs' account would remain the central document of the GBI's investigation, and although its veracity would always be questioned as a work of self-aggrandizement, it was pure Carl Junior. Never had he spoken with greater determination to carve out a monument to his own criminal genius.

According to Carl, his first notions of escape had been in May 1974. During the first part of that month, he'd received a short note from an *Albany Herald* reporter named Charles Postell. In the letter, Postell had expressed a desire to interview Isaacs with the idea of writing a book about his life.

Isaacs agreed to the interview, and Postell arrived at the prison on May 10. After the first interview, there were many others, during which Postell sat listening as Carl, delighted to have such an attentive audience, held forth about his life and crimes.

During the latter part of 1974, Carl even went so far as to tell Postell that he planned to escape. According to Isaacs, Postell replied by bringing up such absurd notions as him flying a helicopter to the prison's fourth floor and snatching Isaacs from the roof, or perhaps sending him a Christmas cake with a gun inside. Despite the idiocy of such notions, Isaacs said that a tacit understanding began to develop between the two that should Isaacs ever attempt an escape, Postell would help in any way he could.

In January 1975, Carl was moved to the fifth floor, then later to Cell Number B-4, once again on the fourth floor. It was at this point, Isaacs said, that he began to work seriously on an escape plan. At that moment, Carl, as he later wrote, "being a realist," determined that he would need assistance in carrying out any escape from Reidsville.

At about that time, Carl began to receive letters from Tami Postell, Charles Postell's daughter, and as relations continued to warm between Isaacs and the entire Postell family, they began to send him the items he occasionally requested, all harmless, things such as pajamas and towels, along with others which, although he saw no immediate need for them, he deemed potentially useful at some later point: glue, tape, and Magic Markers.

During September and October of 1975, according to Isaacs, his relationship with Postell "took on a new perspective." He and Postell were able to speak more freely, while the family circle broadened to include Postell's wife Judy, called Bunki, and a second Postell daughter, Robin.

It was at this time, January 1976, that Postell began to smuggle in miniature bottles of liquor. They talked more openly, Carl about his family, and Postell about his, with "every scrap of information secretly filed away" in Isaacs' mind, as he put it, "for future use."

But by then Postell and his family were not the only outsiders with whom Isaacs was developing a relationship. In March 1976, he began a correspondence with Judy Powell. Powell had glimpsed Carl's picture in a local newspaper, she said, and had fallen in love with him. Carl found this hard to believe, as he wrote, "but my mind was turning over the various avenues of recruiting her to help me."

Judy Powell was placed on Isaacs' approved visiting list, and arrived for her first visit, the "day of reckoning" as Carl called it, during the latter part of May.

During the meeting, Carl made a few nominal requests of Powell to "test her loyalty," and, to his amazement and delight, she obeyed. "The lock had been set," Isaacs later wrote. "It was time to begin."

But not quite.

According to Carl, Postell reacted with outrage at his new friend. He was convinced that she had some ulterior motive for her romantic interest in Carl, he said, and asked for his permission to check her out.

Carl agreed to allow Postell to conduct a "cursory probe" of her background, and promised to delay any further contact with Powell until Postell's investigation was completed.

This was a lie, however, and immediately after Postell's visit, Carl penned a long, detailed letter to Powell detailing Postell's suspicions and intentions. Now Powell was outraged, just as Carl had hoped, and he was able to calm her anxiety by assuring her that he would let her know whatever Postell discovered, and that in any event, it would not come between them.

For the next four weeks, Carl deftly played the two competing parties against each other until finally, with Powell at her wits' end, paranoid, convinced that she was being followed, so frightened that she had become too scared even to visit Isaacs at Reidsville, Carl finally insisted that Postell halt his investigation.

Postell relented, even to the point of declaring that Powell was "on the level and that it would be wise" if Isaacs "latched on to her."

With the matter settled, but in a manner so sudden that Isaacs continued to suspect some kind of ruse on Postell's part, he began to raise the issue of escape with Powell. By late summer she was fully engaged in the plan, and in August she mailed five silver eight-inch hacksaw blades in a box of envelopes from a small town in Alabama.

With Powell indictably committed to his escape, Carl began to work on Postell, telling him of the aid Vinson had already given, and eliciting from him an equal commitment. According to Isaacs, Postell unhesitatingly agreed to be of any assistance he could in Isaacs' impending escape.

With outside assistance now in place, Carl began to work on assistance from within, approaching fellow Death Row inmate Troy Gregg in the fall of 1976.

By then, Carl had devised the basic formula for his escape. His plan was to cut out of his cell through the catwalk bars, then go out a window at the end of the catwalk and on to the roof of the prison. Once on the roof, he intended to lie low until early the following morning, which would have to be a Saturday, leap from the room, and dash to the parking lot where Powell would be waiting in a car. "I realized that it was a grave risk," Carl wrote, "and that my chances of pulling it off were almost nil, but I was very determined to escape."

But if reason would not have been sufficient to deter Isaacs from this plan, a sudden shakedown of A-block was. It was no ordinary, routine shakedown. The officers carried rubber hammers to check the bars for cuts, and as he watched the shakedown progress, Isaacs felt relieved that he had made none in his own bars as yet.

Unnerved by such a sudden, thorough shakedown, and suspicious that the authorities had been alerted by none other than his old friend, Charles Postell, Carl began to formulate a different, and far more elaborate scheme.

But while his plans inside the prison progressed, his outside structure began to collapse. Without explanation, Judy Powell was abruptly excluded from his visitor's list. Bereft of this dedicated lifeline, Carl decided that his next attempt would have to be far more complicated and foolproof than his first one. Accordingly, as he later wrote, it was shortly after that "that the idea in my subconscious mind finally evolved into the greatest plan ever, later to be termed the greatest and most daring escape ever recorded in history."

Two and a half years later, by September 1979, Carl had "worked all the kinks out of the master plan." Now all he needed was to find the men who would be able to pull it off. He had five in mind, only two of whom, Troy Gregg and Johnny Johnson, were actually located on his cell block. The other three, West McCorquodale, David Jarrell, and Tom Fitzgerald were housed elsewhere.

The first task was to get the remaining three men into Isaacs' cell block. Within five days, by having McCorquodale claim that he was having trouble in his relationships with the inmates of his home cell block, Carl had succeeded in having him transferred to Cell Block A.

A month later, David Jarrell was also transferred to A, and not long after that, the third member, Tom Fitzgerald, was also transferred, this time in the middle of the night, to Cell Block A.

Once the escape team was in place, Carl began assembling the tools he deemed necessary to put his plan into operation.

He needed pajamas, black shoes, and belts for each escapee.

With these items, Isaacs, an accomplished tailor, planned to duplicate in the most minute details the uniforms worn by the Reidsville correctional officers.

To accomplish this, however, he needed to get swatches of the actual uniforms in order to duplicate their color. To do this, Carl relied on corruption.

By June 1980, a young correctional officer, Bill Maddox, had for some time been selling small amounts of marijuana to prison inmates. Carl determined that if he could arrange a large marijuana sale, then Maddox would be his, a prison official disastrously compromised, perhaps even faced with imprisonment, a very perilous situation.

But to pull off a large buy, Carl needed money, and, as always, he was broke. To get money, he drew none other than George Dungee, now in failing health and increasingly dim-witted, into a poker game and quickly won over a thousand dollars in IOUs, none of which Dungee could pay. To satisfy the debt, Carl said that he would take Dungee's watch, and Dungee happily agreed.

The watch was now in hand, and valued at over a hundred and fifty dollars. Carl, to avoid compromising himself, had Troy Gregg offer it to Maddox as collateral for thirty dollars' worth of marijuana. Maddox agreed, and the deal was consummated a few days later.

Now fatally compromised, Maddox, over the next few days, supplied Isaacs with a belt loop from his uniform pants along with a piece of his uniform shirt which Carl cut, using a knife handed to him by Maddox.

Bill Maddox was now deeply involved in an escape plan from Death Row. But he was not the only one. A prison trustee now working as a barber, Willie Flynn, had also become involved. A member of the motorcycle gang to which Timothy McCorquodale had belonged, he began supplying Isaacs with an assortment of necessary items.

While the details involved in acquiring dyes to match the uniform swatches supplied by Maddox went forward, so did the least technically complicated element of the escape, the slow, tedious sawing through of the bars along the cell block's catwalk. It was a long, painfully slow process, requiring nearly four hours per bar, top and bottom. As the days passed, two bars each were sawed through in the respective cells of Isaacs, Gregg, and Fitzgerald. Jarrell required three bars, however, while McCorquodale, biggest of them all, demanded no less than four.

While the bars were still being sawed, two pairs of pajamas arrived for McCorquodale. Since only Carl and Jarrell could sew, the other men continued with the bars, while Isaacs and Jarrell concentrated on making exact copies of correctional officer shirts. At various times during this period, Carl would stop work to draw Maddox into long, lingering conversations at his cell, while Jarrell stood nearby, his eyes fixed on the American flag insignia, Bureau of Corrections patch, nameplate, and badge that adorned his uniform, all of which had to be duplicated as part of Isaacs' escape plan.

Once the two men had gotten a clear enough fix on the uniform accessories, they started to work on reproducing them. Isaacs hand-sewed several American flag insignia, secretly cutting squares from the white institutional towels used throughout the prison, then carefully painting in the flag using Magic Markers and ballpoint pens. The borders of the towels served well as the borders of the patches, and were also colored appropriately.

It took five days to make two patches, but when they were done, along with the pajamas Carl now had a grand total of three complete shirts and two patches, all of which he stuffed inside various pillows in the cell block. Only a few days later, Flynn obviated the need to make any further patches when he supplied six authentic flag and correctional officer patches to Isaacs and his men, all of them cleverly concealed beneath the powder in a talcum powder box. Utterly delighted, Isaacs and the other men, as Isaacs later wrote, "gave Willie a big hug and voiced out deep appreciation."

By early June, correctional officer badges had been made from card-board, pieces of a soda can, blue paper, white oil paint, and a blue Magic Marker. The only difficulty had been in making it look shiny, as the actual badges did, a problem Carl corrected by wrapping them very tightly in cellophane, which, as he told Ingram, "was easily obtained from a cigarette pack."

But other aspects of the break were going far too slowly for Carl's own internal pace. The bars were still being sawed each night before the 11:00 P.M. count, a time during which the sound of a nearby television served to conceal the noise. For Isaacs, the whole tedious process was excruciatingly slow.

Not one prone to patience, Isaacs acted. The solution was obvious. He needed more blades.

To get them, he turned once again to Charles Postell, instructing him to buy the blades in Reidsville and hand them over to Minnie and Patti Hunter, McCorquodale's mother and sister. According to Isaacs, Postell also agreed to supply the escapees with guns, drugs (two hundred black beauties, speed) and "a few hundred dollars," all of which were to be placed in a car Minnie Hunter would leave in the prison parking lot.

It was at this time, according to Isaacs, that the ulterior motive he had always suspected in Postell surfaced for the first time when, during a prison visit, Postell advised him that after the escape, Carl should "lay low" until he, Postell, could get a "small cassette recorder and give it to Minnie." There would be plenty of tapes, Postell told him, and "I want you to turn it on as soon as you get in the car." When the tapes were full, they were to be mailed to Postell so that he could reconstruct the escape in a book he would then write.

In the last days of June 1980, final preparations were completed for the escape, though not without a few hitches. Hacksaw blades mailed to four of the escapees were intercepted in the prison mail room on June 25, and as a result strip searches were conducted on Isaacs and Troy Gregg at 7:00 P.M. that evening. Finding nothing, five other cells were shaken down while Isaacs and Gregg sat in their own cells, listening for the first indication that any part of the escape plan had been uncovered.

It never came. During the entire process, despite the intercepted hacksaw blades, no guard had bothered to examine the bars.

The following day, while the men in Cell Block D were laughing at the fact that despite the shakedown, their plans had gone undetected, Carl was told to report to the control office downstairs. Once there, he was told that he had been charged with the illegal possession of instruments of escape and a deadly weapon, the latter nothing more than a pair of scissors. In response to these charges, Carl was taken to disciplinary court on June 25, found guilty of the offenses, and given fourteen days in isolation and ninety days on restricted privileges.

On July 11, Carl was released from the hole and was told that ten hacksaw blades were already en route to the prison, this time concealed in the handle of a portable radio.

The radio arrived on July 18, passed through prison inspection without a blink, and within minutes of its receipt, Isaacs, Gregg, and the others were busily sawing at the bottom bars of their cells.

Once the cell bars had been cut, Carl set about cutting the bars over the window overlooking the prison fire escape. Beginning on the morning of July 19, he worked continually through the weekend, grabbing whatever moments he could to saw, then concealing the saw marks with a concoction of bubble gum and cardboard which he had painted to match the color of the bars.

More pajamas came on July 22, and Carl and Jarrell set to work making the last of the uniform shirts, while continuing to saw through the various cell block bars in any remaining time.

On July 23, the bars on McCorquodale's cell had been completely sawed through, and later that afternoon, Carl, using India ink and black Magic Markers, dyed four pairs of shoes to match the institutional black of the prison staff. That completed, Isaacs turned his talents to fashion-

ing the required six nightstick holders, for which he used pieces of
state-issued belts along with several lengths of coated electrical wire.

The following day, the pace moving inexorably faster as the appointed hour of the escape neared, Carl began making copies of the
metal nameplates that were pinned at the left breast of the uniform
shirts. Using nothing more complicated than cardboard, pieces of aluminum from a soda can, cellophane, and a black writing pen, Carl
constructed identical nameplates, inscribing them with the names,
among others, of his own boyhood heroes, Jesse and Frank James, and
Cole Younger.

Exhilarated by his own daring, Carl took a brief respite from work
to celebrate his cunning. He ordered Maddox to supply him with thirty
dollars' worth of marijuana, then spent the rest of the day, as he wrote,
"just getting high."

On July 25, a pair of headphones arrived for George Dungee. A
package of dark blue dye and a tube of Super Glue were concealed
inside. They were to be used for fashioning and securing the last of the
uniform insignia and nameplates.

Over the next three days the last of the preparations were completed,
down to the minutest detail of sewing stripes on the uniform pants.

On the afternoon of July 27, the day before the planned escape,
Minnie Hunter arrived to tell McCorquodale that everything was ready,
with one exception. According to Issacs, it appeared that Postell had
wavered at the last moment, never sending her any of the supplies he'd
promised Isaacs. There were no pills or guns, not even the cassette
player with which he was supposed to record this magnificent criminal
exploit. To Carl, it appeared that at the last moment, Postell had grown
faint of heart.

But if Postell seemed to be withdrawing from the scheme, there was
plenty of good news to lift Carl's spirits, and McCorquodale was the
bearer of it. The final critical element was now in place, McCorquodale
said; the getaway car had arrived. Another of McCorquodale's relatives
had left it in the parking lot, complete with six changes of clothes in
the truck and a full tank of gas. Minnie and Patti Hunter would be at
the prison the next morning, McCorquodale added, and they would
cause two diversions, one at 4:45 A.M. and another five minutes later.
McCorquodale further informed Isaacs that he had instructed his
mother to call Postell and tell him to meet the escapees in Baxley,

Georgia, at 5:15 A.M., and to have the necessary supplies with him at that time.

A few minutes later, all six of the men who planned to make a daring escape from Death Row in only a few hours watched from a single window on the fourth floor as Minnie and Patti Hunter made their way to the employee parking lot. For the moment all looked well. Then, suddenly, the men realized that the right front tire of the Plymouth, their getaway car, was flat.

For an instant, a cold panic swept through the men who'd gathered in triumph and camaraderie by the window. Then, just as suddenly, their terror was relieved. Clearly, the women in the parking lot had also noticed the flat tire. They were not leaving in their other car. While Patti Hunter remained by the Plymouth, Minnie strolled across the street to a barracks station of the Georgia State Patrol and disappeared inside. Seconds later she reemerged, walked back across the street and waited with Patti until, twenty minutes later, a brown and beige truck arrived. The man inside got out, changed the tire on the Plymouth, then drove out of the parking lot toward downtown Reidsville, the two women following along behind him in the Cutlass they had brought to whisk them away.

A few hours later, just after the 3:00 A.M. count, the last bar in the window above the cell block fire escape was cut through. It was the final, slender barrier between the men and their escape, and with it now eliminated, Isaacs ordered the five others to begin drinking coffee so that they would be wide awake early the next morning when the escape would be carried out. "If someone fell asleep," he wrote, "I made it plain that they would be left behind."

Thirty minutes later, as he lay in his cell excitedly awaiting the moment only two hours away when the escape would be carried out, Carl heard footsteps along the catwalk. Seconds later, a guard stopped in front of his cell. "Pack up your stuff," he said. "You're being transferred this morning."

"I sat on my bed, too stunned to reply," Carl wrote at the end of the narrative he later turned over to Agent Ingram, "my mind racing a thousand miles a second."

In the end, Isaacs opted not to rush the escape, but to take the transfer obediently and let the others go without him. Quietly, he packed his things and headed down the cell block toward the waiting guard. On the way out, he shook each of his partner's hands. "Go, brother," he told them, "make it good."

Several months later, with Troy Gregg dead and the others behind the gleaming white walls of the Great White Elephant in Reidsville, Ingram was leaving Isaacs to return for follow-up interviews with the other escapees. "Got any message for them?" he asked Isaacs as he rose to leave.

Carl nodded. "Yeah," he said with a cold smirk. "Tell 'em I'd like to kick their asses for being out that long and not getting a piece and wasting somebody."

It was a grim and unrepentant message, as cruel, it seemed to Ingram, as it was hopelessly beyond the most determined reaches of rehabilitation. "I thought right then that Carl Isaacs would never rest easy in prison," Ingram remembered, "that this was not the last time he'd try to escape, that as long as there was breath in him, he'd be scheming to be free."

He was right.

Chapter Twenty-six

In the weeks following the Death Row escape, Georgia authorities brought a number of indictments against those individuals Carl had named in the statement he prepared for Agent Ingram. By late August, eleven had been charged, including Minnie Hunter, Timothy McCorquodale's aunt, who had been arrested for aiding in the escape.

By the end of that month, however, that charge had been reduced to the lesser charge of "criminal attempt" to aid an escape, a felony for which she could be sentenced to no more than two and a half years.

Far more striking was the indictment of Charles and Judi Postell for the same crime.

Arrested by GBI agents at their home in Sparks, Georgia, on Wednesday, August 27, Postell and his wife were taken to the Coffee County Jail in Douglas, then released on a five-thousand-dollar bond later that evening.

According to the indictment, the Postells had visited Carl Isaacs on June 18, at which time he had requested fifteen hacksaw blades to aid in his planned escape. In response, the Postells had journeyed to Baxley, Georgia, where Mrs. Postell had purchased ten such blades, all of which she then turned over to Minnie Hunter, who'd mailed them in four separate packages to Isaacs, McCorquodale, Johnson, and Gregg.

Postell admitted that he had received two phone calls from the escapees only a few hours after the escape, but added that he had twice called authorities in Reidsville to report the escape.

As for his arrest, Mr. Postell told reporters that the charges were utterly unsubstantiated, and that they had been made by the GBI in retaliation against articles he had written linking some of the bureau's officials with drug trafficking.

Two weeks later, on November 13, all charges against the Postells were dropped, a decision which District Attorney Dupont Cheney made after it was discovered that Carl Isaacs, who had agreed to testify against the Postells, had made an extortion demand of fifteen thousand dollars in exchange for altering his testimony. "Isaacs' testimony was crucial to the prosecution of the Postells," Cheney told reporters. Now that it was tainted, he added, the case against them could not proceed.

In the meantime, the appeals process for all three of the Alday defendants continued at its own excruciating pace, producing a maddening array of legal maneuvers and countermaneuvers.

On October 31, 1980, approximately two months after the escape from Death Row, the Georgia State Supreme Court refused to review the June 13, 1980, ruling of the Superior Court of Tattnall County denying habeas corpus relief to Wayne Coleman.

A month later, on November 25, the United States District Court for the Southern District of Georgia transferred Isaacs' and Dungee's petitions to the U.S. District Court for the Middle District of Georgia in Columbus.

The following year, on April 27, 1981, the United States Supreme Court denied Coleman's certiorari petition. The petition had asked the court to review an earlier Georgia Supreme Court ruling, which had upheld an even earlier denial of state habeas corpus relief by the Superior Court in Tattnall County.

On July 8, Coleman filed a habeas corpus petition in the U.S. District Court for the Middle District of Georgia, prominently raising the change of venue issue once again.

On October 22, the U.S. District Court for the Middle District of Georgia denied Isaacs' and Dungee's habeas corpus petitions on the merits.

The following month, on November 20, their petition for a rehearing of this petition was denied.

Four months later, on March 11, 1982, the United States District Court for the Middle District of Georgia also denied Wayne Coleman's habeas corpus petitions on the merits.

On June 21, the United States Court of Appeals temporarily remanded Isaacs', Dungee's, and Coleman's appeals back to the Middle

District of Georgia so that additional evidence on the prejudicial pretrial publicity could be gathered.

Part of that evidence consisted of the radio broadcasts which had been transmitted across Seminole County and those adjoining areas from which the Alday juries had been selected. The relevant broadcasts had begun on May 15, the day after the murders, and had continued up to the time of the trials in January 1974, a period of seven months.

It was discovered that tapes of these broadcasts did in fact exist, but that they had never been edited. In order to review them for evidence of community prejudice against the Alday defendants, defense attorneys and their assistants were compelled to listen to the full taped transcripts.

In the end, this was a process that would take almost two and a half years.

During that time, and particularly in 1983, media attention in the form of books and movies reached a crescendo in the Alday murder case.

It amounted to a blitz that left Ernestine and her daughters reeling with bitterness and dismay.

In 1983, Clark Howard's *Brothers in Blood* was published by St. Martin's Press in New York.

Howard had come to Donalsonville the year before and interviewed several members of the Alday family. As Nancy would later say, he had told members of the family that his work on the case would result in "a book your children and grandchildren can be proud of."

The result, however, was far from what either Nancy, her sisters, or Ernestine imagined as a dignified treatment of the Alday case. "I wouldn't even let my children read it," Nancy declared seven years after its publication.

Although Howard had made it clear in an author's note that certain scenes had been dramatically re-created, and that he had used composite characters in his retelling of the story, Nancy and Patricia, who read it first, then warned Ernestine away, found his treatment, particularly of certain members of their family, utterly fanciful.

In addition, certain of the "re-creations" appeared to the Alday sisters as an effort to sensationalize their kindred's suffering. To Nancy and Patricia these accounts appeared purposefully crude, designed to titillate, rather than inform a wider world of their family's suffering and victimization at the hands of Carl Isaacs and the others.

From their point of view, this was bad enough. Even worse from their perspective was the fact that Carl had been made to appear remorseful, while in reality not only had he never expressed the slightest remorse, but he had sought repeatedly, by every word and deed, to wound the Aldays again and again, to reach beyond the bars of his cell and strike at Ernestine and themselves with a cruelty that seemed only to have grown more heartless with the years.

"We wanted just one book in which Carl didn't win," Nancy said in 1990. "Just one book that didn't let him blow himself up again at our expense. Just one book that remembered our Daddy, our brothers, Uncle Aubrey, and Mary."

They did not get it.

And if Nancy and Patricia had felt nothing but distaste for *Brothers in Blood*, it was a mild and carefully restrained response compared to their hatred of yet another work about the murders that also appeared in 1983.

Dead Man Coming was published by the Network Press in Albany, Georgia, and its author was none other than the peripatetic Charles Postell.

Presented in a lurid, blood-spattered cover, the book declared in its hyperbolic reading line that it was the story of "Mass Murderer Carl Isaacs," who "dreams of killing again. Will he?"

Centered exclusively on Carl, the "dead man" of its title, *Dead Man Coming* presented his most outrageous exaggeration of himself. Within its pages, Carl emerges as a young man raped by blacks during a prison riot in Maryland, and who, bent on revenge, then proceeds to murder several blacks in Baltimore City and rape "a couple dozen women," all of this done at a time when he was actually cruising Hillendale with Jennifer and Lori, an interval of aimlessness, boredom, and petty crime that did not even succeed in holding the interest of two teenage girls, a fact Carl had failed to report to his biographer.

By means of such baseless hyperbole, Carl manages to take on a weirdly heroic stature in *Dead Man Coming*, in part a sympathetic and abused child, in part a horrendously cruel adult, but always Carl as Carl wanted others to see him, the criminal mastermind, brilliant, deadly, and remorseless.

As the self-serving portrait of the man who had done them so much harm, Nancy and Patricia found *Dead Man Coming* cruel and unconscionable.

But if the *Atlanta Constitution,* a newspaper that had been quite sympathetic to Postell at the time of his earlier indictment, found such exchanges doubtful and "overwritten" when it reviewed the book, they were far more than a source of literary overkill to the Aldays; they were cruel, humiliating, and unspeakably offensive.

"I wouldn't even read Postell's book," Patricia Alday said in 1990, "not after what people told me was in it, how terrible it was. I just didn't want to feel what I knew I'd feel if I let myself read it, so I just never opened it up."

Nancy, however, read every word. "I would read it, and actually see the people the names meant, Daddy, and my brothers, Mary and Uncle Aubrey, and I would ask myself, 'Why was this written? Why is our family being used like this? Can't we ever just be left alone?' "

Though it was Carl Isaacs who emerged as the villain-hero in written accounts of the Alday murders, it was Billy who came out shining like a knight in armor in the only motion picture made about the case.

Murder One, a film financed and shot in Canada, and released in 1983, gave Billy center stage. It is Billy's voice, decidedly youthful and gentle, that provides the offscreen narration of the film and allows his character to dominate it. Erroneously portrayed as an innocent boy who had never gotten into any trouble with the law prior to the murders, he is swept along by events over which he has no control, and for which he feels nothing but revulsion.

Added to this sympathetic portrait, the film provides a denouement that is pure fiction. For rather than following the facts of the robbery at Mullins Grocery in West Virginia, the film offers a fanciful account in which Billy draws a gun on Carl in order to prevent him from taking a beautiful young girl captive, thus emerging as the heroic agent of her protection, something that, to say the least, never happened, and which struck the surviving Aldays who saw the film as a complete rewriting of events with which they were painfully familiar.

"We could never really understand why the books and the movie seemed to take the side of Carl and Billy and the rest of them," Patricia said years later, "or why we were always made to look, particularly in the movie, like just a bunch of dumb hicks."

It was a view shared by her sister. "I'd read this stuff and see the movie and I'd just ask, 'What about us?' " Nancy said in 1990. "Don't we matter? Doesn't anybody care about what we feel?' "

*   *   *

As Nancy and Patricia saw it, the books and the film dealing with their tragedy were little more than further assaults upon their dignity, as well as either subtle or not-so-subtle defenses of the men who had raped and murdered their closest kin, acts which, in the end, had also robbed them of their ancestral lands. Still, even this was not as damaging as the effect the books and film had on their standing in the community. For among their fellow Seminolians, it became the general belief that members of the Alday family had received large sums of money from the publishers and movie companies who dealt with their story, that large profits had been made by them from the deaths of their relatives, and that the family had actively sought and now secretly enjoyed the fruits of the murders.

The truth was just the opposite. Neither Ernestine nor any of her daughters had ever received a single penny from publishers or motion picture companies.

Nevertheless, the notion that they had received financial rewards from the murders on River Road would linger in Seminole County through the coming years, especially as the cost of the trials and appeals continued to mount. Though utterly unjustified, it would serve to heighten the growing local resentment of trial expenditures, a resentment that, while focused on the defendants, would also wash over to Ernestine and her daughters, driving a secret, painful wedge between them and the community they'd lived in all their lives.

"In the paper, they were always called the 'Alday trials,' " Patricia said. "The 'Alday trials' cost this and that, on and on, as if it was our family that was draining the treasury of Seminole County, not Carl Isaacs, Coleman, and Dungee . . . *but us!*"

That drain was about to escalate unimaginably, but not before the family would be stunned once again by the indefatigable Carl Isaacs.

Chapter Twenty-seven

On November 26, 1985, a correctional officer walking his rounds in Cell House G of the Georgia Classification and Diagnostic Center in Jackson, Georgia, glimpsed something strange in Cell 106 on the prison's new Death Row.

From the catwalk in front of the cell, he noticed a discoloration around the edges of the ventilation screen at the rear of the cell. Using a small metal rod, he poked gently at the discolored material, then watched, thunderstruck, as the entire front portion of the steel reinforced ventilation system tumbled from the wall and crashed to the floor, lifting a wave of loose dust, soap powder, and bits of glue into his widely staring eyes.

In the hole behind the screen, the guard could see that the prisoner assigned to Cell 106 had already succeeded in cutting through layer after layer of screens, louvers, and metal backings, and that he had already penetrated into the plumbing chase behind the cell. Nothing but a single set of thin, steel bars in the skylight above the chase now remained before the escape could be carried out.

The prisoner assigned to Cell 106 was Carl Junior Isaacs.

On December 5, Georgia Bureau of Investigation Agent Robert Ingram journeyed to the Jackson Diagnostic and Classification Center in a déjà vu assignment to determine how Isaacs had managed once again to get within hours of an escape from Georgia's Death Row.

Ingram arrived at 3:20 P.M., and began his interview with Isaacs. Once again, Carl appeared immensely full of himself, reveling in his favorite role of incorrigible outlaw. Thus, after far less prodding than had been required to extract a description of his escape attempt in the 1980 interviews, Carl happily detailed the plan and execution of his second, nearly successful escape attempt.

As he had several years before, Carl had begun his plot by ingratiating himself with various prisoners on his Cell Block, his mind continually tuned to how they might be of assistance.

This time, the mark was Theodore Hall, an inmate housed in the H-4 Cell Block, whom Carl had met in the late spring of 1985.

Hall was a good talker, and so Carl assumed the role of good listener, lounging in his bed for hours while Hall droned on about his family and friends. Suddenly, out of this welter of tedious family detail, Carl's calculating mind latched with a fierce intensity upon a single, minuscule detail. Sam Hall, one of Byron's brothers, was a paraplegic. Paralyzed from the waist down, he went everywhere in a wheelchair.

"Everywhere?" Carl asked.

"Yeah."

"Even here, when he visits you?"

"Yeah."

"He must set that metal detector ringing like hell when he wheels through," Carl said.

"Oh, yeah," Theodore told him, "but nobody notices it, because it's just the chair, you know."

From that moment on, Carl made it his business to get closer and closer to Theodore Hall, finally convincing him not only of his deep friendship but of his willingness to include him in his own brilliant escape plan, one whose details he'd already thought through, and which required only a few small items for its execution, items, which, as it turned out, Sam Hall would be able to supply.

Over the next few weeks, Carl managed to get Sam Hall added to his own visiting list, along with another outside contact, Sylvester Pitts.

On July 20, Pitts and Hall arrived for a visit with Carl and Byron. As a divergence, Theodore, a bit cowardly in his own participation and unwilling to transport contraband into the prison on his person, merely asked to be escorted to the bathroom by the visiting room's only correctional officer, a move that allowed Pitts to retrieve twelve hacksaw blades from one of the hollow bottom bars of Sam Hall's wheelchair.

Once in possession of the saws, Isaacs quickly inserted them into a specially made pocket of his boxer shorts. Later, during the required strip search that was conducted on prisoners after each visit, Carl casually slid his shorts to the floor and let the guard concentrate on his body rather than his clothes.

Back on his cell block, Isaacs hid ten of the blades in a hole underneath the toilet in Hall's cell, 107, while inserting the other two in the shower slide of his own cell, 104.

For the next few months, at times concealing his various hacksaw blades in holes hollowed out in the soles of his shoes, Carl began the difficult and time-consuming process of cutting his way through the vent and into the plumbing chase behind his cell, carefully concealing the cuts beneath a solution of soap, paint, and glue in such a way that it would blend so perfectly with the slats that only the most determined scrutiny would uncover his work.

As the weeks passed, Sam Hall continued to be a regular visitor to Carl and Theodore. Still using his wheelchair as the perfect smuggling machine, he supplied them with additional hacksaw blades, numerous plastic bottles and containers, wire cutters, paint, and finally the escapees' ultimate weapon, Super Glue.

Between visits, the continually interrupted and therefore protracted night work of cutting through to the plumbing chase stretched through July.

On August 17, a few new members of the Hall family arrived at the visiting room, this time with a cake in celebration of Theodore's birthday. During a boisterous round of "Happy Birthday," Sylvester Pitts slipped Carl the second required set of wire cutters.

That night, with the slats now cut completely through, Carl fashioned a false paper vent from the state-furnished writing paper he'd cut to the size of the vent. He attached a second sheet of paper behind it, this one with lines drawn to simulate the screen behind the vent itself, and attached with Band-Aids and chewing gum. With this apparatus in place, Carl no longer had to replace the vent and screen each time the guards approached.

Once the screen had been cut through, Carl filled in its severed parts with a paste he'd made from soap, shaving cream, and toothpaste, then wired it back into position with pipe cleaners he'd purchased from the prison commissary. He then painted the entire ventilation system, the final work so perfect in its execution that in a cell shakedown the following September, no part of it was discovered.

With the failure of the shakedown to reveal his escape effort, Carl felt he had a green light to go forward as quickly and boldly as possible.

As the days passed, he cut through the ventilation system to the metal plate behind it, dug painstakingly around a sewage pipe in the wall, finally penetrated the wall itself, and emerged into the beckoning freedom of the plumbing chase.

At this point, the overall plan was for Theodore Hall and Wayne Coleman to cut through the bars of their cells, then, on the night of the escape, place homemade dummies in their beds, slip down the catwalk to Carl's cell, and from there escape by crawling through the ventilation system and out into the plumbing chase.

Carl knew that sawing through the bars of Coleman and Hall's cells would take many days. To conceal the various stages, he chipped a piece of gray paint from his own bars and, during yet another friendly visit from Sylvester Pitts, handed him the paint and told him to match its color and return with a small amount he could use in the escape.

The following month, the paint arrived, and the last stage of the escape was put into effect.

On the last weekend in October, Pitts furnished Carl with a hand-drawn map of the area of the prison. He also buried a green plastic garbage bag near a stump behind a house only a block or so from the prison. In the bag, Pitts had placed a pair of wire strippers, a T-bar for use in hot-wiring stolen cars, a coat hanger already bent in the shape necessary for opening locked cars, black adhesive tape to be used in breaking into houses, latex gloves, a bag of marijuana, and, last but certainly not least, a .38-caliber revolver.

With everything now set, Carl told his fellow conspirators, Coleman, Hall, and Steven Dennis, a third convict who'd been brought into the plot, that the escape would be made either on Thanksgiving night or at some point during the holiday season. At the appointed time, Carl went on, he would go to the shower, leaving his cell empty. At the same time, Coleman would divert the guard's attention long enough for Hall and Dennis to place dummies in their bunks, and disappear into Carl's cell. A few hours later, at approximately 10:00 P.M., by Carl's estimate, all four of them would crawl through the wall, into the chase, and out one of the exhaust fans to the roof of the prison.

From that point on, it was all speed and derring-do, a quick drop to the ground, a rush to the prison fence, a flash of wire cutters, and away toward the cool blue haven of Canada.

The night before the escape, however, the Jackson Diagnostic correctional officer had glanced to the right as he made his rounds, seen something a bit off-color, and sounded the alarm.

After listening to Isaacs' account, Ingram could hardly believe how close he, Coleman, and the others had come to carrying out their escape. The discovery of the attempt had occurred no more than two or three hours before it was to be put into operation. And unlike the earlier escape, this time Carl himself would have been with them, the brains of the outfit. With him in command, it seemed clear to Ingram that they might well have gone all the way to freedom.

As it turned out, however, Carl Isaacs went nowhere that night. But he was about to.

In early November 1984, nearly a year before the discovery of Carl Isaacs' second escape attempt, evidentiary hearings had finally been held in the Middle District.

Five months later, on March 18, 1985, it denied habeas corpus relief to all three Alday defendants, a ruling that was immediately appealed to the United States Court of Appeals.

By that time, the three convictions and death sentences that had been handed down in Donalsonville over eleven years before had gone through level after level of both the state and federal appeals systems, each time remaining intact.

Then, on December 9, 1985, only ten days after Carl's escape had been thwarted, and nearly twelve and a half years after the murders on River Road, everything abruptly changed. On that day, a three-judge panel of the Eleventh Circuit of the United States Court of Appeals stunned state law enforcement officials by suddenly reversing the general direction of all the appeals that had gone before it. According to the judges, and as cited in their 112-page opinion, instances of "inflammatory and prejudicial pretrial publicity" had so pervaded the local community before and during the trials of Isaacs, Coleman, and Dungee that it had made fair trials impossible.

Because of this impossibility, the judges concluded that each of the defendants should have been granted a change of venue in 1974, when it had first been requested by the defendants' lawyers. Not to have done so, the panel said, had been a fatal, and unconstitutional, judicial error. "If there were no constitutional right to change of venue [in this case]," their opinion declared, "then one can conceive of virtually no case in which a change of venue would be a constitutional necessity."

Thus, in an instant, twelve years of judicial review were overturned, and the convictions and death sentences of Carl Isaacs, Wayne Coleman and George Dungee were set aside despite what the justices called the "overwhelming evidence" of their guilt. To hold otherwise, the panel concluded "would mean an obviously guilty defendant would have no right to a fair trial before an impartial jury; a holding which would be contrary to the well established and fundamental constitutional right of every defendant to a fair trial."

All three defendants were thereby granted new trials.

In Donalsonville, the Aldays sat in stunned silence as the news raced across the state that Georgia's most notorious Death Row inmates had not only delayed their journeys toward the electric chair once again, but that they had been granted wholly new trials.

For the Alday women who remained in Seminole County, the prospect of three new trials came as a stunning blow. Once again, they would become the community's macabre celebrities, their family name emblazoned in the local press, linked to Isaacs, Coleman, and Dungee. At the trials themselves, they would have to confront the faces of the defendants again, sit only a few feet from them, watch silently as they joked with their attorneys. Even worse, however, was the prospect of having to relive the events of May 14 in all their graphic detail.

Still, there was no choice but for at least some members of the family to attend the trials. It would be a much diminished number, however. Bereft of their inheritance, and with the Alday Fund used exclusively for the new sanctuary of the Spring Creek Baptist Church, most of the children simply could not afford to leave their jobs for such long periods. In addition, with the trials being held in three separate locations, all of them located a great distance from Donalsonville, the expenses for food and lodging would be prohibitive. Even Patricia found she simply could not manage it.

Faced with these circumstances, Ernestine made a fateful decision. She would come to the trials herself, stand in for that part of her family that could not afford to do so. Silently, with great dignity and self-restraint, her voice never raised in anger, she would sit in the courtroom to remind the jurors that Ned, Shuggie, Jerry, Jimmy, Aubrey, and Mary Alday had not been forgotten.

"It was an amazingly courageous thing for her to do," prosecutor Charles Ferguson remembered. "It meant that she was going to have to go through it all, the testimony, the pictures, everything she had not been unable to face fifteen years before."

As for the other family members who would accompany her, they would have to do the same, live through it all, but for a second time. "It was like we'd been shot back twelve years," Nancy said. "The rape, the murders; we were going to have to go through it all again."

Over the next few weeks, Georgia officials made numerous appeals contesting this latest ruling. All of them were denied.

Accordingly, on August 18, 1986, Wayne Carl Coleman, George Elder Dungee, and Carl Junior Isaacs were transferred from Death Row to the Chatham County jail in Savannah to await new trials.

A few days later, Superior Court Judge Walter C. MacMillan, Jr., of Sandersville, was appointed to preside over each of the three trials. On August 30, he appointed six new lawyers to defend Isaacs, Coleman, and Dungee.

Within weeks, however, MacMillan was challenged when a motion for his removal as presiding judge was filed by lawyers for Coleman and Dungee. The motion charged that MacMillan was prejudiced against both poor and black defendants.

In response, Judge MacMillan appointed a second jurist, Asa Kelly of Albany, to choose yet a third jurist to decide the issue. Kelly subsequently appointed Blend Taylor, of Brunswick, to conduct a hearing on the motion.

At the hearing held in early September, Steven Bright, Dungee's newly acquired attorney, argued that MacMillan had never had a black law clerk, court reporter, or public defender in his circuit, though its population was forty percent black. In addition, Bright said, MacMillan belonged to the Emanuel County Country Club, which had no black members and practiced racial discrimination.

At the same hearing, lawyers for Coleman charged that MacMillan had called the Georgia Attorney General's Office asking for assistance for the prosecution in the case, while in contrast, public defenders in the judge's circuit had complained in the past about the volume of their caseloads as well as the scarce resources MacMillan permitted to be allocated for their work.

For his part, and out of what he called an "abundance of caution," Seminole County District Attorney Charles Ferguson, whose task it would be to prosecute the three Alday defendants, made no objection to the defense attorneys' arguments, although he thought their motion groundless.

On Monday, October 21, Judge Taylor declared that he found no grounds for removing MacMillan, and denied the motion. Defense lawyers promptly appealed to the Georgia Supreme Court, asking it to overturn Taylor's ruling.

It would take seven months for the supreme court to come to its decision.

But if a terrible silence had fallen over the Georgia State Supreme Court in regard to the Alday defendants, the defendants themselves, particularly Carl Isaacs, were making enough noise to keep the citizenry of Georgia forever in their hearing.

His method was two-pronged.

First, Carl suddenly decided to protest his poor treatment by means of a hunger strike. It began in the Chatham County jail, and authorities there officially listed it as a hunger strike when he missed his ninth consecutive meal.

In fact, Carl was eating all during his "hunger strike," preferring to gobble away at the full forty-three dollars' worth of candy and other junk food he had purchased from the courthouse commissary.

Still, Chatham County authorities decided to take no chances, and Carl was carefully monitored, given daily weigh-ins as well as medical checks of his vital signs.

Far more irritating, however, was Carl's increasing penchant for independent legal maneuvering. In late November, he filed suit against Chatham County for the "inhuman treatment" he alleged he had suffered while in its custody.

A few months later, on March 12, he filed another suit, this one charging that he had been illegally transported from Chatham County, and that all subsequent movement across the state had been illegal. Arguments were heard by a fourth judge, Perry Brennan, on April 2 and dismissed by him a few days later.

Carl was returned to Chatham County's jurisdiction in order to avoid any further lawsuits he might file regarding his right to reside in the area of venue after a change of venue had been granted.

In the meantime, while Carl languished in the Chatham County Jail, and the Georgia Supreme Court continued to ponder the fate of Judge MacMillan, Seminole County was spending a great deal of money to house all three defendants and to pay for their lawyers.

While the original trials had cost approximately fifteen thousand dollars, the hearings and pretrial arguments involved in the retrials had already cost nearly ten thousand in defense fees alone. In addition, the county had spent almost fifteen thousand dollars in jail and court fees.

Still, on the evening of August 21, the Seminole County Board of Commissioners voted a resolution declaring its willingness to assume whatever financial burden was necessary to ensure the prosecution of the defendants even though it might run to a million dollars, and necessitate, as the commission admitted, either a new ad valorem tax or an increase in the mil rate for the already beleaguered people of the county.

Money was also being made on the case, however, the recipient of these funds being Charles Postell. On August 14 the *Donalsonville News* reported that the movie rights to *Dead Man Coming* had been sold to Phoenix Productions. According to the paper, the motion picture production company had pledged a "certain percentage" of its profits to a fund for the Alday Memorial Fund, a pledge of which Ernestine, the fund's indisputable head, was unaware.

Nor could Ernestine anticipate with any confidence that the film would be something of which she could be proud, since, according to the *News,* the script would be written by Postell and a woman named Nancy Sterling, whose previous screen credit, the paper said, was a film called *Rock 'n' Road Trip.*

Finally, during the first week of May, the Georgia State Supreme Court at last rendered judgment on the matter of Judge MacMillan, and in a unanimous decision disqualified him.

Nearly two months later, after an exhaustive and time-consuming search for a judge whose ideas or abilities could not be challenged, Judge Hugh Lawson, Jr., of the Oconee Judicial Circuit was named to replace MacMillan.

By August 13, Lawson had selected Perry, Georgia, a small town in Houston County, to be the site of the first of the defendants' retrials. The defendant in that case would be Carl Junior Isaacs.

For the next year and a half, the various attorneys for the defendants were granted continuances while they worked to develop adequate defenses for their clients. As a result, it was not until January 4, 1988, almost fourteen years to the day of his first trial, that jury selection began in Perry, Georgia, for the trial of Carl Isaacs.

By that time, according to the *Donalsonville News,* the bill for legal fees associated with the defense had reached $135,687, a sum the county could not pay and still operate its various educational, medical, and social service functions. Thus, faced with such an unacceptable decline in county services, the Board of County Commissioners had borrowed $210,000 to offset trial expenses now expected to reach nearly a quarter of a million dollars.

As events would prove, such an amount, though considered astronomical by Seminole County standards, was wildly optimistic. The cost of the retrials had just begun.

"WILL THIS NEVER END?"

Chapter Twenty-eight

D istrict Attorney Charles Ferguson, to whom it now fell to prosecute Isaacs, Coleman, and Dungee, needed only to glance at the previous trial testimony to see exactly how strong a case he had.

"The evidence was absolutely overwhelming," he would say years later, "and it was all still available to us . . . of course with one exception."

That exception was Billy Isaacs. Sixteen years before, Billy had agreed to testify against each of the defendants in exchange for having no murder charges filed against him in the state of Georgia.

Since that time, however, he had been transferred to Allegany County, Maryland, where he, alone among the four men who'd kidnapped Richard Wayne Miller in McConnellsburg, Pennsylvania, had been charged with the various criminal offenses connected to his death.

For those crimes, kidnapping and murder, he had been swiftly tried, convicted, and sentenced to a staggering sixty years in prison, along with five additional years for car theft, all of which were to be served only after he had completed his forty-year sentence in Georgia. If these sentences remained in place, Billy Isaacs would be eligible for parole in slightly more than fifty years. This was not a pleasant prospect for a sixteen-year-old boy, particularly when it seemed entirely possible given their upcoming retrials, that the other Carl and Wayne, each of whom he considered far more culpable than himself, would suffer a fate hardly worse than his own.

"I testified for the state, and then drew one hundred and five years," Billy would say from prison in 1990, "and I didn't kill or rape or kidnap anybody."

Now in his early thirties, no longer a child, and certainly no longer innocent of the law's dark ironies, Billy was well aware that he was not under the slightest obligation to testify against either Carl, Wayne, or George in their upcoming retrials. He had fulfilled his part of the bargain in 1974, and to his mind, the state of Georgia had gotten the better part of the deal, particularly since various Georgia officials had worked vigorously to ensure his later prosecution in Maryland, activities of which he had been unaware in 1974.

Bitter at his treatment and desperately weary of prison, Billy knew that he now had one last card to play. He could trade his testimony for the better deal he felt he deserved, and which had been denied him fifteen years before.

Charles Ferguson knew Billy's situation, too, and in reviewing the case, had even felt some sympathy for him.

"I didn't know Billy as a person," Ferguson recalled, "but looking at what had happened to him in 1974, I was pretty sure he'd want something from us in exchange for his testimony. I was also sure that I couldn't offer him anything."

Except a chance to do the right thing.

Which is precisely what Ferguson did.

"We met in a little room at the prison where Billy was serving his time," Ferguson remembered, "and Billy asked if there was anything I could do for him, and I told him straight out that I couldn't make any deals." Then, in a move whose outcome he could not have known beforehand, Ferguson took out a picture of Ernestine Alday, a woman who, despite her suffering, had never called for Billy's death or raised her voice in vengeance against him.

"Do it for her," Ferguson said.

Billy stared at the picture for a moment, then nodded. "All right, I will," he said.

It was now July 1988. Fifteen years had passed since the murders on River Road. Jimmy Carter, who'd occupied the Georgia governor's mansion at the time of the murders, had ascended to the White House, only to be turned out of it four years later by the Reagan juggernaut. The Watergate scandal, particularly the episode of the Saturday night massacre, which had served to crowd the murders from the national news in 1973, had almost entirely receded from the public mind, its central figure, Richard Nixon, now rising once again to an honored place as elder statesman.

As for the Alday family, much had changed for them as well. As a farming family, they had ceased to be, their 550 acres now in different hands, broken up, subdivided.

Death had claimed some of the survivors on River Road. Bud, last of Ned's farming brothers, was now buried near the rest of them at Spring Creek Baptist Church. Others had simply moved away. Elizabeth had returned to Albany, the child she'd been carrying at the time of the murders now grown into a teenager. Faye, still in high school in 1974, had since married and borne her own children. Norman had retired from the military and settled in the West, returning to Georgia only for short visits.

Alone among the Alday children, Nancy and Patricia remained in Seminole County. But they had also changed. Young women at the time, they had moved into middle age. As for Ernestine, she had turned into an elderly woman, still active, but no longer spry, her movements slow and more ponderous, both her hearing and her eyesight fading noticeably with the passing years.

"We weren't the same anymore," Nancy recalled. "We didn't look the same or feel the same, and yet we were going through the same things again, the trials and the testimony, all of us reliving the murders."

She was right. Things had changed considerably since May 14, 1973. Perhaps more than anything else, the legal process itself had changed in such ways as to greatly extend the amount of time required for a trial.

In marked contrast to the first trial, for example, the actual presentation of evidence in the second trial did not even begin until nearly nine volumes of defense motions and voir dire examination had been completed, a process which, in itself, consumed more time than had been necessary to try all three of the Alday defendants sixteen years before.

Finally, however, on July 3, Ferguson rose to begin the prosecution's case. It was the jury's task, he said, to come to judgment on indictment number 87c-4416-M in the Superior Court of Houston County, Georgia.

After briefly retracing the crimes, he moved through a list of witnesses who were more or less unchanged from those selected and questioned by Peter Zack Geer.

Except for one.

By that time, and with Ferguson's steady encouragement, Ernestine had decided not only to attend Carl's trials, but to testify for the prosecution, a circumstance that Isaacs' attorney, Terry Jackson, found disturbing, since her presence in the courtroom served to heighten the emotional atmosphere of the rest of the Alday family.

"Your honor," Jackson said just as Ernestine was about to answer Ferguson's first question, "your honor, at this time, let the record reflect that the members of the Alday family are in the courtroom and that they are crying and that you can hear it. . . . And we think that this certainly has prejudiced our client's rights."

Jackson then made a motion for a mistrial. When it was denied, he requested that "the Court instruct the bailiff that either the spectators are going to have to be quiet," or that they would be removed from the court.

Outrageous as Jackson's objection seemed to the Aldays seated in the courtroom, the judge heeded it cautiously and issued a firm warning in its behalf. First noting that some of the family members had begun to weep as Ferguson had described the events of May 14, Judge Lawson warned that such displays of emotion would not be tolerated, and that anyone who found it impossible "to remain in the courtroom in a composed and unemotional state" would be asked to leave the room "until their composure can be restored."

Predictably, the judge's warning sent shock waves through the Aldays. They could not believe that their tears could have no place in a courtroom whose walls rang with the suffering of their dearest relatives.

"The Alday family couldn't cry, that's what the judge said," Nancy recalled. "But, as it turned out later, the Isaacs family could cry as much as they wanted. And they did, too. They got up on the stand and cried and cried, and the judge never said a word."

Once the judge had issued his warning, Ernestine, now seventy-three years old, proceeded with her testimony, moving through the late afternoon and early morning hours of May 14 and 15, 1973.

Before leaving the stand, she was shown a series of photographs taken in Jerry Alday's trailer the day after the murders. In one of them, she saw Ned's pipe as it lay in an ashtray on the kitchen table. Utterly composed until then, she suddenly began to cry.

Once Ernestine had left the stand, Ferguson resumed a witness lineup that was little more than a replay of the 1974 trial. Bud Alday testified to his discovery of the bodies, GBI Agent T. R. Bentley to the first investigative efforts the following morning.

As the days progressed, Jerry Godby once again identified Carl Isaacs as the man he'd seen driving Mary Alday's car, while Horace Waters and Ronnie Angel repeated their testimony as to their own roles in the GBI investigation, finally showing the pictures that had been made from the role of negatives he'd found in a small plastic container located in Mary Alday's abandoned car.

One by one, as Ernestine, Nancy, and the others listened from scarcely twenty feet away, he ticked off what the photographs portrayed: a trailer with a neatly trimmed lawn, a mailbox on which the name Alday had been prominently written, a dog in the yard, and finally, a woman working in a flower garden. "Not one thing he named still existed," Nancy remembered. "Not even our name on the deed that held the land. Everything was gone."

Over the next few days, Ferguson continued to call his witnesses, and one by one they gave testimony that traced the development of the investigation as it led inevitably to the final capture of the defendants in the hills of West Virginia.

Finally, at 1:20 P.M. on the afternoon of January 23, 1988, Billy Isaacs, the state's star witness, once again took the stand to testify against his brother.

Now thirty years old, Billy had entirely lost the blush of youth which had surrounded him fifteen years before when he had first taken the stand in Donalsonville. Since that time, the gangly, long-haired teenage boy had entirely faded beneath the slightly wrinkled eyes, the subtly receding hairline, and the added pounds that gave the first suggestions of his approaching middle age.

As for his testimony, it remained the same riveting account it had been when he had first given it so many years before. Sixteen years had not altered a single substantive one of its terrible details.

From only a few feet away, Ernestine and Nancy listened to it all. "And so we went through it again," said Nancy Alday, "everything that happened to my daddy and my brothers, and Uncle Aubrey, and Mary, and I thought to myself, 'Will this never end?' "

Just as in the first trial, Billy had been presented as the prosecution's final witness. But where defense attorneys in Donalsonville had submitted him to a limited, if accusatory, cross-examination, Jackson was determined to use Billy's position on the stand to begin to build his client's defense.

In answer to Jackson's questions, Billy said that "to the best of his knowledge" he had six brothers and five sisters. His father's name was George, he added, and his mother's name was Betty Isaacs "unless she had remarried."

"Now, when you were growing up, did you all live together?" Jackson asked.

"No, sir, we didn't."

"How come?"

"We were all put in different foster homes," Billy replied.

"How old were you when you were first placed in a foster home?"

"Five years of age."

"And was Carl placed in a foster home?" Jackson asked pointedly.

"Yes, he was."

"Did anything occasion you all going to a foster home?"

"I don't know the real reason why my family was broken up," Billy answered. "I do know my mother and father got divorced and the state stepped in and took all of my brothers and sisters as well as me and placed us in foster homes."

As he continued under Jackson's questioning, Billy testified that at one foster home where he, Carl, and Bobby Isaacs had lived, the foster mother had beaten them with shoes and belts or "whatever was handy," and that they had been forced to eat hot peppers and keep them on their tongues.

Under such conditions, of course, running away appeared as the most obvious solution. The Isaacs boys had run away from several such homes, Billy said.

From a discussion of the deplorable conditions of his boyhood, Jackson moved on to certain discrepancies between the testimony Billy had given at the first trial and that which he had just offered in the present case, listing them one by one, even down to Billy's embellishing his current tale with a story of how Carl had been wearing Jerry Alday's cowboy hat and a western-style holster before the murders.

Still, the big question remained Billy himself, his character as a person, and thereby his credibility as a witness.

"Who was holding you hostage in the trailer?" Jackson asked.

"Nobody."

"Did you stop anybody from doing anything in that trailer?"

"No, sir, I did not."

"In fact, you were the lookout, weren't you?"

"Yes, sir."

"What did you think was going to happen to those people when you made that man go into the trailer [after three others had already been murdered]?"

"I wasn't doing any thinking at the time."

"You were a zombie?"

"I was in a state of shock."

"You had a gun?"

"Yes, sir, I did."

"And, in fact, you loaned your gun to somebody to shoot somebody; is that right?"

"Yes, sir."

Jackson then went into any deals Billy might have been offered for his current testimony.

"What did you ask [District Attorney Charles Ferguson] to do for you?" he asked.

"If there was some way that he would make a deal with me for me to be turned loose," Billy answered. "He stated he was not going to make any deals, promises or insinuations in any way whatsoever."

"You hope that Mr. Ferguson does something for you when we finish this?"

"I certainly have lots of hopes that something will be done for me when this is over with," Billy admitted frankly, then added, "that is what has helped keep my sanity for fifteen years, hope."

"That is something to hold onto in prison, isn't it?" Jackson asked softly.

"Yes, it is," Billy told him. "If you lose hope, you might as well go ahead and hang yourself because there is nothing left."

When completed, it was clear that Billy Isaacs' testimony had been nearly identical to that he had given in the first trial. Since that first trial, however, a new "eyewitness" had emerged, one who'd been reluctant to speak in 1973, but who'd spoken more or less ceaselessly since that time.

The witness whose testimony was to be used against Carl Isaacs this time was Carl Isaacs himself.

Chapter Twenty-nine

In December 1976, Carl Isaacs had been contacted by Fleming Fuller, a writer-filmmaker who was doing a television documentary called *Murder One*, the same title he would later use for his screenplay on the Alday murder, which consisted of interviews with various Death Row inmates in Georgia and North Carolina.

While conducting interviews in Reidsville, Fuller learned about Carl Isaacs and the Alday murders, and shortly thereafter Carl agreed to tell his story for Fleming's film. The result was an amazing document, and, from the prosecution's point of view, a damning one. Here was Carl Isaacs staring directly at the camera, his voice entirely emotionless as he gave a chilling, matter-of-fact rendering of the murders on River Road.

"Okay, we pulled around to the back of the trailer," he began. "Wayne got out and . . . I said, 'Check the door,' and he turned the knob on the door."

The unlocked door had opened with no further effort, Carl said, and he and the rest of his gang had then entered and routinely begun ransacking the trailer.

Only this time, there was a complication.

"And then a jeep pulled up," Carl said coolly, his body slouched lazily in his chair, his eyes entirely passive, as if narrating the details of an ordinary day. "When the jeep stopped, the man looked like he was going for a gun . . . and I drew the pistol out of the holster and I threw down on him to freeze."

The men, whose names Carl seemed unable to remember, were Ned and Jerry Alday, and they were immediately marched into the trailer and leaned against what Isaacs referred to as a "countertop."

"Then me and Wayne went to talking, you know, about what we were going to do with them," Carl went on. "So we decided, well, we'll just kill them."

It was not a long conversation. There were no subtleties of moral thought involved. The two men were human beings who could see and tell what they saw. Because of that, they were going to die.

"So after talking with Wayne, I took the youngest one and went in the south bedroom," Carl said. "And Wayne . . . took the other one into the north bedroom. All right. Now I stood there about three or four seconds, you know, waiting to see if I heard a shot. I guess it was like Wayne was waiting on me, and I was waiting on him. And I figured, well, the hell with it. I guess he's waiting on me. So I shot the dude."

As if on a signal, Wayne had also begun firing.

"All right, I come back out," Isaacs said. "As I was coming down the hall, I heard a shot at the other end . . . Wayne hollered. I run through the living room to the kitchen and George was standing by the kitchen door, and he was white as a sheet. Billy was standing in the bedroom door. I run past Billy and asked Wayne what the hell is wrong, you know? And the old man that he had shot was getting up off the bed. I could see blood, and the man had a hole in the back of his head, but the top part of his head was missing, you know, on the front of him . . . So I got my pistol, you know, and cocked it, and shot all the remaining shells . . . on the side of his head. He fell back on the bed. He started to get back up again. You know, and it just blew my mind, you know, I mean, hey, what the hell is this. The man is supposed to be dead. Wayne shot the remaining shells he had."

Carl paused an instant, as if to draw a quick breath, then resumed his grim narrative, his eyes as dull and lusterless as when he'd begun his tale: "All right. I'm trying to load the .22. I can't get it loaded fast enough, because the man is getting up on the bed, and I'm scared shitless. I mean this is the first time I've ever seen anything like this, you know. And I look at George, 'Give me a gun,' you know. He hands me a .32. So I shoot him three times with it, and Wayne shoots him three or four times with the .380. So, you know, he falls back on the bed and he stays there."

Then, while the blue smoke from the revolvers was still floating in the air, the inconceivable began to happen.

"So this green and white pickup truck pulls up in back of the trailer," Carl said.

From the arrival of the pickup, Carl's account unwound almost identically to Billy's earlier testimony, confirming in every detail his younger brother's rendering of the capture and murder of Shuggie and Aubrey Alday.

"I looked at Wayne, I said, 'Well, same way?' " Carl told the unblinking black eye of Fleming Fuller's camera. "And he said, 'Yes, might as well.' So it didn't dawn on me then, but at the time, you know, my pistol was empty. And I took one of them, I can't remember which, into the south bedroom again. And when I walked in, you know, the other dude is sprawled out on the bed. I mean there is blood all over the trailer, all over the floor . . . Anyway, when I got him in the bedroom, you know, he seen the other dude laying there with all this blood. And he turned around and looked at me. And it dawned on me, you know, well, he's going to try to jump me, you know. So I told him, 'Get up on the bed.' . . . And when he laid down, I stepped back and pulled the trigger. And all I could hear was a click, you know. And I turned out of the bedroom and I come walking down the hall . . . So I seen Billy . . . And I grabbed his gun, the .38. I went back to the bedroom, and no sooner than I walked in the door, I looked, you know, where the dude was laying, and his hand was just reaching around a shotgun, a twelve-gauge pump, sitting up in the corner . . . It sort of chilled me, you know. Here I am dumb enough to walk out of that room after leaving him in there, not knowing what's in that room . . . But instead of saying anything to him, I shot him three times. And I come back into the kitchen . . . and George hollered from the living room, 'Here comes somebody.' "

Again, following Billy's earlier testimony in nearly every detail, save for the actual sequence of the murders, Carl described the capture, robbery, and murder of Jimmy Alday, and after that, the arrival in a blue and white Impala of the last of his victims, Mary Campbell Alday.

"She got out of the car before I could stop the tractor and walked over to our car and looked in," Carl said. "I shut the tractor off and run up behind her and grabbed her and told her to just keep walking and there wouldn't be no trouble."

Once in the trailer, Isaacs said, he told Wayne and Billy to begin loading their supplies from Richard Miller's Chevelle to Mary Alday's Impala. Now alone with Mary Alday, save for the gawking presence of George Dungee, Carl's mind began to turn to his own grim satisfactions. "And then it dawned on me, hey, you know, she's a woman . . . So I started feeling her up, and she started to cry about it, talked about please, don't, and all this, you know. And I slapped her, and I told her to shut up. And I took off her clothes, and I was having sex with her when Billy walked in . . . And then Wayne come in . . . and had sex with her. George wanted to have sex with her, and I told him I said, 'Look, we've done took enough damn time, let's go.' "

Continuing in the monotone with which he'd told the preceding events, Carl then went on to describe the last terrible moments of Mary Alday's life, an agony for which, Carl hinted obliquely, she was herself to blame: "Well, when we come out of the trailer, I told her, I said, 'Now, look, don't give us no hassle. It might save your life. Other than that, you're dead.' And I went on to tell her that if you cooperate and do what you're told, we might keep you alive. But it didn't work."

After Fuller's testimony and his reading of Isaacs' interview, Carl's defense attorneys advised the court that they had no witnesses to call on their client's behalf. The court then advised the jury that the defense had the right either to open or to close the arguments in the case, and that it had chosen to close them.

Ferguson rose to make his final arguments. He went over the physical evidence once again, pointedly adding that even without it, they could find the defendant guilty because they could "rely on the words of Carl Isaacs himself."

Once Ferguson had completed his argument, defense attorney Schiavone spoke for the defense. He noted that the jury was required to base its decision on whether or not Carl Isaacs was guilty of each of the six counts of murder, each and every one, and that therefore they had to consider if there was reasonable doubt in the case. He noted that in his interview with Fleming Fuller, Isaacs had told outrageous lies, that there was no blood all over the room, no shotgun for one of the Aldays to reach for, and that Ned Alday had not died beneath a fifteen-shot barrage of gunfire in the bedroom of the Alday trailer. All of that was just Carl's blustering, Schiavone told the court, "material that movie makers take license with . . . so that they can make the most money they possibly can, because they have to draw fans to the theater." Carl's confession, Schiavone declared, was merely "theatrical."

As to Billy Isaacs' testimony, Schiavone deemed it was all a self-serving lie. "But the bottom line and the fundamental truth is that Billy Isaacs was not convicted, nor did he plead guilty, nor did he receive the death sentence, or even life imprisonment for six counts of murder," he said. "That certainly is every reason in the world for him to lie."

"The responsibility is yours," Schiavone concluded. "And remember that each of you have [sic] to make the decision yourself on each count, and you have to determine if it's fact that the State has proved each one beyond a reasonable doubt."

Only a short time later, at 6:45 P.M. on January 25, 1988, fifteen and one half years after the original crime, the jury reached a verdict on case number 87C144461-M, the state of Georgia versus Carl Isaacs.

After deliberation for little more than two hours, they had found him guilty on all six counts of murder.

The penalty phase of Carl Isaacs' second trial began the following day. Ferguson opened his argument for the death penalty by detailing Isaacs' two nearly successful escape attempts, and even had witnesses read Carl's own boastful account of them to the jury.

But it was not only that Isaacs might escape which argued for the imposition of the death penalty, Ferguson said, but the nature of the man himself, one whose unregenerate evil he attempted to demonstrate by calling several witnesses.

The first was Mark Picard, a reporter for WSB-TV in Atlanta. Picard had interviewed Isaacs only a few years after the murders, and during the interview he had discussed the crimes.

"Do you recall any specific reference or conversation with reference to the Alday family?" Ferguson asked.

"I do."

"What do you recall?"

"I recall a question that I asked and his response," Picard answered. "I asked if he had to do it all over again, the Alday killings, would he do it again. He responded that he would. It's been eleven or twelve years," Picard added, "but I recall that clearly because it was one of those moments that sort of sticks in your mind."

To counter the diabolical image of Carl Isaacs that Ferguson had hoped to establish in the minds of the jury, the defense called Shirley Kline to the stand.

A resident of Smithsburg, Maryland, Kline told the court that she had begun corresponding with Carl in 1974. Her son had just been killed in a hit-and-run accident, she said, and at the time she was "confused and messed up." While visiting her mother at a local nursing home, she had read an article in which Betty Isaacs had stated that she did not care for Carl or any of her sons, and that she had "written them off."

In the end, Kline said, she had felt sorry for Carl and had started writing him, beginning a correspondence that had stretched into the years. In addition, she had visited Carl in prison, bringing her husband and daughter along with her. These visits had continued, Kline said, first at Reidsville then at Jackson Diagnostic, and over time Carl had begun to call her "Mom."

Kline went on to say that she and Carl had talked and corresponded about the Bible and other "outside" things. As a result Carl had started doing Bible study courses with her. Later Carl and other inmates had started their own Bible course in prison. In 1979, she said, Carl had written that he had been baptized in her church. Later, he had graduated from the Baptist Christian College in Louisiana, where he'd taken a correspondence course. Continuing his studies, he had finally received a Certificate of Honor, Master of Bible Theology from the International Bible Institute. Since then, Carl had indicated a desire to go even deeper into theology, Kline told the court, an interest which surprised her, she said, since she had always been under the impression he intended to study law.

All of this had convinced Kline that Carl Isaacs was, as she put it, "the kind of person that can reach out and help anyone," since "he's always been outgoing with us, with the whole family."

On January 29, 1988, Ferguson and Jackson made their closing arguments in the penalty phase of the trial.

Isaacs' crimes were "outrageously and wantonly vile, horrible, or inhuman," Ferguson argued. Then he added a final appeal for justice. "Mary Alday won't ever go back to work at the Department of Family and Children Services," he said. "Mrs. Ernestine won't ever sit down to those lunches that they had at her house with Ned and Aubrey and Jerry and Jimmy and Shuggie. Carl Isaacs told them never again. You've got to do that, too. Never again. Never again, Carl Isaacs."

In his argument for Isaacs' life, Terry Jackson described the poverty and abuse Carl had suffered as a child, and in support of which Jackson had previously called two psychologists to testify. Focusing on Isaacs' hatred of his mother, Jackson declared that the rape of Mary Alday had not been a rape at all, but Carl's way of assaulting his own mother. As far as any notion that Carl was some kind of evil genius, nothing could be further from the truth.

"We don't have a mastermind," Jackson told the jury. "We've got a pathetic person who's never felt love, never been able to have any faith in anything. I hope he can have faith in you."

He couldn't.

After deliberating for one hour and fifty-two minutes, the jury found that Carl Junior Isaacs should be put to death.

Accordingly, Judge Lawson asked Isaacs to rise before pronouncing sentence. "All right, Mr. Isaacs," he said then, "it is the sentence and judgment of the court that you suffer death by electrocution at such time and place as may be fixed by the order of this court, the state of Georgia, and the Department of Corrections after the required review of this case by the Supreme Court of Georgia."

Then, as once again required by law, the judge advised Carl Isaacs of his right to appeal.

On February 4, the *Donalsonville News* reprinted an article from the *Houston Home Journal* of Perry, Georgia. It was an interview with Fleming Fuller, the guiding spirit of *Murder One,* conducted by Charles Postell, the author of *Dead Man Coming.*

In the article, Postell noted that Fuller's film had taken only six weeks to complete, and that the filming itself had been done in and around Toronto, Canada, rather than in Georgia.

"I understand that [Seminole County] is nearly bankrupt," Fuller told Postell, "but the city and county fathers there never expressed any interest in a production company coming there and setting up."

This was regrettable, Fuller went on, since it signaled an unfortunate reversal of what had formerly been a vigorous pro-film policy. "I can remember when the Georgia Department of Industry and Trade's film commission went after business," he said, "but I suppose that is a thing of the past."

Neither state nor county governments had offered him any incentives to film *Murder One* in Georgia, Fuller added, whereas the Canadian government had offered "many incentives" to S.C. Entertainment, the film's production company. "We had many people mention the fact that a Georgia movie was being shot in Canada," Fuller told Postell, "but it was the cheapest and best way," since, unlike Georgia, movie investments in Canada were one hundred percent tax deductible.

One week later, on February 11, the *Donalsonville News* reported that the total charges for Carl Isaacs' second trial currently amounted to $69,288.04. Expenditures which the paper meticulously itemized:

$480.00 for prisoner housing for 32 days
$359.32 for medical costs when Isaacs became ill during the trial
$26,681.22 for prisoner transportation and security
$6,470.31 for jail security
$3,645.41 for overtime for patrol staff
$890.00 for county maintenance crews opening and closing doors of courthouse

The *News* added that the second trial would probably end up costing around one hundred thousand dollars, and that an additional four hundred thousand could be expected before the last of the trials had been concluded.

Seminole County was doubtless spending a great deal of money on the retrials, but it was not alone. So were Ernestine, Nancy, and other members of the Alday family who had determined to attend the trials. Though Ernestine's expenses were picked up for the time she was a prosecution witness, all other family members were required to pay their own way. As the trial had dragged on, the bills had begun to mount heavily.

Seeing the Aldays at the trials day after day, realizing the expenses involved in their long stay in Houston County, local citizens created a fund to help ease the drain on personal finances their trial attendance had incurred. By the end of the trial, it had reached three thousand dollars.

"We're going to give it at the Alday Memorial Service on Sunday, March 13," Earl Cheek, the director of the drive, told a reporter. "We are going to give it to them as a love offering. They have already spent much more than that."

And they would have to spend a great deal more.

For on the same day the *Donalsonville News* reported Cheek's remarks, it also informed its readers that Wayne Carl Coleman had been indicted on six counts of murder in Dekalb County the previous Tuesday, and that his retrial had been set for the twenty-first of March.

Chapter Thirty

After three weeks of voir dire testimony, a jury was finally struck in Decatur, Georgia, a small town outside Atlanta, for the retrial of Wayne Coleman.

Sitting at the front of the room, Nancy, who had attended Coleman's first trial, could not believe what she saw as Wayne was led into the room. At forty-one, he appeared old and haggard, his young body now bowed and emaciated, his hair nearly white, all his teeth fallen out. Far from the vigorous twenty-six-year-old man of fifteen years before, Coleman now presented the dismaying picture of a broken, middle-aged man. "He didn't look like the same man anymore," Nancy remembered. "He just looked plain pitiful." Even more alarming, from her perspective, was the fact that the jury would never know the lanky, grinning youth of the first trial. Instead they would come to judgment upon someone else entirely, an emaciated old man who seemed hardly able to hold his head up. Watching him amble to his seat, then ease himself awkwardly into it, his bony arms hanging limply at his sides, she feared that someone on the jury would feel sorry for him, would think that he had suffered enough, perhaps might even work to set him free.

Opening statements were offered on April 25, Charles Ferguson for the prosecution, and court-appointed attorney Thomas West, a staunch southern liberal and active opponent of the death penalty, for the defense.

West had grown up in rural Georgia, and he still retained vivid memories of reading about executions in the local paper. They had always been of some unfortunate character with a name like Willie or Leroy, whom West knew to be either poor or black, or, in most cases, both, and who had been given no legal defense before their executions.

As for Wayne Coleman, West was determined to provide him with the full-scale defense he believed to have been lacking in the first trial, and which would concentrate on demonstrating that there was little evidence that Coleman himself had actually murdered anyone. Beyond that, West hoped to offer a vision of Coleman as a witless follower of Carl Isaacs, and to offer testimony designed to mitigate his criminal responsibility in the murders themselves.

It was a strategy that West began with his opening statement on April 25. "Carl Isaacs is one of the most manipulative persons you will ever meet," he declared.

As for Billy, he was of a piece with his brother. "The state will present Billy Isaacs as a choirboy," West told the jury, "but he's exactly like Carl, a killer, a manipulator who cut a deal with the state."

In contrast to his half-brothers, West told the jury, Wayne Coleman was afflicted with "a personality so passive, so easily manipulated, that he'd do anything for his brothers." Because of that, he added, "the defense will show that every time Carl assigns Wayne to kill someone, he isn't able to do it, and Carl has to run in and finish the job."

After opening statements, Ferguson presented a case for the prosecution that was more or less identical to that which had been offered in 1973, again relying on physical evidence and Billy Isaacs' eyewitness testimony, along with Coleman's own confession of the crimes, to establish his guilt.

To these witnesses, neither West nor his cocounsel, Robert Citronberg, offered much cross-examination, since the defense's intention had never been to contest the fact that Coleman had been involved in the murders on River Road.

The defense became more aggressive on April 29, however, when it called William Dickenson, a clinical psychiatrist whose specialty was, as he told the jury, the science of psychologically evaluating people charged with crimes.

In this capacity Dickenson had spent approximately twelve hours with Carl Isaacs, during which time he had administered a great many psychological tests.

Under Citronberg's questioning, Dickenson described the various psychological examinations he had given Carl Isaacs, and the general nature of their results.

They were hardly flattering.

"Carl Isaacs is a very rigid person," Dickenson told the jury, "not very flexible in dealing with his environment."

In addition, Dickenson said, Carl had failed to "show the normal range of emotions." Instead, he had demonstrated a propensity toward numerous "fears, insecurities, strong feelings of inadequacy, lots of tendencies to be compulsive and obsessive."

Even more alarming, Carl had shown "very, very strong underlying feelings of hostility," particularly toward authority figures and women.

But Carl could be charming too, Dickenson added, and very manipulative, especially when he needed to "gain something."

In order to gain the most from his social interactions, Dickenson said, Carl would naturally surround himself with inferiors, "passive, dependent, yielding, inadequate" people like, for example, Wayne Coleman, whose below-average IQ range of 70 to 80 was decidedly inferior to Carl's of 95 to 110.

Now moving from a psychological evaluation of Carl Isaacs to one of Coleman himself, the defense called Dr. Howard Albrecht, a local clinical psychologist.

Albrecht had first met Coleman on November 24, 1987, then again on December 9, for a total of approximately twelve hours of psychological testing. During this time, he had administered a battery of psychological tests. Since mid-March, he had met with Coleman twice a week for a total of fifteen sessions of two hours each, meetings which he described as "very stressful" for Coleman.

As to the test results, Albrecht went on, they had revealed a decidedly deprived character in both emotional and intellectual terms. Coleman had a low-range intelligence, along with what Albrecht described as a "weak fund of common cultural information." Coleman, it seemed, had not known who wrote *Hamlet*.

In addition, Dr. Albrecht said, Coleman's powers of concentration were extremely poor, as was his social judgment. As a result, he could no more work out simple mathematical problems than he could plan his day. His reading ability was at a fourth-grade level, his mathematical ability a year lower than that.

But if Coleman was no whiz kid, neither was he much of an inspiration as a human being. "I found him to be a depressed individual," Albrecht told the jury, "probably depressed characterologically, by which I mean, not only as a result of his situation of being imprisoned or facing a possible death penalty, but that he had probably always been

depressed all his life, with this depression relating to a very pronounced
sense of loss and deprivation."

Wayne was "a very lonely" person, Albrecht added, who had suffered
a deprived early life, one "in which there was not very much in terms
of attention, affection, and nurturance from any parental figures."

This had resulted in a personality that was "depressed, possibly sui-
cidal, very suspicious, and paranoid."

It was also what the doctor called a "borderline personality," one
lacking the structure that might have helped Coleman gain a cohesive
sense of himself as a person. Consequently, Coleman had a poor sense
of his own identity, which, in turn, made him a "passive individual
. . . a follower," one particularly susceptible to the suggestions of family
members, particularly superior family members, particularly Carl Junior
Isaacs.

Still, according to Albrecht, Wayne would not just do anything
anyone told him to. For example, testify in his own defense. Coleman
could not do that, Albrecht said, because he was a frightened person,
terrified of getting on the stand. Forced to do so, he would have what
Albrecht described as a "panic attack."

At the conclusion of Albrecht's testimony, the defense completed its
case, then sat back to await the jury's verdict.

It was not long in coming.

At 8:10 P.M., after a dinner of take-out hamburgers, the jury sent
word that it had reached a verdict. They had found Wayne Carl Coleman guilty of six counts of murder.

The penalty phase began the day after the jury's verdict with West's
questioning of Dr. Albrecht.

"Can you tell me what effect, if any, a history of deprivation at an
early age has on the development of an individual adult personality?"
he asked.

"The predominant effect it had was to make Wayne very distrust-
ful," Albrecht replied. "He lost his natural father before he was born,
then lost George Isaacs, a father figure to him, very precipitously."

According to Albrecht, this would make Coleman "leery of authority,
at times somewhat rebellious, not having been able to work through a
very good challenging phase of adolescence that is necessary in order
to become an adult."

West mentioned the elements within Coleman's history of deprivation, his begging on the streets and living in sharecropper shacks. "What effect does that have on the personality?" he asked.

Albrecht replied that it would make Coleman withdrawn and reluctant to have relationships with others "in the same way that the survivors of the Nazi holocaust, when tested, revealed a lack of willingness to become involved with others."

West moved on to Coleman's passivity.

"Doctor, you testified that Wayne was passive. Can you tell me why he would, for example, confess to seven homicides . . . and that his brothers had no hand in it?"

"I can't underestimate the extent to which Wayne experiences brotherly love toward his younger brothers," Albrecht answered.

According to Albrecht, Coleman's earliest dream had been of a fire that had suddenly broken out in one of the "shacks" the family lived in. The fire had started where the stovepipe met the roof, and Coleman had taken his brother out of the burning house. The "fire" in the house, Albrecht added, was probably indicative of its turmoil, the pervasive alcoholism and abuse.

This early fantasy, with its sense of protection, had been a theme played throughout Coleman's life, Albrecht told the jury, and it had ended in his taking the blame for all six of the Alday murders.

"Is Wayne able to point his finger at his brothers and say that they actually did it?" West asked.

Albrecht's answer was unequivocal. "Wayne would not do that," he said.

As to Coleman's failure to testify, Albrecht told the jury that he recalled "one very touching comment Wayne made to me about the victims."

"What did he say about the victims?"

"He said, 'Well, they didn't have a chance to give their last words. Why should I?' "

"Doctor, what does that comment tell you about Wayne Coleman?"

"That he still feels guilt for what happened," Albrecht answered. "After the crime he described for me a period when he was incarcerated, and he was extremely distraught. And he describes getting so disturbed that he got down on his knees and prayed for God's forgiveness. And he says he feels that eventually God forgave him. I don't believe Wayne Coleman has forgiven himself."

*   *   *

Nor should he, Charles Ferguson thought, as he rose to cross-examine Dr. Albrecht.

"Now you said that you feel that Wayne has a lot of feeling for other people?" he asked.

"Yes."

"Would that feeling that he has for other people be consistent with him leaving a young woman nude in the woods and abandoning her body and leaving it there? Is that consistent with feeling for others?"

"I cannot answer that," Albrecht replied. "I think that's up to this jury to decide. If I had a cold, he'd ask me about how I was feeling—a concern for me as a person, and for others."

From her place in the courtroom, Nancy could hardly contain her contempt for Albrecht's testimony, particularly his description of the man who'd killed her father, three of her brothers, and her uncle, who had raped her sister-in-law, then participated in her murder, as a kind, concerned person. Always the most volatile of the Alday sisters, and having far less of the religious faith that guided her mother toward gentleness, acceptance, and forgiveness, Nancy had finally reached the boiling point, her grief at last overshadowed by her rage. "I'd like to have shown him a few pictures from the trailer and the woods," she told Ernestine as they left the courtroom a short time later, "and let him tell me how concerned a human being Wayne Coleman was."

Albrecht's testimony had irritated Nancy; that which followed it positively made her squirm.

After weeks of effort, West had finally persuaded Coleman's mother, Betty Isaacs, to testify in her son's behalf.

"Wayne was a good boy," she told the jury. "He worked on the farms. He helped—done everything he could do. He never done nothing wrong."

"Did he obey you?" West asked.

"Yes, he did," Mrs. Isaacs replied. "Got along real good with his brothers and sisters."

"While he was living with you, was he ever in trouble?"

"Not no serious trouble, no."

"What kind of kid was Carl?"

"He was rough," Mrs. Isaacs said. "He wouldn't listen to nobody. You tell him something, he wouldn't listen."

"If you put Wayne and Billy and Carl in a pot, who would the leader be?"

"Carl. He could talk people into things."

"Do you think that Carl could pull the trigger and kill somebody?"

"Yes."

"Do you think that Billy could?"

"Yes."

"Could Wayne pull the trigger?"

"No," Mrs. Isaacs said, "because he was never that kind of a boy."

It was a view of Coleman that his sister Ruth confirmed when she followed Betty Isaacs to the stand.

"What kind of kid was Wayne when he was growing up?" Citronberg asked.

"He was well-respected. A good boy."

"Was he a loud child or a quiet child?"

"He was quiet."

"What kind of kid was Carl?"

"He was mean, vicious."

"Do you think Carl could pull the trigger and shoot somebody?"

"Yes."

"Do you think Billy could pull the trigger and shoot somebody?"

"Yes."

"Do you think Wayne could pull the trigger and shoot somebody?"

"No."

"Why is that?"

"Because he was quiet."

"Do you love Wayne?"

"Yes," Ruth replied, "I do."

Then, suddenly, she began to cry, and as she did so, Nancy noticed that rather than raising any objection to her weeping, as defense attorneys had done in the case of their own tears, Citronberg let it go on for quite some time before finally turning to the court.

"Do we have any tissues, Your Honor?" he asked gently.

As it turned out, the court did not.

In the final moments of the penalty phase, Ferguson faced the jury and declared in a short statement that most of the defense's case for a life sentence for Coleman was just "so much smoke."

"I don't blame Betty Isaacs and Ruth Isaacs for telling you they don't want Wayne executed," he went on, "but Jerry Alday didn't want to die. Ned Alday didn't want to die. Aubrey Alday didn't want to die. Shuggie Alday didn't want to die. Jimmy Alday didn't want to die. And Mary Alday didn't want to die."

Once Ferguson had concluded, Tom West made his final argument for sparing Coleman's life.

"Smoke screen?" he asked. "You tell me if it's a smoke screen to bring in a man's mother when the state is trying to take his life and to tell what kind of a person he is."

West added that he had never contested the fact that six people had been murdered, but that he had only tried to discover "why in the world that happened—who was responsible. Who was the leader? Who was the follower? Who was abused? Whose arm was twisted? Whose idea was it? That's what we've been trying to do in the defense in this case."

Such things were not important to the prosecution, West continued, because the state "didn't care who did it or why or whether Wayne Coleman may just have been cowering in the back while the leader did the killing."

That is precisely what Coleman had done, West concluded. "I'm not saying that Wayne is innocent," he told the jury. "I'm not saying that he's not guilty in the sense that you have found him guilty. But, if we're going to decide who lives and who dies, don't you want to base that on more than just the fact that he was there?"

"Who was the real guilty party in this case?" West asked. "Carl Isaacs. Carl Isaacs has been tried a second time and found guilty of six murders and sentenced to death again. Don't worry about the guilty not being punished in this case."

As for Coleman: "Let him live out his life," West implored the jury. "You've heard testimony about what he has not had in life." Still, despite his background, Coleman had in a sense triumphed over it far more than his brothers had. "Somehow, Wayne maintained his humanity," West said, then asked the jury to spare his life.

"If any one of you feel that a life sentence is appropriate, that's it," he said, "and I'd ask you to allow him to live."

As she watched the jury file silently from the room, Nancy wondered if West had reached that one solitary person who would spare Wayne Coleman's life.

It would be longer than any of them could have imagined before they found out.

Both during the trial, and after it, as one day lengthened slowly into another while the jury continued its unexpectedly protracted deliberations concerning the fate of Wayne Coleman, Ernestine and Nancy remained in Decatur, the two of them cooped up in their room at the local Day's Inn. It was a situation made infinitely worse by the fact that members of Coleman's family had been booked into the same small motel. "We were always running into Betty Isaacs, Carl Isaacs' mother, and Coleman's sisters," Nancy remembered. "And they would give us these terrible looks, like they thought that we were the ones who'd killed their people, instead of the way it really was."

At the ice and soda machines, or in the laundry, or simply as they strolled to their cars in the motel parking lot, Ernestine and Nancy would sometimes feel themselves under the hostile glare of Betty Isaacs or one of her daughters. "We never wished any harm on Mrs. Isaacs and her daughters that came down to testify in Decatur," Ernestine later said. "We'd never said a word against them. But the fact is, it was her boys that came down here and killed my husband and my boys, not the other way around."

At 10:20 A.M. on Tuesday, May 11, a full six days after the final arguments in the penalty phase had been concluded, and following a record thirty-five hours of continuous deliberation, the foreman of the jury sent a note to the judge which declared tersely: "We are unable to agree upon a sentence."

That simple statement was the culmination of seemingly endless days of deliberation during which the jury room had been rocked by bursts of argument, screams, and weeping as a single juror held out against the imposition of the death penalty.

According to later reports, it had been a stalemate from the beginning, when, upon entering the jury room, one of the jurors, a twenty-two-year-old woman who had been a small child at the time of the murders, announced unequivocally that she would not vote for the death sentence.

Despite the juror's inflexible statement, deliberations had continued, struggling on through Mother's Day in what the *Atlanta Constitution* later called "a marathon that experts say is unequaled in modern death penalty deliberations in Georgia."

By the sixth day, however, the deadlock had become obvious. A mistrial was therefore declared by Judge Lawson, and under Georgia law, this meant that Coleman would get a life sentence. He would be eligible for parole in fifteen years.

"Wayne's satisfied that the jury spared his life," West told reporters at the end of the proceedings. For that reason, he added, any further appeal would be a waste of time.

With news of the hung jury, Ernestine once more moved toward a serene acceptance. Nancy, however, was less sanguine. Spiritually exhausted and economically depleted by the lengthy trial and subsequent jury deliberations, she packed the car solemnly and prepared for the eight-hour drive back to Donalsonville. It was not a pleasant journey, but in some sense, it was at least a welcome one. "We all really needed some relief," Nancy said in 1990. "By the time that trial was over, I felt like I'd been staring at Wayne Coleman all my life."

It was but a short respite, however, for only a few weeks after returning to Seminole County, Nancy and Ernestine began their preparations to attend the trial of George Dungee, next in line to be prosecuted.

But it was a trial that never happened.

In 1988, the Georgia General Assembly had decreed that mentally retarded individuals could not be executed in Georgia. At the same time, it officially judged mentally retarded people to be those whose I.Q. tested lower than 70.

Repeatedly given I.Q. tests, George Dungee had never scored higher than 68.

Thus, on July 14, 1988, Dungee pleaded guilty by reason of mental retardation to six counts of murder before the Superior Court of Muscogee County in Columbus. He was sentenced to six consecutive life terms.

With Wayne Coleman and George Dungee now spared the death penalty, only Carl Isaacs remained with the shadow of the gallows still before him.

On March 20, 1989, his attorneys filed a 764-page brief with the Georgia State Supreme Court in an initial appeal action whose continuing process would last for at least eight to thirteen years.

It might also continue indefinitely.

In the meantime, Ernestine, Nancy, and Patricia Alday remain in an odd state of ambiguity and suspension. For them, "justice," as Ernestine always called it, is no longer at issue. Only closure is, only the sense that the legal process that resulted from the slaughter of May 14, 1973, will eventually come to an end while some of those who survived it are still alive.

As the months pass, and Carl Isaacs' appeals stagger through the various layers of the judicial system, Ernestine, now seventy-five years old, rocks in her padded rocker and lets her eyes move from one photograph to the next, from Ned, to Shuggie, then on to Jerry, Jimmy, Aubrey, Mary. "Not a day goes by I don't think of them," she tells what she considers the last of the reporters who will bother to write about the tragedy on River Road. "Tell everybody that. Tell them not a day goes by."

Each morning Patricia rises at the same early hour, then drives to the small brick building that houses the Seminole County Department of Family and Children Services in downtown Donalsonville. "I see all these terrible things that happen in families around here," she says, "all the abuse, sexual and every other kind. And I think of my father and my brothers, and I think how good they were, even better than I could have known at the time."

At her job at the local marina, Nancy watches the long white boats glide up and down Lake Seminole, then lifts her eyes upward to catch the flight of the cattle egrets that soar above it. "Daddy and all of them really loved the lake," she says simply, as if there is nothing more to say.

Both as individuals and as the remnants of an unspeakably wounded family, the mood that surrounds Ernestine and her daughters is one of weariness and retirement, a sense that all their passion has been spent. Though yearning for some final settlement to the tragedy they suffered, they no longer expect it. Still, they fight off bitterness as best they can, as if clinging to the words they chose to have inscribed on Mary Alday's grave:

Love can hope, where reason would despair.